MW01670517

Bible Truth Revealed

by

Kerensa Grigson

Published by

Bible Truth Revealed

Copyright © 2015 Bible Truth Revealed
All rights reserved.

First Printing: 2015

Photo copyright - see credits for image ownership

ISBN: 978-0-9941997-4-4

www.bibletruthrevealed.com

This book is dedicated to

the three dignitaries of the Godhead

the Father, Son and Holy Ghost.

It is the author's sincere prayer that the Gospel message contained in this book be scattered around the globe like the leaves of autumn. From the continents of Asia, Africa, and South America to the islands of the sea, the message of Christ our salvation is to be proclaimed. And when that work is done, the Lord's promise is, He will surely come and take us home. Matthew 24:14.

Preface

When I was a child of just eight years old, I read the story of Noah's Ark in the Bible at church for the first time. I was absolutely astonished at the detail regarding the construction of the ship. Ever after, I was searching for archaeological evidence of the Ark.

In 2008 I joined an archaeological expedition to the Noah's Ark site near Dogubayazit in Eastern Turkey. Sitting on the bow of the ship for the first time, I was truly amazed by the sheer size of the vessel, and I really did feel that I was standing upon a very ancient ship near the top of a mountain.

After the Noah's Ark expedition, I visited the sites for the Red Sea Crossing, the Garden Tomb and Sodom and Gomorrah. Later in 2008, after returning from my archaeological expedition, I was inspired to tell the world what I had seen. I began collating my research into PowerPoints and gave presentations to various churches in Western Australia.

Early 2014, my personal ministry extended into co-publishing books with a friend. Later that year, my idea for the book *Bible Truth Revealed* began to form in my mind. This project was a monumental task that involved collating the best information from my presentations (based on my personal research and the research of many others) and rewriting it into easy to read text.

Bible Truth Revealed was written in four sections, namely, Noah's Ark, The Red Sea Crossing, Calvary's Hidden Secret (the Garden Tomb of Jesus) and the lost cities of Sodom and Gomorrah. Each section has two subsections: archaeological evidence and theology (including Bible texts). The theology sections were inspired by the writings of Ellet Waggoner and Alonzo Jones.

Each of these four main sections include many photographs from my expedition (you will note I appear in some of them). In 2013 I visited Jerusalem a second time to collect more photographs.

Bible Truth Revealed is non-denominational and has been written for Christians, non-Christians and atheists to reveal Bible truth and to show that sites in the Bible really do exist. The latter may find the archaeological sections interesting, but hopefully they will read the Bible stories and develop a close relationship with God.

Unfortunately, some television documentaries and many in the scientific establishment dismiss the real site of Noah's Ark and other biblical sites without proper research and knowledge. *Bible Truth Revealed* attempts to clarify the facts and dispel the myths from such documentaries by providing credible scientific and historical evidence for these sites.

It is my sincere wish that in reading this book you will come to believe in the Bible and find God as your friend and saviour.

The Author

Contents

SECTION 1 - NOAH'S ARK

SECTION 2 - THE EXODUS

SECTION 3 - CALVARY'S HIDDEN SECRET

SECTION 4 - SODOM & GOMORRAH

Noah's Ark

PART 1 - THE STORY OF THE FLOOD

IN THE BEGINNING

> God created man in his own image, in the image of God created he him; male and female created he them. Genesis 1:27

> Lo, this only have I found, that God hath made man upright; but they have sought out many inventions. Ecclesiastes 7:29

In the beginning, God made man upright, in His own image. From the very beginning man was created standing tall and straight. God distinguished man from other animals including apes. This small detail will forever be a safeguard against new theories of man's origin.

> God made man and fashioned him with His hands. Psalm 119:73

> The LORD God formed man of the dust of the ground, and breathed into his nostrils the breath of life; and man became a living soul. Genesis 2:7

In this scripture we are told that God formed man out of the dust of the ground and breathed into him the breath of life.

> God's energy is still exerted in upholding the objects of His creation. It is not because the mechanism that has once been set in motion continues to act by its own inherent energy that the pulse beats and breath follows breath; but every breath, every pulsation of the heart, is an evidence of the all-pervading care of Him in whom "we live, and move, and have our being" (Acts 17:28).
> *Patriarchs and Prophets*, p.115

GOD'S CREATIVE POWER

> Canst thou by searching find out God? canst thou find out the Almighty unto perfection? It is as high as heaven; what canst thou do? deeper than hell; what canst thou know? Job 11:7-8

God's work of creation is a mystery that has never been revealed to men. Human science will never discover His secrets. As His existence is incomprehensible, so is

His creative power. Nevertheless He reveals to us through His word the vital things we need to know.

LARGE IN STATURE

> There were giants in the earth in those days. Genesis 6:4

People living before the flood were larger in stature than people living today. Man has degenerated and become smaller over the millennia.

PEOPLE BEFORE THE FLOOD LIVED LONGER

> And all the days of Methuselah were nine hundred sixty and nine years: and he died. Genesis 5:27

The Bible reveals that the antediluvians (people living before the flood) lived much longer than people today. For example Methuselah, the grandfather of Noah, lived to be 969 years of age. Living to such a great age these men knew virtually no bounds to the acquisition of knowledge. (See also *Antiquities of the Jews* by Flavius Josephus, Chapter 3. Para 9.)

HIGHLY CIVILISED

> Zillah, she also bare Tubalcain, an instructor of every artificer in brass and iron: and the sister of Tubalcain was Naamah. Genesis 4:22

The antediluvians were highly civilised and skilled in metallurgy. The Bible records that Tubalcain, the sixth descendant from Cain, instructed craftsman in brass and iron.

THE NAMES OF THE TEN PATRIARCHS WHO LIVED BEFORE THE FLOOD

There were ten patriarchs who lived before the flood. These men were teachers of righteousness and they worshipped the true God in their generations.

According to Vigouroux, in *Dictionnaire de la bible*, the tradition of ten ancient ancestors is found also with other races; e.g. among the Hindus, with their ten *Pitris* or forefathers, comprising Brahma and the nine Bramadikas; among the ancient Germans and Scandinavians, with their belief in the ten ancestors of Odin, etc.

The names of the patriarchs were prophetic. When the meaning of these names are combined in sequence according to birth there is a prophecy of Christ. The patriarchs looked forward to Christ's day. "Enoch also, the seventh from Adam, prophesied... saying, Behold, the Lord cometh with ten thousands of his saints to execute judgment upon all, and to convince all that are ungodly among them of all their ungodly deeds which they have ungodly committed, and of all their hard speeches which ungodly sinners have spoken against him" (Jude 14). SEE TABLE ON PAGE 16.

The prophecy was a promise that Christ would be our substitute and surety.

THE HISTORY OF CAIN AND ABEL

Adam and Eve had two sons and to outward appearance they were brethren. Abel expressed faith in the Saviour through a blood sacrifice. Cain brought only the fruit of his own labours and refused to recognise the need of a Redeemer. Abel was accepted. Cain was rejected.

There are only two belief systems in this world, both originating with Cain and Abel. The one that feels their insufficiency and depends upon the blood of Christ; and the other who feel they can save themselves through their own works. SEE TABLE ON PAGE 17.

THE WORD OF GOD IS INFALLIBLE

> God... cannot lie. Titus 1:2

> All scripture is given by inspiration of God. 2 Timothy 3:16

We can depend on the word of God. The scriptures are a record of the world's history, chronicled by God Himself. If "God cannot lie" and "every word of God is pure" (Proverbs 30:5) then we must accept the biblical account of the creation as fact.

WHY DID GOD FLOOD THE EARTH AND DESTROY THE ANTEDILUVIANS?

> God saw that the wickedness of man was great in the earth, and that every imagination of the thoughts of his heart was only evil continually. Genesis 6:5

The descendants of Cain in successive generations became increasingly wicked. Violence and bloodshed filled the earth. The longer men lived the more hardened in sin they became. God, grieved with the sorrow and suffering, sent the deluge to put a check on the evil.

THE SONS OF GOD

> There were giants in the earth in those days; and also after that, when the sons of God came in unto the daughters of men, and they bare children to them, the same became mighty men which were of old, men of renown. Genesis 6:4

The *Book of Enoch* describes a super race of giant humans called Nephilim – the offspring of the "sons of God" and the "daughters of men" before the Deluge. The *Book of Enoch* is not included in the Bible and the term Nephilim is not mentioned in scripture once, yet many are convinced by this story that demonic angels interbred with human females to create a super race of people. A careful reading of Genesis 6:4 however, explains that the giants already existed *before* the sons of God came in unto the daughters of men. The Bible also clarifies that angels cannot procreate (Matthew 22:30); and that the term "sons of God" is only used in reference to those who have accepted God's Covenant (John 1:12; Romans 8:14; Philippians 2:15; 1 John 3:2).

Christ Prophesied by the Patriarch's Names

Name	Bible Dictionary	"Who's Who?"	Strong's Concordance	Summary
Adam	red,ground	man	H120 ruddy, human being, mankind	a human being, ground of mankind
Seth	appoint, compensate	founder	H8352 put, substituted (to place)	is appointed, put in place, as a substitute that compensates
Enos	man, mankind	mortal	H583 a mortal	for mortal man/mankind
Cainan	meaning unknown	none	H7018 fixed (a nest, chamber/dwelling [erect, nestle, build, occupy])	a fixed dwelling place
Mahalaleel	God shines forth	God's praise	H4111 praise of God	for God's praise and outraying
Jared	servant	descent	H3382 a descent (to descend, go down, fall, bring down)	God's servant, who descended, went down
Enoch	initiated, dedicated	dedicated	H2585 intitiated (to narrow, discipline)	who obediently dedicated himself
Methuselah	man of the javelin	man of the javelin	man of a dart (an adult, a man; a missile, a shoot, a branch)	to be the shoot and branch that was pierced and brought
Lamech	meaning unknown	H3929 from uncertain root		(strength and)
Noah	rest, relief	rest	H5146 quiet	quiet rest; which allowed
Shem	renown	renown	8035 name (honor, authority, character)	honor
Ham	hot	hot	H2526 hot	passion and
Japheth	none	he enlarges	H3315 expansions (to open, roomy)	blessing

A human being, ground of mankind is appointed, put in place, as a substitute that compensates for mortal man/mankind. A fixed dwelling place for God's praise and out raying, God's servant, who descended, went down, obediently dedicating himself to be the shoot and branch that was pierced, brought (strength and) quiet rest; which allowed - honor, passion and blessing.

Nelson's Illustrated Bible Dictionary, Who's Who in the Bible by Jane Comay and Ronald Brownrigg, Strong's Concordance

Prophecy of Cain's Descendants

Name	Bible Dictionary	"Who's Who?"	Strong's Concordance	Summary
Cain	possessed	spear	H7014 a lance (as striking fast)	the swift striking lance of self gotten righteousness produces
Enoch	initiated, dedicated	dedicated	H2585 initiated (to narrow, discipline)	wandering a narrow, disclipining initiation by God, in the form of
Irad	wild donkey	fleet	H5897 fugitive (to sequester)	a quick hiding-away, separating
Mehujael	smitten by God	smitten	H4232 smitten of God (stroke, rub, erase)	discipline, stroking (cleaning up) of
Methusael	name of God	(see Methuselah) "man of the javelin"	H4967 man who is of God	those called by God; which brings
Lamech	meaning unknown	strong	H3929 from uncertain root	strength
Jabal	nomadic	stream	H2989 a stream (to flow)	detachment from the physical flow of life
Jubal	playing	sound	H3106 a stream	music
Tubal-Cain	the smith (of cutting instruments)	none [tubal=tumult]	H8423 offspring of Cain	weapons against sin, and
Naamah	lovely, beautiful	pleasing	H5279 pleasantness (pleas-ure)	loveliness, beauty and pleasure

The swift striking lance of self-gotten righteousness produces a narrow, disciplining initiation by God, in the form of a quick hiding-away, separating discipline, a stroking (cleaning up) of those called by God; which brings strength, detachment from the physical flow of life, music, weapons against sin, and loveliness, beauty and pleasure.

Nelson's Illustrated Bible Dictionary, "Who's Who in the Bible" by Jane Comay and Ronald Brownrigg, Strong's Concordance

INTERMARRIAGE CORRUPTED THE SONS OF GOD

The Bible records that Cain's descendants were city dwellers (Genesis 4:17) and that Seth's descendants lived in the mountains as herdsmen and shepherds. As the cities expanded to the foothills of the mountains, the descendants of Seth saw that the daughters of Cain were fair and began to intermingle with them.

The intermarriage between the true worshippers of God with the heathen corrupted the simple faith received from their fathers. The standards of God were compromised until they became so degraded that eventually they worshipped the creation instead of the Creator. Noah, his grandfather and other patriarchs from that line maintained the true worship amidst the prevailing apostasy.

120 YEARS PROBATION

> The LORD said, My spirit shall not always strive with man, for that he also is flesh: yet his days shall be an hundred and twenty years. Genesis 6:3

> The longsuffering of God waited in the days of Noah, while the ark was a preparing, wherein few, that is, eight souls were saved by water. 1 Peter 3:20

God saw that there was only wickedness in man's heart continually and that the earth was filled with violence. The condition of society so deeply grieved Him that He came to regret making man (Genesis 6:6). But Noah was just and perfect in his generation and found grace in God's sight so God instructed him to build an Ark for his family.

PROCLAIMING THE MESSAGE OF WARNING

While Noah gave the warning message to the world, his works testified of his sincerity. Through the building of the Ark his faith was perfected and made evident. Everything he possessed was invested in the project and every blow of his hammer was a witness to those who came to marvel at the strange sight.

In the time of Noah there had never been a flood before, neither had it ever rained because the earth was watered by a mist (Genesis 2:6). Noah had to take God at His word.

THE WORLD GIVEN TIME TO REPENT

> The Lord is not slack concerning his promise, as some men count slackness; but is longsuffering to us-ward, not willing that any should perish, but that all should come to repentance. 2 Peter 3:9

> Say unto them, As I live, saith the Lord GOD, I have no pleasure in the death

> of the wicked; but that the wicked turn from his way and live: turn ye, turn ye from your evil ways; for why will ye die, O house of Israel? Ezekiel 33:11

120 years is no short time to rethink one's own direction in life and to make necessary changes for a more positive future. If they had repented and believed the message, God would have turned aside the judgment as He did with Nineveh. But the people were not willing to humble themselves and accept God's offer of salvation. They loved their pleasures and their sins too much, and would not change, therefore sealing their destruction.

WHAT MADE NOAH DIFFERENT?

> By faith Noah, being warned of God of things not yet seen, moved with fear, prepared an ark to the saving of his house; by the which he condemned the world, and became heir of the righteousness which is by faith. Hebrews 11:7

Noah took God seriously and believed that He was going to execute the judgment He had foretold. He had a personal sense of accountability and sought the favour of God.

> Faith has nothing to do with feelings. The promises of God are true no matter how we feel. In those waves of despair we must never cherish the thought that we cannot approach God. If we confess our sin He is faithful and just to forgive our sin (1 John 1:9).

MOCKERS AND SCOFFERS

> Behold, there went out a sower to sow:... And...as he sowed... some fell on stony ground, where it had not much earth; and immediately it sprang up, because it had no depth of earth: But when the sun was up, it was scorched; and because it had no root, it withered away. Mark 4:3-6

The boldest and most defiant scoffers were those who had once believed the warning that Noah gave and began to reform their lives. But they had renounced their faith because of the persecution from family and friends. Despite the universal ridicule, Noah's firm trust in God's word fortified him against it.

MY LORD DELAYETH HIS COMING

> If that servant say in his heart, My lord delayeth his coming; and shall begin to beat the menservants and maidens, and to eat and drink, and to be drunken; The lord of that servant will come in a day when he looketh not for him, and at an hour when he is not aware, and will cut him in sunder, and will appoint him his portion with the unbelievers. And that servant, which knew his lord's will, and prepared not himself, neither did according to his will, shall be beaten

with many stripes. Luke 12:45-47

God's faithful servants proclaim the soon coming of Christ because by doing so they have made a personal choice to hasten His return. Those who believe His appearing is afar off are likened to a wicked servant because they prefer the pleasures of this world and by their actions say, "My lord delayeth His coming."

WATCH AND WAIT

> But of that day and that hour knoweth no man, no, not the angels which are in heaven, neither the Son, but the Father. Take ye heed, watch and pray: for ye know not when the time is. Mark 13:32-33

> Behold, I come as a thief. Blessed is he that watcheth, and keepeth his garments, lest he walk naked, and they see his shame. Revelation 16:15

Noah did not know the day the flood would come but he did know the month and the year. When he saw the animals guided into the Ark by an unseen hand he knew the time was near. Christ has commissioned us to watch and wait, observing the signs of His second appearing so that the event does not catch us off-guard. The scriptures and the prophecies foretell His soon coming and no one need be in the dark.

AS IN THE DAYS OF NOAH

> As it was in the days of Noe, so shall it be also in the days of the Son of man. They did eat, they drank, they married wives, they were given in marriage, until the day that Noe entered into the ark, and the flood came, and destroyed them all. Luke 17:26-27

While the world was preoccupied with its pleasures and entertainment, Noah was building for eternity.

SCOFFERS IN THE LAST DAYS

> Knowing this first, that there shall come in the last days scoffers, walking after their own lusts, And saying, Where is the promise of his coming? for since the fathers fell asleep, all things continue as they were from the beginning of the creation. For this they willingly are ignorant of, that by the word of God the heavens were of old, and the earth standing out of the water and in the water: Whereby the world that then was, being overflowed with water, perish ed. 2 Peter 3:3-6

The theory of evolution directly contradicts the word of God. Christ said, "Blessed are the meek and lowly." Evolution declares that only the fittest will survive. God's word says man has become degraded by sin. Evolution says man is evolving into a superior species.

Fig. A4 – Philosophers gazing in astonishment.

Men are always coming up with new theories and speculations that do away with the existence of God because if they were to acknowledge God, there is a personal accountability before a judgment.

Others twist the word of God to say things that it does not say. They take the literal meaning of the word and place a spiritualistic interpretation upon it.

THE ANIMALS ENTER THE ARK

> They went in unto Noah into the ark, two and two of all flesh, wherein is the breath of life. And they that went in, went in male and female of all flesh, as God had commanded him: and the LORD shut him in. Genesis 7:15-16

Multitudes looked on with astonishment as a divine hand guided the animals two by two into the Ark. Of the clean animals they went in by sevens. One was for a sacrifice on the other side of the flood, and the other six to ensure a bountiful supply of food. Once Noah, his family and the animals had entered the Ark the door was shut.

NOAH SEVERELY TESTED

> It came to pass after seven days, that the waters of the flood were upon the earth. Genesis 7:10

It did not rain immediately after Noah entered the Ark. For seven days the people gathered round about it with their taunts and jeers while no sign of the coming flood appeared. This was a severe test for Noah and his family. The apparent delay made the antediluvians even more certain Noah was a fanatic and that the flood would never happen.

SUDDEN DESTRUCTION

> For yourselves know perfectly that the day of the Lord so cometh as a thief in the night. For when they shall say, Peace and safety; then sudden destruction cometh upon them, as travail upon a woman with child; and they shall not escape. 1 Thessalonians 5:2-3

Multitudes in our day are making the same mistake as those before the flood. They are saying, "Peace and safety," not realising that sudden destruction is about to burst upon them.

Science agrees with creation

- In 1961 Professor John C. Whitcomb and Dr Henry M. Morris published a book called ***The Genesis Flood: The Biblical Record and Its Scientific Implications***. This book recognised the inadequacies of uniformitarianism and evolution which presuppose that the earth's environmental conditions have always remained predictable and stable; and instead presented a biblically-based system of creationism and catastrophism.
- Robert V Gentry, a nuclear physicist was convinced that radioactive halos might be "the key" to determining the young age of the Earth, and vindicating flood geology. In his book ***Creation's Tiny Mystery*** (2003) he scientifically proves, by measuring the rate of decay of radioactive halos in the earth's granite rocks, that these rocks were the product of instantaneous creation as opposed to rock that was formed by hot magma over long ages.
- ***The Evolution Cruncher*** (2001) by Vance Ferrel B.A. M.A. is a compilation of scientific facts which disprove the evolution theory. Vance presents strong evidence for the young age of the earth, intelligent design of all life forms and the unreliability of carbon-dating, among other evidences.

AN EXAMPLE OF THE DIALOGUE BETWEEN NOAH AND THE ANTEDILUVIANS

The sons of men assembled together, about seven hundred thousand men and women, and they came unto Noah to the Ark. And they called to Noah, saying, "Open for us that we may come to thee in the Ark and wherefore shall we die?"

And Noah, with a loud voice, answered them from the Ark, saying, "Have you not all rebelled against the Lord, and said that he does not exist? (Isn't that like evolutionists today?) And therefore the Lord brought upon you this evil, to destroy and cut you off from the face of the earth.

Is this the thing that I spoke to you of one hundred and twenty years back, and you would not hearken to the voice of the Lord, and now do you desire to live upon earth?"

And they said to Noah, "We are ready to return to the Lord; only open for us that we may live and not die."

And Noah answered them, saying, "Behold now that you see the trouble of your souls, (now that you see the flood) you wish to return to the Lord, why did you not return during these hundred and twenty years, which the Lord granted you as the determined period? But now you come and tell me this on account of the trouble of your souls, now also the Lord will not listen to you, neither will he give ear to you on this day, so that you will not now succeed in your wishes."

And the sons of men approached in order to break into the Ark, to come in on account of the rain, for they could not bear the rain upon them. And the Lord sent all the beasts and animals that stood round the Ark. And the beasts overpowered them and drove them from that place and every man went his way and they again scattered themselves upon the face of the earth.

Book of Jasher

The ferocity of the storm was cataclysmic. Mountains were ripped from their foundations and hurled great distances burying entire forests beneath their mass. Gigantic cracks opened up in the earth's surface and water from the subterranean chambers violently erupted into the air. Seething volcanoes bubbled beneath the sea pouring forth molten lava and shaping anew the earth's face. As the waters arose the people bound themselves to large beasts with their children in the hope that they would flee to higher ground. Above all the commotion of the earth's upheaval was heard the wails of despair from the perishing.

HIS STRANGE ACT

> For the LORD shall rise up as in mount Perazim, he shall be wroth as in the valley of Gibeon, that he may do his work, his strange work; and bring to pass his act, his strange act. Now therefore be ye not mockers, lest your bands be made strong: for I have heard from the Lord GOD of hosts a consumption, even determined upon the whole earth. Isaiah 28:21-22

God takes no delight in destroying His own creation. For the sake of a righteous few He forebears long with the wicked and permits them to live out their sinful course. But when their wickedness escalates to such a point that it threatens to extinguish the entire human race as it did with the antediluvians, His level of forbearance is reached and He must intervene to put a check on sin. Therefore it was in mercy that God sent the flood.

THE ARK'S VOYAGE

For forty days it continued to rain and the earth spewed forth its fountains until the waters had risen fifteen cubits (7.9 metres) above the highest mountains. Every creature on the dry land perished and every living substance was destroyed. Only Noah and his family remained alive in the Ark. For five months the Ark was tossed to and fro on the raging waters and the occupants of the Ark feared for their lives. In the seventh month on the seventeenth day of the month (150 days from when the flood began) the Ark rested upon the mountains of Ararat. The waters gradually receded until the first day of the tenth month (73 days later) when the tops of the mountains were uncovered.

Forty days later, Noah opened the window of the Ark and sent forth a raven which flew back and forth. Seven days later Noah released a dove which found nothing and returned to the Ark. Seven days after that he sent it out again and it returned with an olive leaf in its mouth. The following week it was released once more and never returned.

In the sixth hundred and first year, in the first month, the first day of the month the waters were dried up from off the earth and Noah removed the covering of the Ark. And in the second month, on the twenty seventh day of the month God commanded Noah, his family and the animals to go forth from the Ark, multiply and be fruitful upon the earth. In total Noah and his family were in the Ark for one Jewish calendar year and ten days (370 days).

THE RAINBOW

> As I have sworn that the waters of Noah should no more go over the earth; so have I sworn that I would not be wroth with thee, nor rebuke thee. For the mountains shall depart, and the hills be removed; but My kindness shall not depart from thee, neither shall the covenant of My peace be removed, saith Jehovah that hath mercy on thee. Isaiah 54:9-10

In gratitude to God for preserving his life and the life of his family, Noah built an altar and sacrificed one of each of the clean animals. This offering pleased God who promised that He would never flood the entire earth again. As a reminder, He placed the rainbow in the sky.

Linked to the bow of promise was the assurance of God's Covenant of Peace with Noah. This was the promise of the mercy of God through Christ and an inheritance among the saints.

> The rainbow of promise encircling the throne on high is an everlasting testimony that "God so loved the world, that He gave His only-begotten Son, that whosoever believeth in Him should not perish, but have everlasting life." John 3:16. It testifies to the universe that God will never forsake His people in their struggle with evil. It is an assurance to us of strength and protection as long as the throne itself shall endure. *The Desire of Ages*, p.493
>
> "Behold, a throne was set in heaven, and one sat on the throne... There was a rainbow round about the throne, in sight like unto an emerald." Revelation 4:2-3. When man by his great wickedness invites the divine judgments, the Saviour, interceding with the Father in his behalf, points to the bow in the clouds, to the rainbow around the throne and above His own head, as a token of the mercy of God toward the repentant sinner. *Patriarchs and Prophets*, p.107

THE FAITH OF NOAH

> By faith Noah, being warned of God of things not yet seen, moved with fear, prepared an ark to the saving of his house; by the which he condemned the world, and became heir of the righteousness which is by faith. Hebrews 11:7

> And spared not the old world, but saved Noah the eighth person, a preacher of righteousness, bringing in the flood upon the world of the ungodly. 2 Peter 2:5

When Noah was yet childless, the Lord had declared that only Noah, his family and the animals would survive the flood (Genesis 6:18). In this Covenant God gave Noah the promise that he would have a posterity and that through his posterity the world's redeemer would come. Despite the foreknowledge that he and his family would be the only survivors of the flood, Noah still faithfully proclaimed the warning message for 120 years as a witness against the ungodly, and in the hope that some might yet be saved.

Several centuries later God gave Noah's descendant Abraham, who was also yet childless, the same promise of a posterity through which the seed (the Messiah) would come. Both Noah and Abraham believed that God had a special purpose for their life, and because of this God was able to work in and through them to sup-

Fig. A6 – God is seeking faithful Noahs today.

ply the very fact. Abraham, like Noah, chose to receive God's word as a personal prophecy of his own life, and as a consequence God chose him to be the father of many nations and the spiritual father of His church. God is also recruiting Noahs, Abrahams and Elijahs in our day but He leaves the choice with us as to whether we will choose to be the one or not. The book of Acts declares, "It shall come to pass in the last days, saith God, I will pour out of my Spirit upon all flesh: and your sons and your daughters shall prophesy, and your young men shall see visions, and your old men shall dream dreams" (Acts 2:17). Will we choose to be the one to fulfil this promise? This is what Noah and Abraham did and this is what made their faith so great.

A SECOND CHANCE

> And I will put enmity between thee and the woman, and between thy seed and her seed; it shall bruise thy head, and thou shalt bruise his heel.
>
> Genesis 3:15

In the Garden of Eden God gave the promise that the woman's seed would bruise the serpents head (Genesis 3:15). This was the promise of Christ. Noah knew that Christ had not yet been born and that in order for God to keep His promise He would have to preserve His life and the life of His children during the flood. Christ was the lamb slain from the foundation of the world. If Christ had not made this pledge to die for the human race, there would never have been a second probation. It was only due to the love of Christ that Noah and his family were preserved in the earth.

VISIBLE EVIDENCES VERSUS FAITH

> Now faith is the substance of things hoped for, the evidence of things not seen. Hebrews 11:1

> Seest thou how faith wrought with his works, and by works was faith made perfect? James 2:22

In the days before the flood God commanded Noah to build a large visible Ark as an evidence of His saving love and mercy to reach the repentant sinner. For 120 years the Ark stood a visible witness against the wicked inhabitants of the earth, yet it did not cultivate a saving faith in those who saw it. Noah faithfully carried out the work God had given him to do and in trying to save others his own faith was established. Saving faith is no different today. When we do all that is in our power to save others we are in reality saving ourselves. While faith itself is not tangible, it will produce tangible results.

Fig. A7 – Noah's three sons.

A NEW BEGINNING

All human beings are made up of the same DNA but the variety of characteristics between races was all contained in the gene pool of Noah. It is also likely that when the people dispersed over the face of the earth after the destruction of Babel, the gene pool in the dispersed groups became narrower and more concentrated, resulting in the distinguishing features of all the different cultures we have today. Interestingly we see a reversal of this as the world is becoming more multicultural and national boundaries are being corroded away. The unique features of each race are beginning to blend.

DISPERSION OF THE DESCENDANTS OF THE SONS OF NOAH

> And God blessed Noah and his sons, and said unto them, Be fruitful, and multiply, and replenish the earth.
> Genesis 9:1

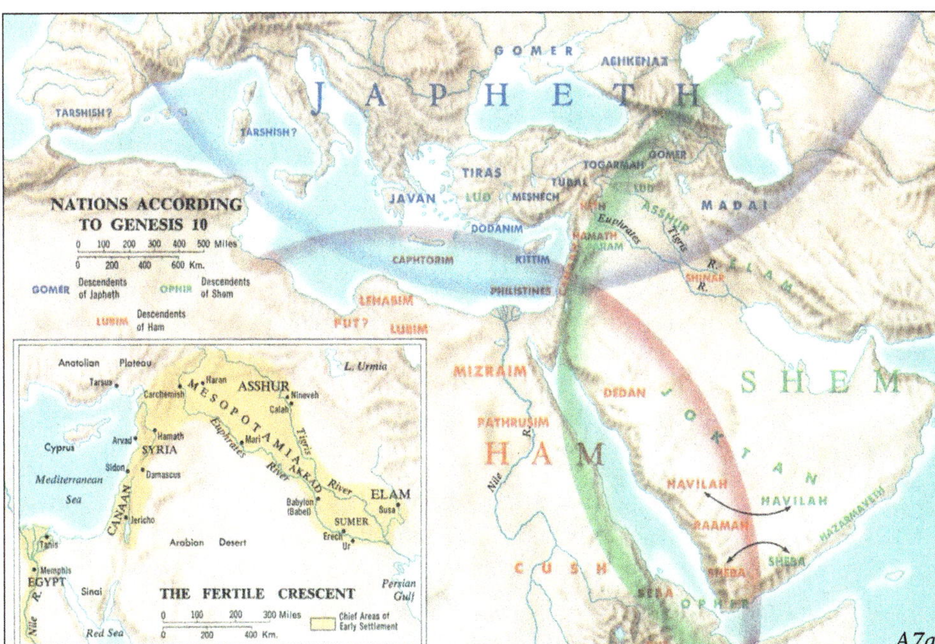

PART 2 - ARCHAEOLOGY AND GEOGRAPHICS OF THE ARK

An archaeological inquest into Noah's Ark on Mount Judi in Eastern Turkey

Noah's Ark is located in the politically volatile region of eastern Turkey close to the border of north-west Iran. The Ark itself rests just outside a small village called Uzengili which is 19 kilometres south-east of the city of Dogubayazit.

HISTORICAL ACCOUNTS OF THE ARK'S LANDING SITE

There are several historical accounts of where the Ark landed:

- The Bible records that the Ark came to land in the mountains of Ararat (plural). Genesis 8:4.
- The Koran states that the Ark came to land in the mountain of Al-Judi
- The Epic of Gilgamesh, recorded on both ancient Mesopotamian and Sumerian tablets describes the boat as coming to rest on the peak of Nisir.

The place where Noah's Ark came to rest fits all three descriptions. It is one of the sister mountains of Ararat; one of its peaks is called Mount Judi (Al-Judi); and the modern day village of Uzengili, located only 500 metres south-west of the Ark, was formerly called Nasir (Nisir).

WHY THE ARK DID NOT LAND ON MT ARARAT

Mount Ararat is a steep volcanic mountain which stands 5,137 metres high and 25 kilometres wide at the base. In the year 1840 there was a volcanic eruption which blew a gigantic hole out of the north-eastern side of the mountain. This triggered a landslide destroying several villages. Although Mt Ararat stands the highest mountain in the region today, it may not always have towered at such a great height. When an active volcano erupts it can grow upwards as lava spills forth hardening into new external layers. Therefore it is entirely possible that during the time of Noah, Mt Ararat was a much smaller mountain adding to its own height over several millennia through volcanic eruptions.

The Bible states that the Ark came to rest in the mountains (plural) of Ararat. This means that the Ark came to rest upon one of the mountains in the region of Ararat but not necessarily Mt Ararat itself.

THE LOCATION OF NOAH'S ARK

Uzengili is a small village located 19 kilometres south-east of Dogubayazit, a major centre in the Ağrı Province, the eastern-most district of Turkey. Mt Ararat, the largest volcanic cone on the continent of Asia, is approximately 25 kilometres north.

THE LANDING SITE OF THE ARK

After its treacherous voyage on the flooded earth, the Ark finally came to rest on Mount Judi in a tight cul-de-sac at the top of a valley which extends down towards the village of Uzengili. The highest point of Mount Judi is marked by a large limestone ridge located approximately 1 kilometre to the east of the landing site. This limestone ridge is called "The Wall of Heaven".

A11

MOUNT JUDI AND THE WALL OF HEAVEN

To the right of the limestone ridge are crescent shaped mountains creating a cul-de-sac which provided a safe port for the Ark, protecting it from strong winds and external elements. It is believed this site was the original resting place of the Ark when the waters subsided.

Fig. A12 – Kerensa beside the original landing site with the Wall of Heaven behind.

At one time there was an active volcano between the cul-de-sac and the wall of heaven which erupted. The subsequent mud and lava flow swept the Ark from its original landing site to its current location approximately 1.5 kilometres down the valley. The remains of petrified rib timbers from the hull of the Ark as well as man-made rock ballasts were found near the entrance of the cul-de-sac.

THE STONE STELA ENGRAVING

In the late 1970's a stone Stela was found erected on one of the peaks that form the cul-de-sac. The Stela was engraved with inscriptions in three ancient languages. Only one of the languages, ancient cuneiform, was translatable.

Also engraved upon the Stela was a panoramic view of the resting place of the Ark. It depicted a mountain standing adjacent to a limestone ridge near a boat with eight people in it. A raven was carved above the boat in two stages of flight. This

A13

A14

supports the biblical account of a raven flying back and forth for seven days until the waters were dried up off the earth (Genesis 8:7). Shortly after its discovery the Stela was taken apart and the stones were cemented into a boundary marker (see figure A15). Several years later this was disassembled and reconstructed into a new boundary marker with the engravings facing inward. By 1988, the structure had been destroyed.

Fig. A15 – On the Stela above the tail end of the Ark can be seen with a raven flying above it. The stone far right is inscribed with an ancient language.

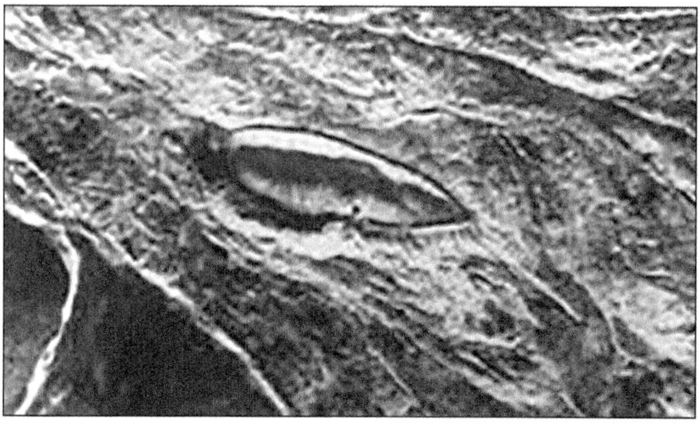

Fig. A16 – This aerial photograph was taken by Colonel Darupinar in 1959 while surveying the region. To his trained eye the Ark shape resembled a ship. From comparing satelite photos with the Stela we can see that the Ark was not square but built according to modern ship-building techniques.

THE TENDUREK VOLCANIC FORMATION

The engraving on the Stela reveals that an ancient volcano once stood between the limestone ridge and the Ark's landing site. This volcano, known as the *Tendurek formation* no longer exists today. But it does provide a vital clue as to how the Ark became dislodged from near the top of the mountain and came to rest at its present-day location 1.5 kilometres further down the mountain.

One theory is that when the Tendurek formation erupted, fissures opened up in the earth pouring forth rivers of mud. As the mud spilled over into the valley, the Ark was swept from its original landing site and carried down the mountain side where it impacted a large rock on the starboard (right) side. The mud continued to flow downhill swinging the Ark around approximately 200-220° but without dislodging it from the rock.

BIBLICAL PLACE NAMES

There are a number of places in the local area with names that date back to antiquity. These names reflect the story of the flood and suggest that the area was once submerged in water.

A	*Yigityatagi*	Heroes Anchorage	**E**	*Kargaconmaz*	The crow won't land
B	*Mahser*	The Last Judgment	**F**	*Daronynk*	Where the oars were reversed
C	*Mahsur*	Raised from the dead	**G**	*Nasar*	To make a presentation of sacrifice
D	*Ziyaret*	Voluntary Pilgrimage	**H**	*Al Judi*	The High Place

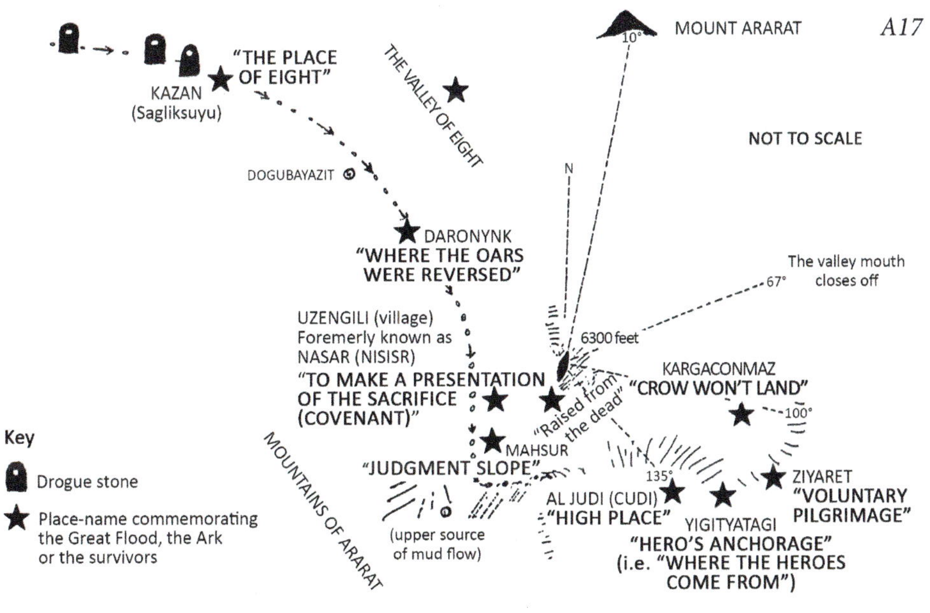

ARK FOUND IN 1959 AERIAL SURVEY

The boat shaped object was discovered in October 1959 by a Turkish pilot named Colonel Darupinar who was undertaking an aerial survey of the region. To his trained eye the boat shaped object gave the appearance of a man-made ship and was facing the wrong direction for it to be a natural geological formation formed by a mud-slide.

Fig. A18 – The boat formation was first brought to public attention the following year in a 1960 edition of Life Magazine.

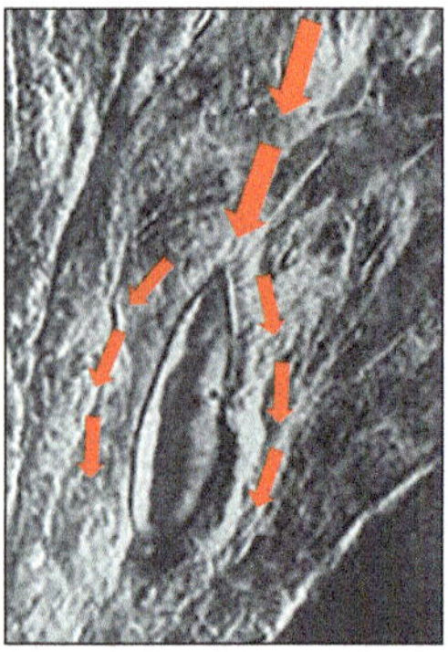

THE ARK IS NOT A NATURAL GEOLOGICAL FORMATION

The fact that the sharp ended bow is uphill from the rounded stern eliminates the possibility of this shape being formed on this mountain by mud-flow. In nature, the round end always faces into the mud-flow and the flow leaves at the sharp end.

Fig. A19 – Showing the direction of the mudflow around the Ark.

1978 EARTHQUAKE

In 1978 an earthquake raised the Ark out of the ground approximately five metres. There was no damage to nearby villages.

Fig. A20,A21– Before and after the earthquake of 1978.

Fig. A22,A23 – Before and after the earthquake of 1978.

24

25

26

A27

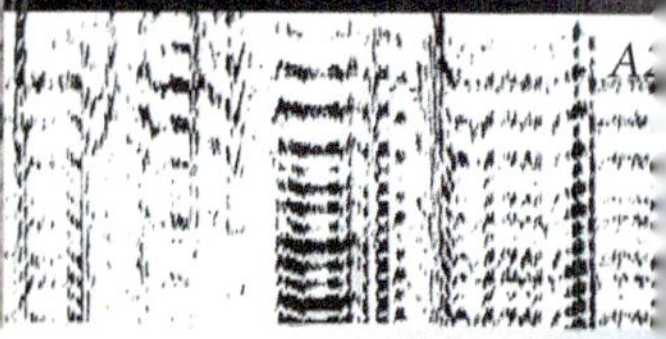

A30

SCANNING THE ARK

In the years 1985-1986 Bible researcher and explorer Ron Wyatt attracted academic interest in the Darupinar site and multiple scans were conducted by a team of professionals. Measurements were made of the arrangement of iron locations detected in the Ark using subsurface radar units, metal detectors, frequency generators, etc.

The subsurface scans revealed walls, chambers, a door near the south end, and ramps. There are chambers with deck support timbers intact along the western side. The model below illustrates the results of the scans.

Fig. A33,A34 – Two large round water tanks 4.27 metres high and 7.31 metres across with metal bands around them near the bow.

LENGTH OF THE ARK

> This is the fashion which thou shalt make it of: The length of the ark shall be three hundred cubits, the breadth of it fifty cubits, and the height of it thirty cubits.
> Genesis 6:15

Subsurface radar detected iron cross-sections at regular intervals, indicating the location of bulkheads. These locations were marked (see figures a31 & a32). The total length of the Ark was carefully measured using these results at 515 feet or 157 metres. The Egyptian cubit is 20.6 inches. 300 Egyptian cubits is equal to 515 feet which is the exact length of the Ark, as described in the Genesis account.

THE ARK A FEAT OF MATHEMATICAL ENGINEERING BRILLIANCE

515 feet (300 cubits) is 6,180 inches. This number is based on "*Phi*".

It was soon realised from the scans that the Ark was constructed using the mathematical formulas of *Phi* and *Pi*.

Pi is the ratio of a circle's circumference to its diameter and is expressed as 3.142 divided by 2.

Phi is a composite of golden rectangles that can be joined to form a logarithmic spiral as seen in giant galaxies, tiny shells and the inward curve of a wave when it breaks. It is also used by engineers in the construction of the hull of a ship. *Phi* is expressed as **1.618**. The golden rule of *Phi* is that each proceeding rectangle in the curve is 1.618 times greater than the one before it and this sequence forms a natural curve. (See figure A35.)

Fig. A35 – Fibonacci Logarithmic Spiral based on Phi.

A36

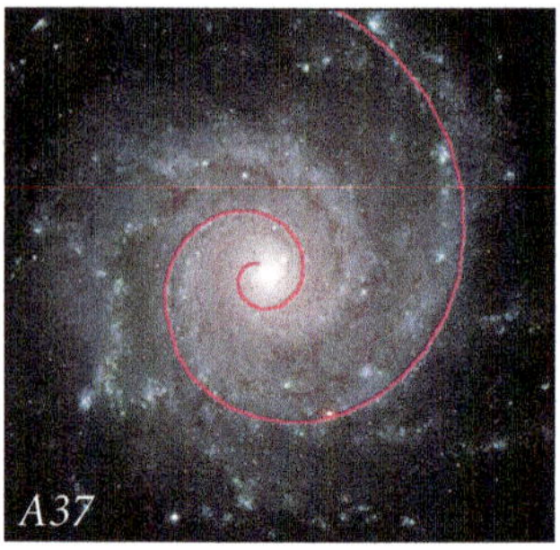

A37

The principle of "phi" was used in the designing of the Ark. Once the length and the required deck area were determined, Noah knew exactly how wide to built his vessel and where to locate the Moon Pool.

Phi is used today in the construction of ships hulls to minimise water turbulence. The ratios of Phi and Pi are evident in every major aspect of the Ark's construction. Precise mathematical relationships of this kind are not the result of chance. Yet here in this design there is not one relationship but five. There can be little doubt that this structure was built by man and whoever designed it applied principles of mathematics and hydrodynamics that were not fully known again for almost 5000 years.

If you subscribe a rectangle around the boat-shaped object, if you divide the actual area of the artefact into that rectangle you get 1.618 (Phi). If you say the length is 300 cubits and you divide that length into the area of the deck you get 49.7 cubits. Therefore the average width of the Ark is 50 cubits. Based on the dimensions I think this was the artefact. I think this was Noah's Ark.

Sam Windsor, Marine Engineer

THE ARK'S CONSTRUCTION BASED ON "PHI"

1.	The length of the Ark at Uzengili and the length of the Ark as recorded in the Bible are identical: **6180** inches.	**6180**
2.	The horizontal curve of the "bow" was on the spiral **6180**.	**6180**
3.	The length of the "first room" was greater than the width of the central "corridor" by a difference of **.6180**.	**6180**
4.	The length of the "second room" along the "corridor" was greater than three times the width of the "corridor" by a difference of **.6180**.	**6180**
5.	The difference between the position of the main transverse dividing "wall" and the total length of the formation was **.6180**.	**6180**
6.	If the Ark was built according to the ratio of **.6180**, and the average width was 50 cubits or 85.8333 feet, then we would expect the widest point of the Ark to be 138 feet. This is the exact measurement of the widest beam of the Ark at Uzengili.	**6180**
7.	The biblical height of the Ark was **618.0** inches	**6180**

DEPTH OF THE ARK

No depth measurements could be determined from the Ark. However marine engineering and naval architecture indicate an average depth of 30 cubits or 15.45 metres based on the following calculation by Sam Windsor:

> The total area inside of the "deck edge outline" was 7,112,113 square inches. The area of the deck is then the desired 6,350,400 square inches. This area, multiplied by 1.61803399 is the area of the circumscribed rectangle or 10,275,163 square inches. The rectangle width (and maximum beam of the vessel) is this larger area (10,275,163) divided by the desired length of 6180 inches. This was how Noah decided how wide to build his vessel. The width of the rectangle is 1663 inches, 79.17 great Babylonian cubits, 80.73 Egyptian Cubits or 138 1/2 feet!
>
> Genesis records the depth to be 30 cubits. 1663 divided by the square of phi (2.6180), produces 635 inches, 30.24 great Babylonian cubits or 30.82 Egyptian cubits. A depth of 30 cubits would agree with the Genesis account.
>
> The average width of the Ark was computed at 49.85 cubits. The probable average depth was about 30 cubits. If the actual average depth were 30.8 cubits, the average width versus the average depth was another phi ratio.
>
> Sam Windsor

AVERAGE WIDTH OF THE ARK

In 1991 Sam Windsor, an American marine engineer, prepared a computer program of the Ark artefact, and entered the data from the survey. He calculated the average width to be 1,027 inches, or 85.6 feet., or 49.85 cubits. 49.85 cubits is very close to 50 cubits, which is the width dimension given in Genesis.

THE VOLUME OF THE ARK

> This boat-shaped formation was found to be, at maximum beam, 137.3 feet wide, or approximately 80.71 cubits. The Genesis account has the Ark's width at 50 cubits, seemingly in contradiction. But in ancient times the width of a boat was specified in terms of its storage capacity or the cubic volume of water it displaced which had nothing to do with its true shape.
>
> This means that the Genesis account is a volumetric measurement of a boat-shaped artefact. This is normal in naval architecture. In our age, nobody cites the size of a vessel by length, but rather by tons of displaced water. This, too, is a volumetric measure. Such is the method of measurement for volume for sea-going vessels.
>
> Donald Patten

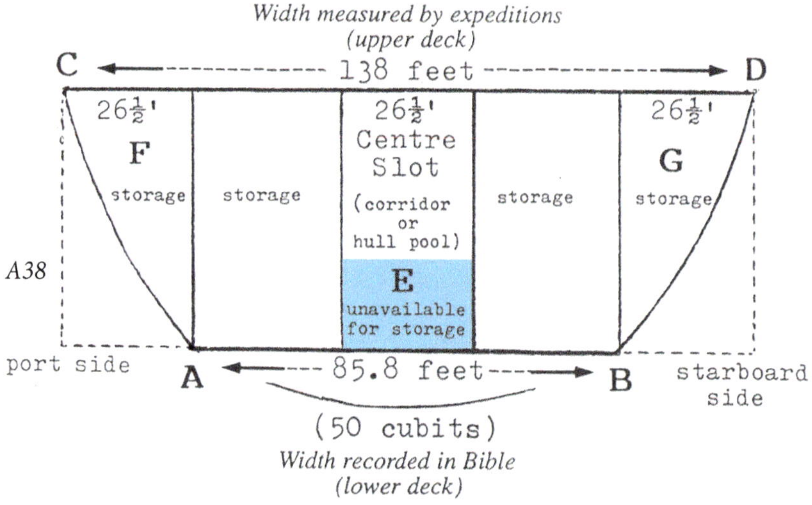

MOON-POOL

> The presence, size and location of the moon pool indicates extremely sophisticated vessel design.
>
> Sam Windsor

A rectangular hole was found in the hull of the ship. The experts identified this as a "moon-pool" which served the purpose of:

NOTE: Please note that the widest beam measurement taken by Donald Patten (137.3 feet) differs slightly to the widest beam measurement taken by Sam Windsor (138.5 feet) by approximately 1 foot. This is because Donald Patten took his measurement from the second widest beam.

- Hydraulic brake – to slow the Ark down.
- Sewerage system – as rainwater was permitted to fall into the Ark it would have flushed out the animal compartments and all the residue through the moon-pool.
- Air ventilation system – the water moving up and down inside the moon pool would have been like a piston moving up and down, in and out forcing air into the ship.
- Ballast – stabilising the ship in rough seas.

THE ARK WAS NOT A BOX

A box is only ¼ as stable as a tapered boat. Had the Ark been a long rectangle it would have capsized in a rough sea... As the hull shape becomes more rectangular, the metacentre rises so high that even small rolls result in tremendous force righting the vessel... A reed raft in the shape of the artefact southeast of Dogubayazit, Turkey, is four times more stable than is the traditional 50 cubit beam.

Sam Windsor

THE DESIGN OF THE ARK WAS SUCCESSFUL

The design of the Ark was successful. The shape provided maneuverability, stability, low structural stress, good sea keeping characteristics, forced air ventilation (wave action in the moon pool), overboard discharge without side scuppers (holes in the sides, or freeing ports, with swinging plates), etc. It employed iron in its construction but avoided long electrical conductors from roof to sea.

Sam Windsor

SIZE COMPARISON

A39

Queen Mary 2 - 345 metres

Titanic - 269 metres

Noah's Ark - 137 metres, double decker bus and an elephant

A4

A41

A4

A44,A45

A4

EVIDENCE OF VERTICAL RIB TIMBERS

Fig. A46 – Along the sides of the Ark vertical rib timbers are exposed at regular intervals. Remarkably the vertical timbers are still erect preserving the original shape of the boat.
Fig. A48 – Below is a sketch of the vertical timbers at the bow on the port side.

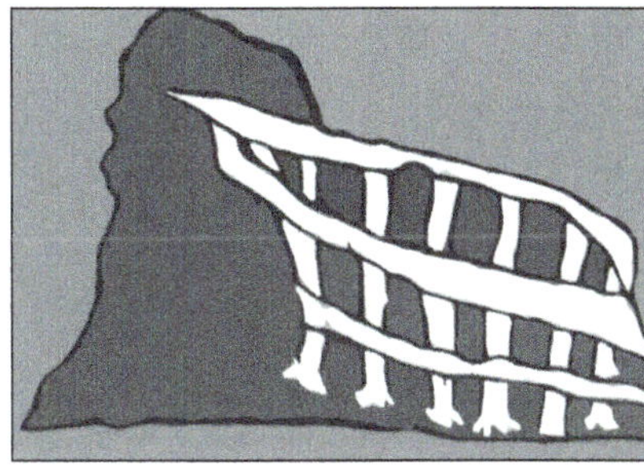

FISSURES

Fig. A47 – Fissures or cracks between the vertical rib timbers are perpendicular to the mudflow going around the Ark. This is evidence that the Ark is not a natural formation.

A50

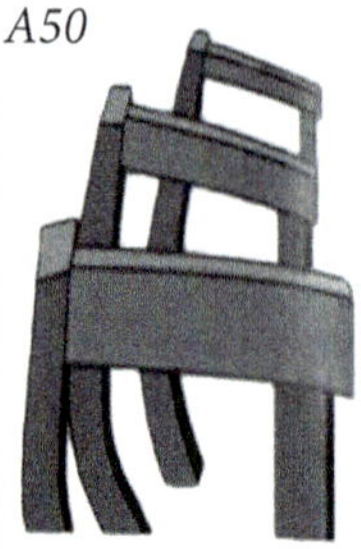

EVIDENCE OF HORIZONTAL DECK TIMBERS

The ends of petrified deck support timbers can be seen protruding out of the external walls of the Ark at regular intervals. Four internal protrusions on the inside wall of the port side once supported beams which extended out to the middle of the deck. There are corresponding protrusions on the other side. The petrified remains of five vertical posts extending along the port side from the stern have also been measured at regular intervals.

A51

A52

A53

56
A57
A58
59

LAMINATED WOOD SPECIMEN

> Make thee an ark of gopher wood; rooms shalt thou make in the ark, and shalt pitch it within and without with pitch. Genesis 6:14

In 1986 a piece of laminated deck timber about one foot long was located approximately one metre below the surface. The specimen was taken back to the United States and analysed at Galbraith Laboratories Inc.. The wood specimen contained traces of organic carbon which proved that it was once made of living matter which has since turned to stone through petrification. See figures A61 and A62.

9/16/87 Noahs Ark Sample			
	% Calcium	0.073	
	% Iron	13.04	
	% Carbon	0.71	0.64
	% CO_3 calculated as Carbon	0.0081	

A60

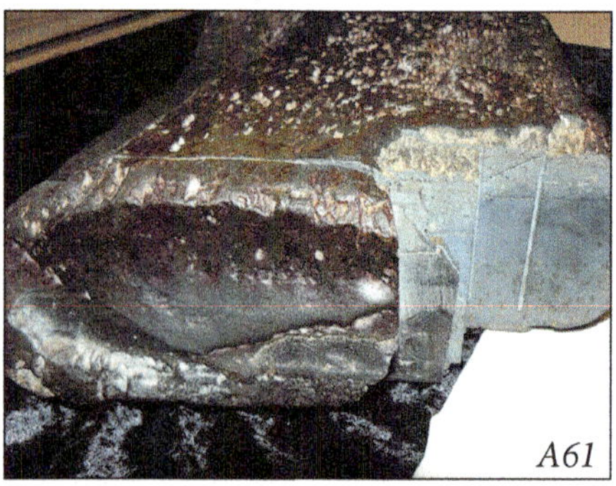

A61

A62

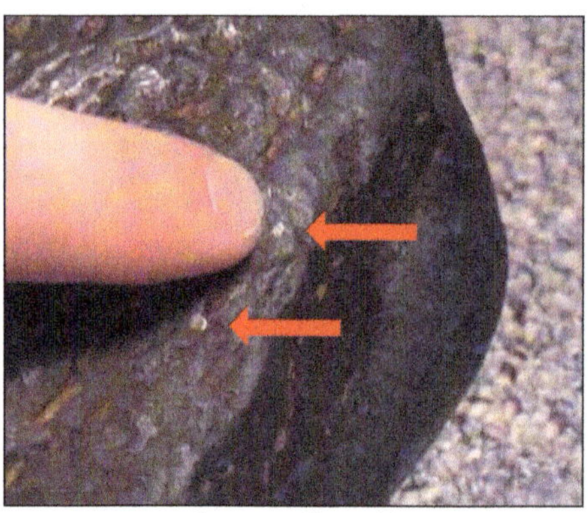

Fig. A63 – Nails are still visible.

PITCH

Berosus was a Chaldean priest, philosopher and astronomer for the King of Uruk in modern day Iraq. In 290 B.C. he was taken captive by one of Alexander the Great's generals and was forced to reveal the location of the Ark. In his description he mentioned that pilgrims visited the Ark and carried off pieces of bitumen. This is evidence that the Ark was accessible, unlike Mt Ararat which is steep and dangerous to ascend.

> It is said there is still some part of this ship in Armenia at the mountain of the Cordyaeans; and that some people carry off pieces of the bitumen (pitch), which they take away, and use chiefly as amulets for the averting of mischiefs.
>
> Berosus the Chaldean

A65

METAL ALLOYS ON THE ARK

Tubal-Cain an instructor of every craftsman in bronze and iron. Genesis 4:22

The Ark is laden with evidence that metal was used in its construction. A crescent shaped washer was discovered and analysed at Galbrath Laboratories in 2001. It was found to contain high levels of iron, titanium and alumina. Some of these metal alloys occur in nature but not in such high concentrations in the shape of a man-made washer or rivet. See figures A67 and A68.

SAMPLE ID	LAB ID	ANALYSIS	RESULT(S)	
Ark-Rivet	I-1897	Iron	8.38	%
		Aluminum	8.35	%
		Titanium	1.59	%

A66

A67

A68

A69

A7

A7

A71-A73

A74

A76

A7

In 2001 the metal remains of a rivet shaft was also analysed at Galbraith Laboratories and showed high traces of iron, aluminium, titanium and magnesium. The mix of these metals does not occur naturally. See figure A78.

SAMPLE ID	LAB ID	ANALYSIS	RESULT(S)	
Ark-Rod	J-9175	Aluminum	8.08	%
		Iron	8.24	%
		Titanium	1.34	%
		Magnesium	3.82	%

A78

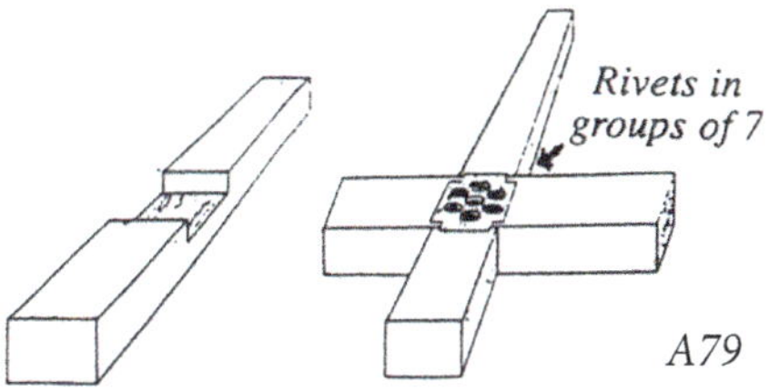

A79

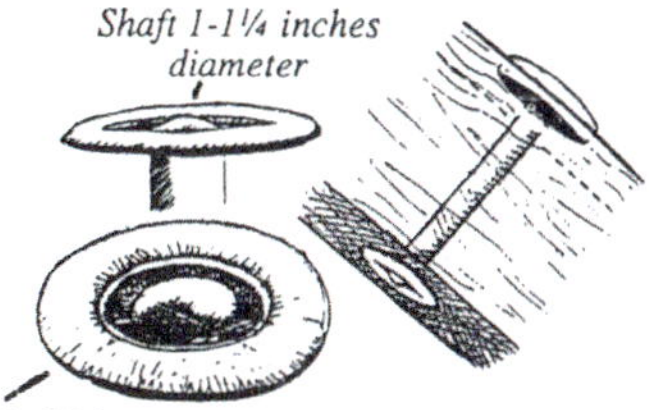

A80

Other important finds included:

- A metal plate which would have contained seven rivets to fasten the intersection of vertical and horizontal beams. See figure A69.
- Metal caps on vertical posts on the exterior walls of the Ark. The metal caps were struck while hot leaving an X imprint. See figure A74.

According to Genesis 4:22 the people living before the flood had a knowledge of metallurgy and we can logically conclude that these skills would have been used in the construction of the Ark. These metal objects appear to be special markers that God has preserved as evidence that this is the Ark.

FINDINGS OF THE EXPERTS

Dr John Baumgardner, a physicist at Los Alamos Laboratories during the 1980's, confirmed that there was iron on the Ark. While holding a portion of a broken angle bracket in his fingers he stated:

> It's striking in the fact of its angular character. It has some preferred planes on the object on the outside as well as the inside. This inner portion appears to be silica replacement of something. This would represent, if the interpretation is correct, a portion of an angle bracket and we see a corner of it here. It's interesting that it apparently still displays the grain structure of the iron. I would say it has the character of cast iron. It appears this is pure iron oxide here, this outer portion.
>
> I think that there is a zero probability that it's a natural object. It certainly is a man-made object. This has to be a man made structure, it's full of metal. The metal has a regular pattern to it and the size of the thing and the shape of the thing is such that it's almost certainly a large boat. Dr. John Baumgardner

David Fasold was a marine salvage expert who conducted a geological survey of the Ark in 1985-86 with a metal detector and a molecular frequency generator. He was instrumental in locating the discrete positions of iron masses approximately 53cms apart in lines, both longitudinal and transverse proving that a man-made grid-like pattern of iron existed on the Ark. Stakes were driven at the loci of the iron and surveyor's ribbon was laid on the ground over the stakes. The distance between the ribbon centre lines were measured where the transverse lines intersected longitudinal lines. Only iron based metal locations were used for this measuring activity, the intersections demarking what would have been former beam and bulkhead supports (upright partition between compartments in ships) laid out in clear geometric patterns.

> There are approximately 5,400 discrete iron masses on the ship. While four are quite large, approximately 1.44m in diameter, the majority are small. David Fasold reported 85% pure manganese nodules were found in the Ark. The maximum purity of natural manganese nodules is 25%. Manganese of greater purity can be obtained only by electrolysis. Sam Windsor

Sam Windsor identified the Ark was patterned after a modern boat frame design.

> The modern lofting procedure [pattern] is that used for "balanced foil shapes" in NACA (National Aeronautical Civil Administration) curves. See "Theory of Wing Sections" by Ira H. Abbott and Albert E. Von Doenhoff, Dover Publications, Inc., New York, N.Y. The procedure produces a striking similarity to the dimensions of the arrangement of the steel masses in the formation. The similarity is so striking, in fact, as to cast into absurdity any notion that chance or "natural causes" are involved in the shape of the formation. Sam Windsor

> "Chance" is as good an explanation for this formation as it is for an orangutan being able to assemble an operating battleship from spare parts. Sam Windsor

Joe Rosetta, Vice President of Geo Survey Systems, when reviewing a scan of the Ark stated:

> These lines are too periodic to be random natural type interfaces. It must be a man-made structure. Joe Rosetta

THE REMAINS OF A POTSHERD

In 1998 a potsherd was discovered near the Ark with an engraving of a man with a hammer wearing a crown. There is an ancient cuneiform inscription on the crown which is translated "Noah". (Figures A81,A82.)

On the reverse side of the potsherd there is an engraving of a man releasing two birds. (Figures A83,A84.)

The ancient potsherd is evidence that pilgrims once came to visit the Ark on Mount Judi and that souvenirs were sold there.

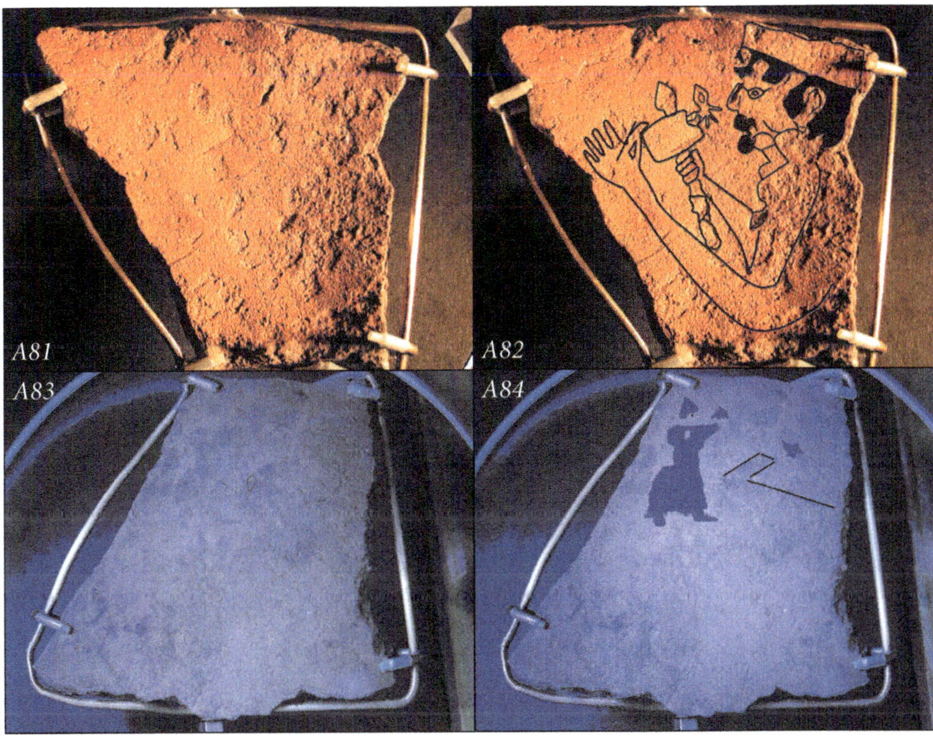

A81 A82 A83 A84

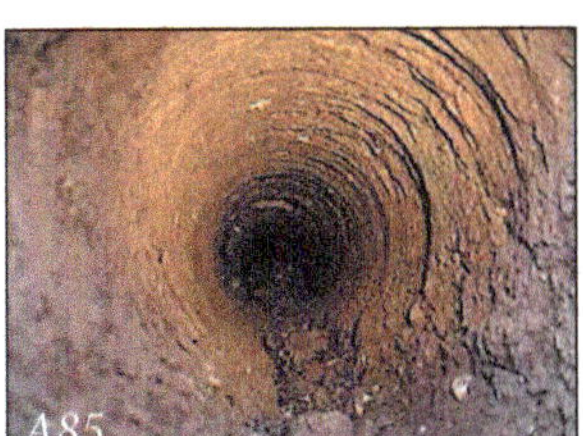

A85

FOSSILISED ANIMAL REMAINS

The remains of a petrified deer antler, large wild cat hair and an animal dropping were extracted from a hole drilled into the belly of the ship. This is evidence that exotic animals were carried on the Ark.

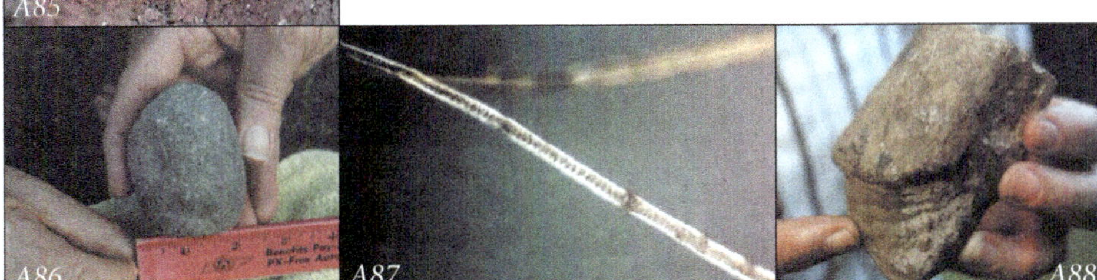

A86 A87 A88

A90

Government confirms: "This is Noah's Ark"

A91

A92

NOAH'S ARK NATIONAL PARK

In 1987 the Turkish Government opened Noah's Ark National Park, officially recognising the Ark. A sign was erected at the bottom of Mount Judi beside the highway to direct tourists to the Ark. The sign reads "*Nuhun Gemisi*" in Turkish which means "Noah's Boat" in English (figure A93).

The visitors centre hosts a display of petrified shells and corals found on the summit of Mount Judi, which is over 2000 metres above sea level. This is evidence that the mountain was once completely submerged under water and that the flood was of world-wide extent. A collection of fossilised pieces of wood found on the Ark are also exhibited (figure A98).

A93

FOSSIL EVIDENCE

In 2008 several coral samples and a shell were photographed at the top of Mount Judi about 1 kilometre above the visitor's centre, towards the peak.

A94

A95

A96

A97

A98

THE AMOMUM PLANT

There is a plant that grows on the site of the Ark that does not grow anywhere else in the world. In ancient times it was said this plant possessed unique qualities that would make old men youthful. The Jewish historian Josephus wrote of the Amoma plant in Turkey and it is also described in the Epic of Gilgamesh.

> When Monobazus was grown old, and saw that he had but a little time to live, he had a mind to come to the sight of his son before he died. So he sent for him, and embraced him after the most affectionate manner, and bestowed on him the country called Carra; it was a soil that bare amomum in great plenty: there are also in it the remains of that Ark, wherein it is related that Noah escaped the deluge, and where they are still shown to such as are desirous to see them. Josephus, *Antiquities*, Book 20, Chap. 2, Para. 2

The Epic of Gilgamesh is a legend recorded on several ancient tablets. In the story, the warrior Gilgamesh, goes in search of a man named Uta-Napishtim to learn the secret of eternal life. Uta-Napishtim (a man who survived a world-wide deluge with his family), then tells Gilgamesh of a plant that will restore him to his youthful condition which, after finding it at the last, Gilgamesh loses to a wily serpent.

> (Then answered) Uta-Napishtim to him, (yea) [to] Gilgamesh [spake he]:
> "Gilgamesh, (hither) didst come (all) aweary with rowing; (O, tell me),
> What shall I give thee (as a gift) wherewith to return to thy country?
> Gigamesh, I will reveal thee a hidden matter... I'll tell thee:
> There is a plant like a thorn with its root (?) [deep down in the ocean],
> Like unto those of the briar (in sooth) its prickles will scratch [thee],
> (Yet) if thy hand reach this plant, [thou'lt surely find life (everlasting)]."
> (Then) when Gilgamesh heard this, he loosen'd [his girdle about him],
> Bound heavy stones [on his feet], which dragg'd him down to the sea-deeps,
> [Found he the plant]; as he seized on the plant, its prickles did scratch him.
> Cut he the heavy stones [from his feet] that again it restore him unto its shore
> Gilgamesh spake to him, (yea), to the boatman Ur-shanabi (this-wise):
> "(Nay, but) this plant is a plant of great wonder (?), Ur-shanabi," said he,
> "Whereby a man may attain his desire – I'll take it to Erech,
> The high walled and give it to eat [unto...].
> 'Greybeard-who-turneth-to-man-in-his-prime' is its name and I'll eat it.
> I myself, that again I may come to my youthful condition.
>
> *Epic of Gilgamesh*, Tablet 11, Column 1, Lines 263- 282. Translated by R. Compbell Thompson

THE BABYLONIAN FLOOD TABLETS

Several clay tablets from Iraq, housed in the British Museum, recount the story of the flood.

The Epic of Gilgamesh was a poem written well before the Iliad of Homer. It is the oldest poem ever found and has been recorded on multiple clay tablets by several successive ancient empires including the Akkadians, the Hittites and the Assyrians. It was likely committed to clay sometime between 2750 and 2500 B.C.. The saga involves the transformation of a bad king into a good one, a friendship between two men, and the quest for eternal life. Despite being written from a pagan perspective, the text supports the Biblical account of a global deluge.

A100

The Flood Tablet - Tablet No. 11

The Flood Tablet (7th Century B.C.), is perhaps the most famous of all the cuneiform tablets. It is the eleventh tablet of the Gilgamesh Epic, and describes how the gods sent a flood to destroy the world. Like Noah, Uta-Napishtim was forewarned and built an Ark to house and preserve living things. After the flood he sent out birds to look for dry land.

The Yale Tablet - Tablet No. 3

Clay tablet reproducing an episode of the Epic of Gilgamesh (Old Babylonian period, ca. 1800 B.C.). The Yale Gilgamesh Tablet is one of the most important manuscripts of this epic poem from ancient Iraq.

A101

A102

The Epic of Atra-hasis

Old Babylonian, written in year 12 of Ammisaduqa, king of Babylon 1635 B.C.. This tablet is one of three which contained the Epic of Atrahasis, hero of the Babylonian flood story. It recounts how the gods, after several attempts to destroy mankind, which had been making too much noise for their comfort, eventually arranged for a flood to drown the world. The god of wisdom, Enki, surreptitiously warned his devotee Atrahasis of what was to happen, thereby enabling him to prepare a boat in which he, his household and his animals were saved.

CRYPTIC SECRET BY BEROSUS

In 290 B.C., Berosus the Chaldean, high priest to the king of Uruk (modern-day Iraq), formed a cryptic teaser which contained the co-ordinates for the Ark's location.

Berosus said, "The Ark is five stades in length and two stades in breadth."

In ancient times a right angle triangle would be used to describe the geographic location of an object.

Decoding the crypt

The"stades" Berosus referred to are in fact two angles of a right angle triangle.

The "5" ratio is the biggest and represents the 90° angle.

The "2" ratio is smaller and represents the 36° angle.

The "3" ratio [5 - 2 = 3] is therefore [90° - 36° = 54°] the 54°angle.

The Persian prime meridian at Persepolis

During the time of Berosus the prime meridian went through the Persian capital, Persepolis (in modern-day Iran). The Tomb of King Darius was built beside the Persian prime meridian.

When Berosus gave the co-ordinates for the right-angle triangle, he used the area of King Darius' tomb as the starting point for the 90° angle of the right angle triangle.

The Persian prime meridian on the world map is 52°50' E (longitude) which we take as the commencement point for calculating the Ark's longitude.

In his cryptic teaser, Berosus converted the length of Noah's Ark in feet to minutes of the sun's arc west of the Persian prime meridian.

Calculating the longitude

300 Egyptian cubits = 515 feet or 515 minutes [515/60 = 8°35'] of the sun's arc west of Persepolis. Therefore 52°50' E - 8°35' E = 44°15' E. This co-ordinate is the longitude for Noah's Ark.

Two ways of calculating the latitude

The latitude of the Tomb of king Darius is 30°00'N. When you add the length of Noah's Ark to the height of the Ark you get [515 feet + 51 feet = 566 feet]. Converting 566 feet to minutes is 9°26' [566/60 = 9°26']. By adding 9°26' N to 30°00' N you arrive at the latitude of Noah's Ark which is 39°26' N.

In the right angle triangle the longitude of [44°15' E] would be intercepted by a line of 36° originating from the tomb of king Darius [52°50' E; 30°00' N]. This also arrives at a latitude of [39°26' N] on the world map.

The co-ordinates [44°15' E; 39°26' N] are therefore the co-ordinates of the Ark. Berosus' crypt proves that the ancients knew that the world was round and had calculated the circumference of the earth as 360° as we do today. See Isaiah 40:22.

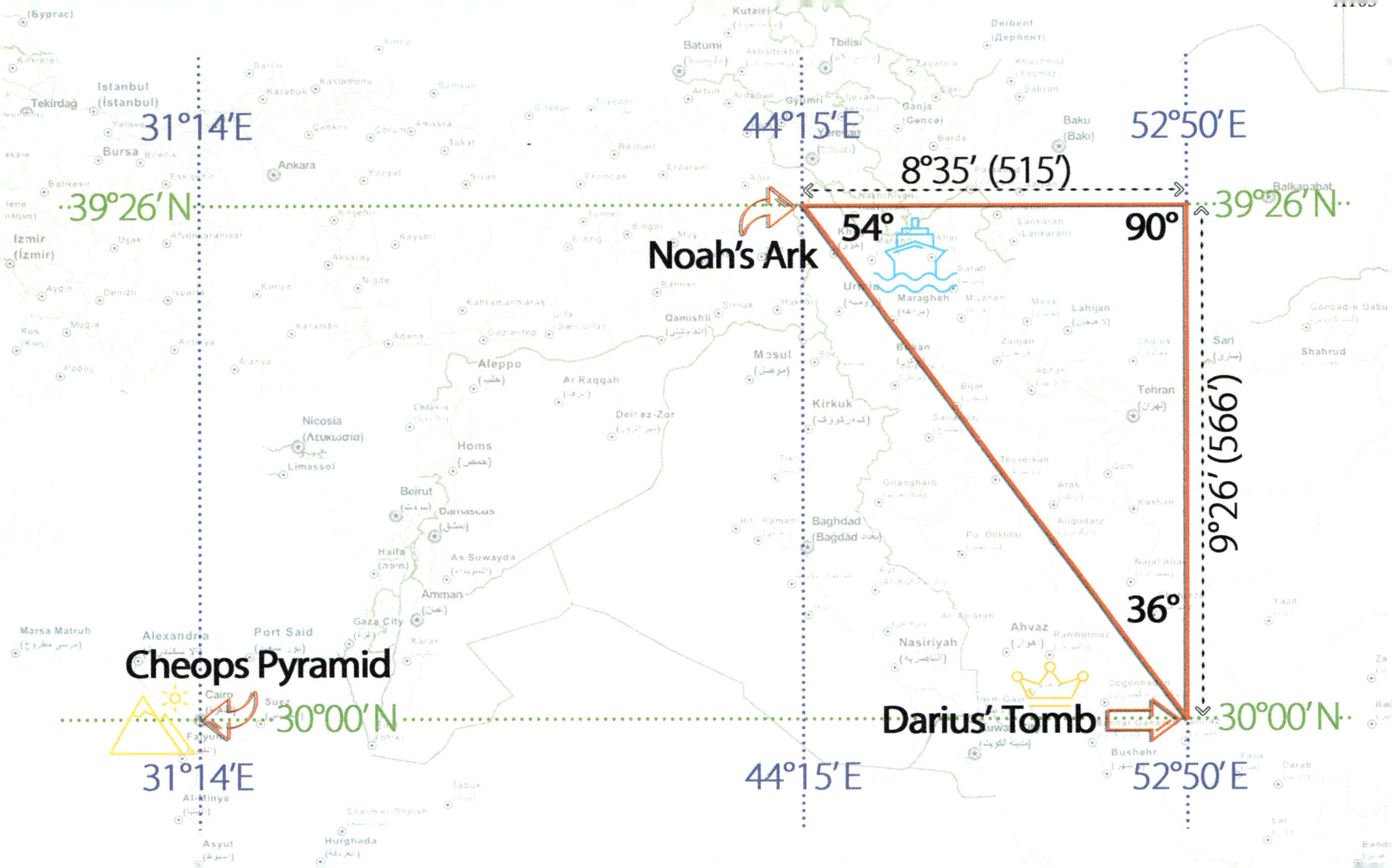

31°14′E
44°15′E
52°50′E
8°35′ (515′)
39°26′N
39°26′N
Noah's Ark
54°
90°
9°26′ (566′)
36°
Cheops Pyramid
30°00′N
Darius' Tomb
30°00′N
31°14′E
44°15′E
52°50′E

THE CHEOPS PYRAMID IN LOCATION TO THE ARK

Persians and Babylonians

The Persians buried their kings an Ark's length and an Ark's height (in minutes of the sun's arc west) from Noah's Ark. This means the ancient builders of Persepolis knew the location of the Ark.

Egyptians

The Cheops Pyramid at Giza is located on the same latitude as the tomb of King Darius 30°00′ N and is located an Ark's height and length [515 feet + 51 feet = 566 feet] from the latitude of the Ark [39°26 N]. This is no coincidence. The Egyptians built the Cheops pyramid in reference to the location of Noah's Ark. (Figure A103.)

The Cheops Pyramid

The Cheops Pyramid is located in the centre of the world's land-mass. If the earth is divided into four quarters originating at Cheops, the land-mass in each quarter is the same. Evidently, after the earth was divided in the days of Peleg the ancients surveyed the entire earth.

Cheops pyramid built on the mathematical ratio of "Phi"

> While Fibonacci is credited with the "discovery" of the golden ratio, the number has long been known to appear in at least one other place on earth as a monument to ancient technology. This unique number can be obtained by dividing the area of the surfaces of the Great Pyramid of Giza by the area of the pyramid's base. (The perimeter of that monument, when divided by its height gives the value of 2 times *pi*. There is a slight discrepancy between the values of *pi* and *phi* produced by assuming all surfaces are "flat planes". This discrepancy was eliminated by the builders when they dished [con-caved] the surfaces slightly to increase the surface area.) Sam Windsor

EARTH DIVIDED IN THE DAYS OF PELEG

> Unto Eber were born two sons: the name of one was Peleg; for in his days was the earth divided; and his brother's name was Joktan. Genesis 10:25

Only a few hundred years after the flood, Nimrod (the great grandson of Noah through the line of Ham), built the tower of Babel and attempted to unify the earth's inhabitants in an apostate religion. God placed a check on this rebellion by confounding the languages of the people so that they were scattered abroad. (Genesis 11:6-9.)

As the families removed further from the centre of civilisation, the gene pool became more limited. There were less people to intermix and breed with so the genetics became more concentrated. Also, as they proceeded further from civilisation, less knowledge of technology and civilisation was retained in their memory.

During the life-time of Peleg (the great, great grandson of Noah through the line of Shem), the earth, which was one great central land mass, was divided and broken up into seven continents. This effectually scattered the people.

FLOOD LEGENDS

There are numerous stories of the flood found in legends and myths throughout the world which have been handed down from antiquity. Estimates range from 300 to as many as 80,000. The majority of these include the account of people being saved in a boat. While the accounts differ according to the local cultures and beliefs, they do testify to the fact that there once was a great flood.

The Greeks

The ancient Greek myth *Deucalion* tells the story of the son of Prometheus and his wife Pyrrha, who were the only survivors after the Greek God Zeus punished mankind by sending a flood. They sailed in a box for nine days, which after the ninth day, rested upon a mountain called Parnassus, which is a mountain chain in the middle of Greece.

The Native Americans

The Cherokee Indians tell of a dog that warned his master about a coming flood. The dog instructed him to build a boat and put in it all that he would save, before a great rain comes and floods the land.

An Alaskan tribe, the Tlinget, remember a great flood which covered all their homes. They saved themselves by making a great raft by tying all their boats together until a magician ordered the sea to calm and the flood to dry up.

The Acagchememe Indians of Southern California have several songs that refer to a great deluge that filled the valleys and covered the mountains destroying nearly all the human race, except for a few who were saved at the top of a mountain.

The Indigenous Australians

One tribe in New South Wales has an oral tradition passed down from generation to generation which describes how their ancestor spirit (who created everything and gave life) got mad because they broke his laws. In his wrath he sent a cyclone and rain until the whole earth was flooded except for the top of a hill. Everyone drowned except for a few survivors who made it to the top of the hill.

The Chinese Language

The story of creation, the flood and the teachings of the Gospel are embedded in the Chinese language. The following are examples:

洪	=	氵	+	共	(	廾	+	一	+	八	)
Flood		*Water*		*Total*		*Together*		*Earth*		*Eight*	

船	=	舟	+	八	+	口
Large Boat		*Vessel*		*Eight*		*People*

義	=	羊	+	我	(	七	+	手	)
Righteous-ness		*Sheep*		*Me*		*Knife*		*Hand*	

Left – Kerensa beside a drogue stone 2 metres high, 1.4 metres at its widest point and 0.60 metres thick at its base.

Opposite page:

Top right – the first anchor stone cut loose on a small hill to the north of Sagliksuyu. The hole at the top of the stone is broken, clearly exposing the drill curve.

Centre left – drogue stone located north-east of the village.

Centre right – a local village boy standing next to two broken drogue stones that have been used as tomb-stones in their cemetery.

Bottom right – Most famous drogue stone. Local village children playing around it.

ANCHOR STONES

Sagliksuyu is a small Kurdish village in the region of Kazan, located approximately 10 kilometres north-west of the city of Dogubayazit. In 1977 several large anchor stones were found in the area of the village. It is believed that there were up to 24 of these drogue stones that were tied to the bottom of the Ark.

Anchor stones

The Bible states in Genesis 7:24 that the waters prevailed on the earth for an hundred and fifty days and that after this period the waters abated or calmed. The anchor stones in the region are an evidence that the Ark entered a safe haven of calmer waters in the valley of the mountains of Ararat.

The use of anchor stones

> In ancient times anchor stones were used to stabilise boats in rough seas. As the boat was being pushed forward, the surface area of the anchor stones being trailed through the water restricted the movement of the boat so that the line was always taut.
>
> David Fasold

The special design of anchor stones

Anchor stones have a hole at one end for a rope and they have a special shape for minimising turbulence through the water.

Visited by religious pilgrims

For thousands of years religious pilgrims visited this region of Ararat. It was known that these anchor stones were related to the story of the Ark of Noah.

105

106

A107

108

CURVED HOLES IN THE ANCHOR STONES

The distinguishing feature of an anchor stone is the drilled hole at the top. The curved drill holes in the anchor stones in the area of Kazan are especially unique because they were drilled on an angle of curvature in relation to the size, weight and density of each stone. The smaller stones, for example had tighter curved holes with a smaller radius to keep the rope taut underwater. The larger stones had slightly larger holes on less of a curvature to achieve the same effect. Additionally, the inner part of the hole was larger than the outer so that when a knot was placed in the centre of the hole the water would cause the knot to swell to ensure the rope did not slide. The curved drill holes also prevented the ropes from fraying.

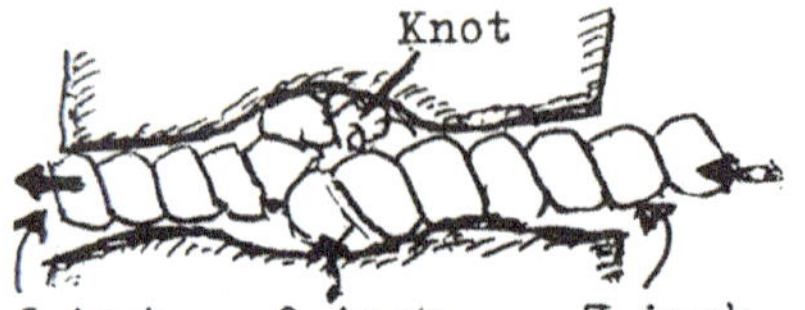

A109

Expert opinion

Sam Windsor was a nationally recognised expert in ship structures and fluid dynamics. He specialised in determining the cause of maritime accidents and in an interview he gave his qualified opinion on the anchor stones at Kazan:

> There are curved drilled holes in the rock. I don't know how we would do it. We only see curved drilled rock in one other place of the world and that is the Mayan temples in Central America. The holes are drilled in curves through the thick end and the holes vary in diameter. It's interesting that the hole diameters correspond to the size of the stone. If the stone is a 4 tonne stone I measured a 3 inch diameter hole on a 9 inch radius of curvature. But when the diameter was 4 ½ inches the stone I was looking at was about 10 tonnes and the radius of the curvature of the hole was 12 inches. Sam Windsor

A110

What they would have looked like

The scans of Noah's Ark showed several beams protruding out from the stern. The anchor stones would have been secured by a rope to these beams.

The holes of the anchor stones were drilled at the top, to the left, right or centre depending on their position underneath the boat.

Conclusion

The anchor stones at Sagliksuyu provide yet another evidence because they are unique in the world and could only be the right dimensions for the Ark.

111

A112

113

114

A115

THE VILLAGE OF SAGLIKSUYU

The remains of an ancient wall

Remnants of an ancient wall that once fortified the village still remain. The stones used in the construction of the wall are too large and heavy for modern day humans to lift. The ancient wall once had a ceramic mural of the Noah's Ark flood story. Tiny fragments of the tiles can still be found scattered amidst the stone rubble in Sagliksuyu. The local villagers keep a number of these tiles in their homes.

Two large stones with a human figure engraved upon them were removed from the top portion of the wall by the villagers. See images A119 and A123.

A116

A117

A118

Ancient building

In 1977 an ancient building was discovered at the foot of the hills to the north-east of the village. The building had thick stone walls approximately ninety centimetres in depth. The windows were narrow on the inside, funnelling out wide on the outside. Shortly after the building was surveyed it was destroyed, leaving only a foundation of rubble.

Noah's wife

The Bible does not name Noah's wife, however according to the book of Jasher, Noah married a woman called Naamah. This book records that Noah refrained from taking a wife because he knew the deluge was coming. But God instructed him to take a wife anyway and beget children. He was 498 years old at the time he married Naamah, who was 580 years old.

The tomb-stone and grave of Noah's wife

Beside the ruined building lie the remains of an elongated trench approximately five metres long, two metres wide and one metre deep. In 1977 there was a tombstone at this site which had an engraving on it of a rainbow encircling eight people and a boat riding upon a wave (see figure A117). Seven people on the tombstone had their eyes open except for Noah's wife whose head was bowed down with her eyes shut. As she was the only one with her eyes closed it is believed this was her grave.

119

A120

121

122

A123

Naamah's grave looted

The find was immediately reported to antiquity and that very night the grave and all its contents were looted. All that remains of the grave today is the trench. While none of the grave's contents, including the location of a sarcophagus can be confirmed, various finger bones found beside the grave indicate that Naamah was approximately 12 feet (3.7m) tall.

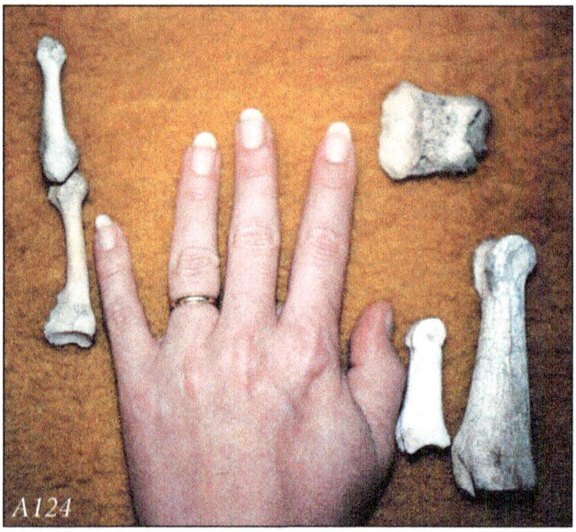
A124

Child's thumb bone

The bone close to the lady's thumb belonged to a child. Anthropologists can tell this was a child's thumb because it hasn't developed properly at the join. The thumb bone next to the child's bone is three times the size. This gives an indication of how large these people were.

Large female skull

At the time of the discovery in 1977, a large female skull twice the size of a woman's skull today, appeared in the foyer of a hotel in Dogubayazit. It was showcased behind a glass screen for one year before it suddenly vanished. Another unusual item from antiquity surfaced on the black market at about the same time. A very large female gold bodice decorated with large precious stones sold for $1,000,000.

Ancient boundary stones

To the south of the grave site along the foot hills there is a long tine of boundary markers in a curved row. The stones are large and appear to be ancient boundary markers. They are set close to a paved water channel.

A125

PETRIFIED TREE BARK - WINDOW OF THE ARK

A window shalt thou make to the ark, and in a cubit shalt thou finish it above.

Genesis 6:16

The ark rested in the seventh month, on the seventeenth day of the month, upon the mountains of Ararat. The waters decreased continually until the tenth month: in the tenth month, on the first day of the month, were the tops of the mountains seen. And it came to pass at the end of forty days, that Noah opened the window of the ark which he had made: And he sent forth a raven, which went forth to and fro, until the waters were dried up from off the earth.

Genesis 8:4-7

South-west of the village of Sagliksuyu rests a solitary object on a gentle sloping mound. The remains of a petrified tree bark approximately 2.5 metres long, 1.2 metres wide and 0.5 metres deep seems extraordinarily out of place on the desolate, dusty plain. The exterior of the object is rippled like tree bark, grey in colour, and has the appearance of stone. The object is solid inside but chimes like tin when tapped with a small piece of stone.

A126

A127

THE STORY OF NOAH REMOVING THE WINDOW OF THE ARK

Noah and his family had been at sea for nine months and longed to walk upon the earth again. As the waters abated Noah, still unable to view the situation outside, took a leap of faith and pushed the window out of its position plunging it into the sea. The quest for land began with the release of a raven but still another three weeks would pass before a dove returned with a fig leaf in its mouth bringing an occasion for much rejoicing. One month later, Noah removed the covering of the Ark. This also required much faith as once the covering was removed it could not be placed back on again. As Noah poked his head out of the top of the Ark for the first time in almost a year, he now had a full view of the glorious mountain tops around him. Gazing upon the face of the earth and seeing that the ground was dry, his faith was rewarded. As he had waited for God's command to enter the Ark he now patiently waited for His special directions to depart.

EXPERT CONCLUSION

> The boat shaped formation I examined... appears to have had sea keeping features appropriate to both its mission and to materials in use for vessels at the time in which it was built. These are not the result of a "natural formation"... Consider the probability that nature might provide a "dirt, iron and rock" formation with all of the following properties:
>
> 1. It is a ship shaped form, in three dimensions.
> 2. It has a moon pool of just the right size and shape to control hogging and sagging by reducing forward buoyancy without sacrificing stability.
> 3. The moon pool provides overboard drainage without compromisig deck flooding and provides "forced venting".
> 4. The moon pool is wide enough to provide protected anchor handling.
> 5. The moon pool is located far enough back to permit dragging a sea anchor and flailing anchor with the bow held forward. Yet it is far enough forward to allow the vessel to turn without putting the vessel in irons.
> 6. The moon pool is positioned to retard forward motion caused by wind,

A128

without reversing the orientation of the vessel.

7. There are incrementally located iron nodules in about 5,400 places showing lineal patterns corresponding both in regularity and position to transverse and longitudinal members or scantlings of a "shaped" hull.
8. There are repeated relationships among dimensions of the ratio phi (one dimension divided by another being 1.62, 1.62 squared or cubed, etc.) This is a number that was also fascinating to the builders of the great pyramid of Giza, an unlikely coincidence.
9. The anchors found are sized and located appropriate to the vessel size and mission and they were left in the valley floor upstream of the beaching site.
10. The gentle grade of the beach site is the only such site at its elevation east of the anchor stones' location which would accommodate a large [boat] where it could be successfully off loaded. All other such large, "beach like" landing sites are at lake bottom elevations.
11. The technique used to drill the holes in the stones is evidenced only in ancient artefacts, and was achieved by a process unknown even to this day.
12. The site location corresponds to ancient folklore and literary descriptions of the flood event.
13. The site location is within 1/2 mile of the longitude and latitude given in triangulation co-ordinates by Berosus relative to the tomb of Darius near Persopolis.

Sam Windsor

> Now all the writers of barbarian histories make mention of this flood, and of this ark; among whom is Berosus the Chaldean... Hieronymus the Egyptian also, who wrote the Phoenician Antiquities, and Mnaseas... Nay, Nicolaus of Damascus, in his ninety-sixth book, hath a particular relation about them and a great many more, make mention of the same. Flavius Josephus, ***Antiquities,*** Chapter 3. Para 6.

GOD'S RAINBOW COVENANT

I do set my bow in the cloud, and it shall be for a token of a covenant between me and the earth. Genesis 9:13

Fig. A129 – Kerensa, a rainbow and the town of Sagliksuyu behind.

Section 2

THE EXODUS

ARCHAEOLOGICAL PROOF FOR THE EXODUS

The Bible records that during the life of Moses, approximately 3,500 years ago, the Children of Israel made their exodus from Egypt, the land of their captivity, to embark on a journey through the wilderness to Mt Sinai, and then on to the Promised Land. If the Biblical narrative is true, then we would expect this monumental event to be verifiable through historical records and archaeological remains. Since the early 1980's, compelling archaeological evidence has surfaced attesting to the credibility of the Biblical account. It is the prerogative of this book to build a solid and compelling case for the Exodus.

THE SPIRITUAL LESSON

> Now all these things happened unto them for ensamples: and they are written for our admonition, upon whom the ends of the world are come.
>
> 1 Corinthians 10:11

> For unto us was the gospel preached, as well as unto them: but the word preached did not profit them, not being mixed with faith in them that heard it.
>
> Hebrews 4:2

In addition to the archaeological inquest, this book will take you on a spiritual journey out of Egypt and into the wilderness, to reveal how the Everlasting Gospel of Jesus Christ was preached to the Israelites, as it is to us today.

PROMISE OF RELEASE FROM EGYPTIAN BONDAGE IN THE FOURTH GENERATION

The Bible states in Genesis 15:16 that Abraham was instructed by God to make a sacrifice. After offering up the sacrifice, Abraham fell into a deep sleep and was shown in vision that his seed would be a stranger in a land that was not theirs, and would go into bondage. In verse 16 God reveals to Abraham that his seed will come out of captivity in the fourth generation. Abraham was about eighty-five years old when he had this vision.

GENEALOGY OF ISHMAEL AND ISAAC

Abraham was seventy-five years old when He departed from Haran, in southern

Turkey, into the land of Canaan (Genesis 12:4). Another important clue about Abraham's age is given in Genesis 16:3 which states that Sarah, Abraham's wife, took Hagar her maid, an Egyptian, after Abram had dwelt ten years in the land of Canaan, and gave her to her husband Abraham to be his wife. We can therefore conclude that Abraham was eighty-five years old when he received the vision of the 400 year prophecy, and in the same year Ishmael was conceived with Hagar. In Genesis 16:16 it states that Abraham was eighty-six years old when Hagar bare Ishmael. Fourteen years later, Sarah would give birth to Isaac, the child of promise, when Abraham was one hundred years old (Genesis 21:5.)

The prophecy of the 430 years (Galatians 3:17) began when Abraham left Haran and came into Canaan when he was seventy-five years old. And the 400 year prophecy confirming the affliction of Israel until the fourth generation was given to Abraham when he was eighty-five years old (Genesis 15:13). However the affliction of Israel did not actually commence until twenty years later when Ishmael mocked Isaac after he had been weaned from the breast. In the Bible the 430 and 400 year time prophecies both terminate in the same year. When God repeats a prophecy we know it is important. When a parent tells their child to do something twice, the second command reinforces what was said the first time.

While there is conjecture between Biblical historians as to the exact date of the Exodus, I believe the year of the Exodus to be 1491 B.C..

PART 1 - THE STORY OF JOSEPH

Jacob was the grandson of Abraham. He loved God and desired to serve Him but after deceiving his brother Esau out of the birthright, he fled as a fugitive to the land of Haran where he worked for his uncle, Laban. Jacob worked seven years for Laban and then married his two daughters Leah and Rachel. The posterity from these wives and their two handmaids was twelve sons. (Genesis 30-32.)

Jacob was blessed by God with many sons. His favourite wife Rachel was barren for many years and this caused them both great sorrow. Finally, in the seventh year of their marriage Rachel conceived and bore a son called Joseph who became the pride and joy of the aged patriarch.

As the son of his favourite wife, Jacob loved Joseph more than all his other sons and unwisely lavished affection upon him. One day Jacob presented Joseph with an expensive coat of many colours. Coats of this kind were only worn by people of distinction and this excited the jealousy of the other brothers who feared that their father might

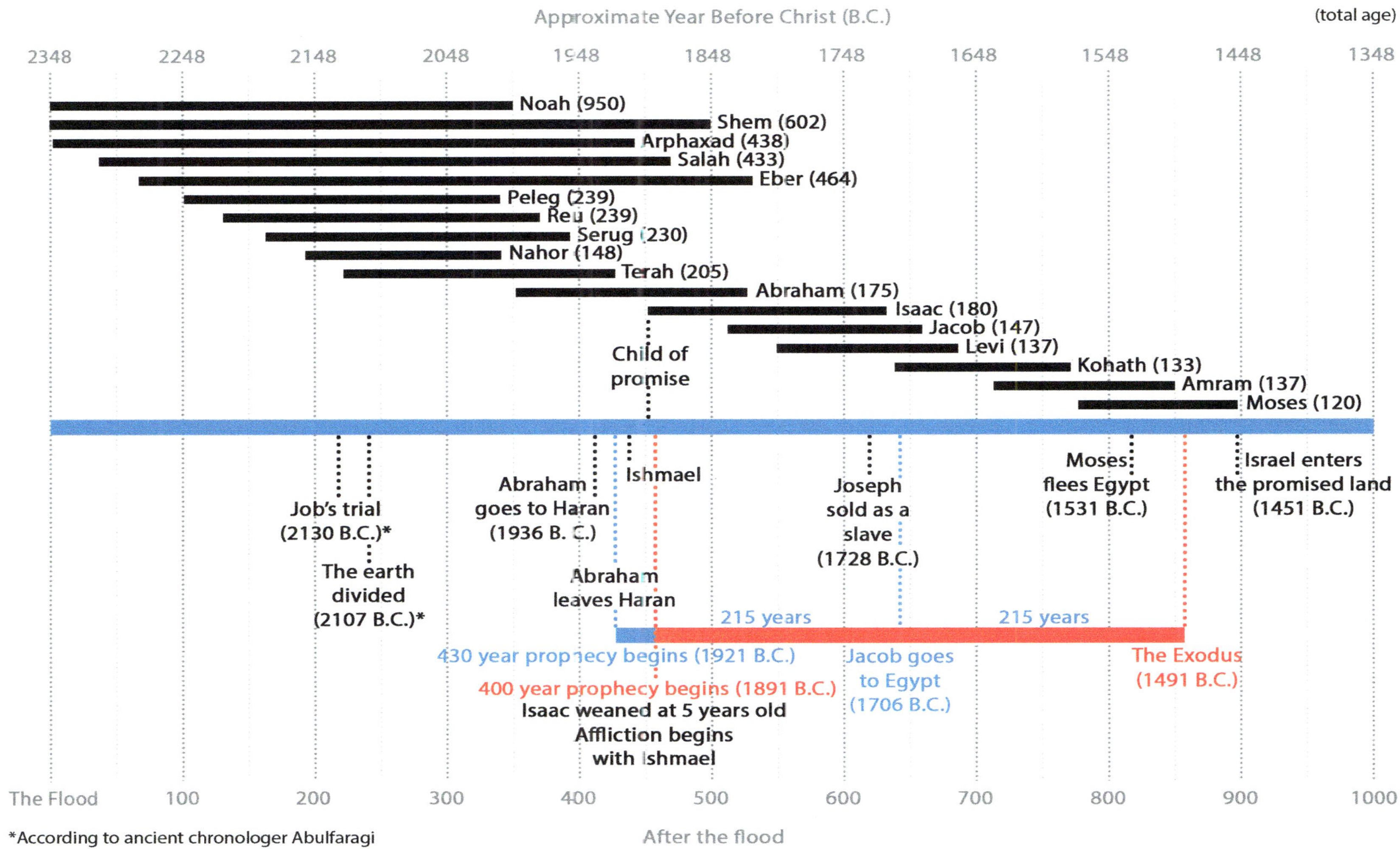

*According to ancient chronologer Abulfaragi

bestow upon Joseph the birthright belonging to the oldest son.

The anger of the brothers was aroused one day as Joseph told them of a dream that he had had. "Behold," he said, "we were binding sheaves in the field, and, lo, my sheaf arose, and also stood upright; and, behold, your sheaves stood round about, and made obeisance to my sheaf." The brothers received the dream as Joseph claiming that he would one day rule over them. Jacob openly rebuked Joseph for telling the dream but secretly he pondered its meaning. (Genesis 37:8-11.)

The sons of Jacob were shepherds tending to large flocks. Their work often required them to be away from home for several months at a time. On one occasion they had gone to Shechem and after a lengthy absence Jacob sought to hear word from them. Joseph was asked by his father to go to Shechem on foot (about 80 kilometres away) to find them. Upon reaching Shechem Joseph was told by a local man that his brothers had moved on to Dothan (21 kilometres further away). Tired, hungry and weary from the long journey Joseph pressed on and his heart became merry at the thought of being reconciled with his brothers.

When Joseph finally found his brothers he immediately discerned their satanic hatred of him. They had been careful to conceal their real feelings in front of their father but now exercised no restraint. Had Jacob known of his sons' real feelings towards Joseph He would never have sent him on this mission. (Genesis 37:18-22.)

The brothers purposed to kill Joseph but Reuben intervened by suggesting they throw him into a pit, planning to come back later and let him out. As the oldest son, Reuben had forfeited his birthright. Enraged by Jacob's affections to Rachel's handmaid Bilhah, after her death, Reuben defiled Bilhah to turn his father's affections to his mother, Leah. Simeon was the main instigator in the crime against Joseph because with Reuben having disqualified himself for the birthright, he felt his position as the next oldest was threatened by Joseph being the first-born of Jacob's favourite wife.

> And it came to pass, when Joseph was come unto his brethren, that they stripped Joseph out of his coat, his coat of many colours that was on him; And they took him, and cast him into a pit: and the pit was empty, there was no water in it.
> Genesis 37:23-24

> And Judah Said come, let us sell him to the Ishmeelites, and let not our hand be upon him; for he is our brother and our flesh. And his brethren were content.
> Genesis 37:18

While Simeon and Levi were contending for the birthright, as the fourth oldest son Judah had resigned himself to the fact that the birthright would never be bestowed on him and therefore saw no advantage in killing Joseph. It is important to note that even though Judah never pursued the birthright, the right to the birth of Christ through his progeny was bestowed upon him.

JOSEPH WAS A TYPE OF CHRIST

> And they took Joseph's coat, and killed a kid of the goats, and dipped the coat in the blood; And they sent the coat of many colours, and they brought it to their father; and said, This have we found: know now whether it be thy son's coat or no. And he knew it, and said, It is my son's coat; an evil beast hath devoured him; Joseph is without doubt rent in pieces. And Jacob rent his clothes, and put sackcloth upon his loins, and mourned for his son many days. And all his sons and all his daughters rose up to comfort him; but he refused to be comforted; and he said, For I will go down into the grave unto my son mourning. Thus his father wept for him. And the Midianites sold him into Egypt unto Potiphar, an officer of Pharaoh's, and captain of the guard. Genesis 37:31-36

JOSEPH'S MULTI-COLOURED COAT AND THE RAINBOW

Joseph's coat of many colours is a symbol of the Everlasting Covenant represented by the colours of the rainbow. When Jacob fled from Esau and lay down in sorrow upon the plain at Bethel, the Lord had confirmed His Covenant with him through a dream in which he saw God at the top of a ladder with a rainbow about Him. Jacob bestowed the coat upon Joseph as a reminder of God's promise to him.

> I do set my bow in the cloud, and it shall be for a token of a covenant between me and the earth. And it shall come to pass, when I bring a cloud over the earth, that the bow shall be seen in the cloud: And I will remember my covenant, which is between me and you and every living creature of all flesh; and the waters shall no more become a flood to destroy all flesh. And the bow shall be in the cloud; and I will look upon it, that I may remember the everlasting covenant between God and every living creature of all flesh that is upon the earth. And God said unto Noah, This is the token of the covenant, which I have established between me and all flesh that is upon the earth. Genesis 9:13-17

The colours of the rainbow in the sky represent the colours round about the throne of God. Jesus points to the bow as a token of God's mercy toward the repentant sinner.

> The revelator declares, "Behold, a throne was set in heaven, and one sat on the throne... There was a rainbow round about the throne, in sight like unto an emerald." Revelation 4:2-3. When man by his great wickedness invites the divine judgments, the Saviour, interceding with the Father in his behalf, points to the bow in the clouds, to the rainbow around the throne and above His own head, as a token of the mercy of God toward the repentant sinner. *Patriarchs & Prophets*, p.107

> The rainbow of promise encircling the throne on high is an everlasting testimony... to the universe that God will never forsake His people in their struggle with evil. It is an assurance to us of strength and protection as long as the throne itself shall endure. *The Desire of Ages*, p.493

JOSEPH'S MULTI-COLOURED COAT A SYMBOL OF CHRIST'S IMPARTED LIFE

The coat worn by Joseph symbolised the beautiful character of Christ. Joseph's lovely Christlike character was a perpetual rebuke to his brethren. His fidelity to God kindled Satan's wrath against him through the brothers. In like manner, the Jewish leaders had a satanic hatred towards Jesus because His sinless life was a reproof to their evil deeds and hypocrisy.

PARALLELS BETWEEN JOSEPH AND CHRIST

Joseph was thrown into a dark pit. Christ also was thrown into the pit of sin and misery when He left His lofty position in heaven, came down to this earth and took upon Himself our humanity.

Once the coat had been seized and stripped from Joseph it was torn by the brothers to make it appear that an animal had attacked Joseph. This tearing of the coat signified Christ's flesh and His heart being torn at Calvary when He took upon Himself the guilt of sin and its penalty for the human race.

Joseph and his father Jacob both suffered from a broken heart in the tragedy of their separation.

In like manner, Christ died of a broken heart (Psalm 40:12). At the very time Christ died the veil in the sanctuary was ripped from the top to the bottom. Our Heavenly Father, distraught with grief, ripped that veil apart with righteous indignation. The Father's own heart had been broken and ripped in two by the death of His only Son. The separation at Calvary between the Father and Son caused them both immense suffering and pain.

Joseph's coat was torn and dipped in the blood of a kid. This represented the Everlasting Covenant being confirmed by the blood of Jesus at Calvary (the Lamb slain from the foundation of the world. Revelation 13:8).

This symbol also met its fulfillment after Christ had given up the ghost when a soldier pierced Him in the side and there came out a stream of blood and water (John 19:33-35). Calvary was foreshadowed by the story of Joseph and his multi-coloured coat.

The eleven brothers of Joseph represented the founding pillars of the church, yet they attempted to kill him. During Christ's ministry, the Jewish leadership sought to condemn and sentence Jesus to death.

When the brothers went to Egypt during the drought to buy wheat and corn, "Joseph knew his brethren, but they knew not him" (Genesis 42:8). Jesus "came unto His own, and His own received Him not" (John 1:11).

Jacob was totally grief stricken at the loss of his beloved son Joseph, and it left a permament scar upon his life. In heaven Christ pleaded before the Father to permit Him to come to this earth to redeem sinners. Yet it was a struggle even with the King of the universe to yield up His Son to die for the guilty race. The depths and mystery of this love we will explore in heaven for endless ages.

For God so loved the world, that He gave His only-begotten Son, that whoso-

> ever believeth in Him should not perish, but have everlasting life. John 3:16

In Gethsemane Christ prayed, "O My Father, if this cup may not pass away from Me, except I drink it, Thy will be done." His humanity shrunk from the sacrifice of His life. In that experience, God suffered with His Son and in mercy sent an angel, not to take the cup from Christ's hand but to strengthen Him to drink it with the assurance of His love.

JOSEPH SOLD AS A SLAVE

> Then there passed by Midianites merchantmen; and they drew and lifted up Joseph out of the pit, and sold Joseph to the Ishmaelites for twenty pieces of silver: and they brought Joseph into Egypt. Genesis 37:28

Joseph's brothers sold him as a slave for twenty pieces of silver to the Ishmaelites. Christ was betrayed by one of his own brethren, Judas, for thirty pieces of silver. In both instances it was the cost of a slave (Zechariah 11:12-13, Matthew 26:15).

Joseph was only a young man of seventeen years of age when he was betrayed by his own brothers and sold as a slave for twenty pieces of silver. The thought of never seeing his beloved father again and his little brother Benjamin broke his heart. Alone and friendless, he was grief stricken and terrified.

> In this terrible experience Joseph learnt of His own weakness. He realised that through being indulged by his father certain faults had been encouraged in him that might now be corrected. He was becoming self-sufficient and exacting. Accustomed to the tenderness of his father's care, he felt that he was unprepared to cope with the difficulties before him, in the bitter, uncared-for life of a stranger and a slave. Then his thoughts turned to his father's God. Joseph believed that the God of his fathers would be his God. He then and there gave himself fully to the Lord, and he prayed that the Keeper of Israel would be with him in the land of his exile.
>
> His soul thrilled with the high resolve to prove himself true to God--under all circumstances to act as became a subject of the King of heaven. He would serve the Lord with undivided heart; he would meet the trials of his lot with fortitude and perform every duty with fidelity. One day's experience had been the turning point in Joseph's life. Its terrible calamity had transformed him from a petted child to a man, thoughtful, courageous, and self-possessed. *Patriarchs and Prophets*, p.214

JOSEPH IN EGYPT

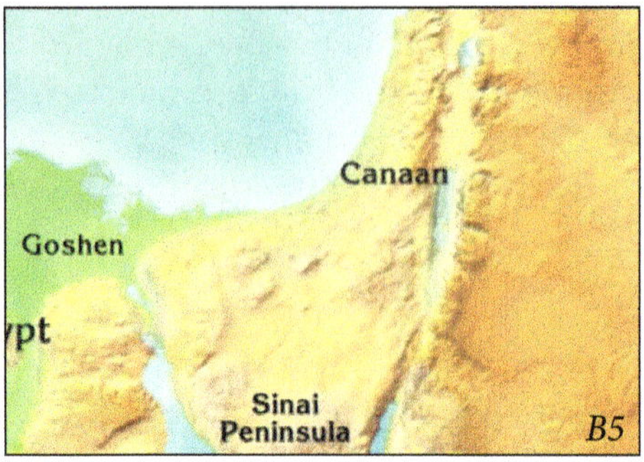

It was a long journey of about 350 kilometres from Canaan to Egypt.

> The Midianites sold him into Egypt unto Potiphar, an officer of Pharaoh's, and captain of the guard. Genesis 37:36

When the Midianites came to Egypt they sold Joseph to a man named Potiphar who was captain of the King's guard. Joseph remained in his service for ten years. Here amidst the idolatry of Egypt and exposed to many temptations, Joseph preserved his simplicity and his fidelity to God. He was not ashamed of the religion of his fathers, and he made no effort to hide the fact that he was a worshipper of Jehovah.

> And his master [Potiphar] saw that the LORD was with Joseph, and that the LORD made all that he did to prosper in his hand. Genesis 39:2

> The marked prosperity which attended everything placed under Joseph's care was not the result of a direct miracle; but his industry, care, and energy were crowned with the divine blessing. Joseph attributed his success to the favor of God and even his idolatrous master accepted this as the secret of his unparalleled prosperity.
>
> Joseph's gentleness and fidelity won the heart of the chief captain, who came to regard him as a son rather than a slave. The youth was brought in contact with men of rank and learning, and he acquired a knowledge of science, of languages, and of affairs--an education needful to the future prime minister of Egypt. *Conflict and Courage*, p.74

POTIPHER'S WIFE TEMPTS JOSEPH

As time elapsed Potiphar's wife accused Joseph of a vile crime.

> It came to pass after these things, that his master's wife cast her eyes upon Joseph; and she said, Lie with me. But he refused, and said unto his master's wife, Behold, my master wotteth not what is with me in the house, and he hath committed all that he hath to my hand; And it came to pass, as she spake to Joseph day by day, that he hearkened not unto her, to lie by her, or to be with her. And it came to pass about this time, that Joseph went into the house to do his business; and there was none of the men of the house there within. And she caught him by his garment, saying, Lie with me: and he left his garment in her hand, and fled, and got him out. And it came to pass, when she saw that he had left his garment in her hand, and was fled forth, that she

> called unto the men of her house, and spake unto them, saying, See he hath brought in an Hebrew unto us to mock us; he came in unto me to lie with me, and I cried with a loud voice. Genesis 39:7-14

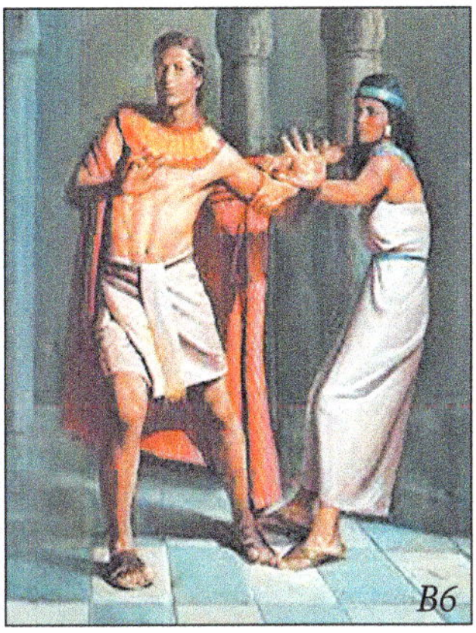

The temptation from Potiphar's wife came upon Joseph swiftly and suddenly, but he determined in his heart not to yield but to remain faithful to God. Although Joseph was suffering wrong he did not do wrong and therefore he remained under God's protection.

> She laid up his garment by her, until his lord came home. And she spake unto him according to these words, saying, The Hebrew servant, which thou hast brought unto us, came in unto me to mock me. Genesis 39:16-17

Potiphar's wife presented Joseph's garment to her husband as evidence that he had attempted to assault her. Had Potiphar believed his wife, Joseph would have been immediately put to death but instead he was seized by guards and taken to Pharaoh's prison-house. Joseph's imprisonment attested to his innocence.

JOSEPH IN PRISON

> Joseph's master took him, and put him into the prison, a place where the king's prisoners were bound: and he was there in the prison. Genesis 39:20

Potiphar was the captain of the king's guard and Joseph was cast into the dungeon below Potiphar's house.

> The LORD was with Joseph and showed him mercy, and gave him favour in the sight of the keeper of the prison. And the keeper of the prison committed to Joseph's hand all the prisoners that were in the prison; and whatsoever they did there, he was the doer of it. The keeper of the prison looked not to anything that was under his hand; because the LORD was with him, and that which he did, the LORD made it to prosper. Genesis 39:21-23

Even in the prison, God was with Joseph and He became a blessing to everyone around him. Forgetting his own problems, he showed pity and compassion to those who were suffering and offered words of sympathy to relieve the oppressed. Wherever Joseph went he proved faithful in the everyday, little things of life. It was his unswerving obedience to God in these little things that qualified him for greater trusts. Through servitude and imprisonment, under wrong and affliction, the beautiful character of Christ was being developed in Joseph.

THE DREAM OF THE BUTLER AND THE BAKER

The king's butler and the king's baker had been thrown into prison for some offence. One morning Joseph noticed that the two men appeared very sad. Upon making inquiry, they informed him of their remarkable dreams and that they were anxious to learn the significance. Joseph responded, "Do not interpretations belong to God?" "Tell me the dreams," he said. As each man related their dream Joseph noted their import. The king's butler described how he saw three vines clustered with beautiful grapes. He then pressed the juice from the grapes into a cup and placed it in Pharaoh's hand to drink from. The baker saw in his dream three bread baskets upon his head and the birds flew and picked the bread from the baskets. Joseph explained that in three days' time the butler would be reinstated to his position and that the baker would be put to death at the king's command. In both cases the events occurred as foretold.

On the third day when the butler was released from prison Joseph entreated him to remember his case before the king and said, "Think on me." Although every particular of the dream was fulfilled he forgot his promise to Joseph.

PHARAOH'S DREAM

Two more long years in the prison passed and Joseph was about to give up hope, when the prison gates were finally opened. Pharaoh had a dream that none of his magicians could interpret. It was then that the butler remembered Joseph. Feeling remorseful for his forgetfulness and ingratitude, the butler revealed to Pharaoh how his own dream and that of the baker had been interpreted by Joseph and fulfilled. It was humiliating to Pharaoh that his magicians were unable to interpret the meaning of his dreams, nevertheless he summonsed Joseph to the palace.

> Pharaoh said unto Joseph, In my dream, behold, I stood upon the bank of the river: And, behold, there came up out of the river seven kine, fat-fleshed and well favoured; and they fed in a meadow: And, behold, seven other kine came up after them, poor and very ill favoured and lean-fleshed, such as I never saw in all the land of Egypt for badness: And the lean and the ill favoured kine did eat up the first seven fat kine: And when they had eaten them up, it could not be known that they had eaten them; but they were still ill favoured, as at the beginning. So I awoke.
>
> Genesis 41:17-21

Pharaoh was perplexed because after the thin cows had eaten the fat cows, the thin cows remained thin.

Pharaoh returned to his sleep and dreamed again.

I saw in my dream, and, behold, seven ears came up in one stalk, full and good: And, behold, seven ears, withered, thin, and blasted with the east wind, sprung up after them: And the thin ears devoured the seven good ears: and I told this unto the magicians; but there was none that could declare it to me.

Genesis 41:23-24

JOSEPH INTERPRETS THE DREAM:

Joseph said unto Pharaoh, The dream of Pharaoh is one: God hath showed Pharaoh what he is about to do. The seven good kine are seven years; and the seven good ears are seven years: the dream is one. And the seven thin and ill favoured kine that came up after them are seven years; and the seven empty ears blasted with the east wind shall be seven years of famine. This is the thing which I have spoken unto Pharaoh: What God is about to do he showeth unto Pharaoh. Behold, there come seven years of great plenty throughout all the land of Egypt: And there shall arise after them seven years of famine; and all the plenty shall be forgotten in the land of Egypt; and the famine shall consume the land; And the plenty shall not be known in the land by reason of that famine following; for it shall be very grievous. And for that the dream was doubled unto Pharaoh twice; it is because the thing is established by God, and God will shortly bring it to pass. Genesis 41:25-32

Joseph explains to Pharaoh that both dreams have one and the same meaning. There will be seven years of plenty followed by seven years of famine.

JOSEPH'S COUNSEL LEADS TO HIS EXALTATION

Now therefore let Pharaoh look out a man discreet and wise, and set him over the land of Egypt. Let Pharaoh do this, and let him appoint officers over the land, and take up the fifth part of the land of Egypt in the seven plenteous years. And let them gather all the food of those good years that come, and lay up corn under the hand of Pharaoh, and let them keep food in the cities. And that food shall be for store to the land against the seven years of famine, which shall be in the land of Egypt; that the land perish not through the famine. And the thing was good in the eyes of Pharaoh, and in the eyes of all his servants. And Pharaoh said unto his servants, Can we find such a one as this is, a man in whom the Spirit of God is? And Pharaoh said unto Joseph, Forasmuch as God hath showed thee all this, there is none so discreet and wise as thou art: Thou shalt be over my house, and according unto thy word shall all my people be ruled: only in the throne will I be greater than thou. Genesis 41:33-40

Pharaoh discerns that Joseph has a superior religion and is connected to a God with a higher power. He places Joseph second in command and declares that only in the throne will he be greater than Joseph.

THE SEVEN YEARS OF FAMINE

In fulfilment of Pharaoh's dream, the seven years of plenty brought a bountiful harvest. Joseph made preparations to store the excess grain for the famine which was to follow. This famine was of world-wide extent and Joseph's family in Canaan were severely affected. Jacob heard that there was grain in Egypt and commanded his sons to go and buy supplies. As governor of Egypt, Joseph personally oversaw the sale and distribution of food at the granaries. When the brothers came before Joseph to buy grain he immediately recognised them, but they knew him not.

> Now when Jacob saw that there was corn in Egypt, he said, Behold, I have heard that there is corn in Egypt: get you down thither, and buy for us from thence; that we may live, and not die. And Joseph's ten brethren went down to buy corn in Egypt. And Joseph was the governor over the land, and he it was that sold to all the people of the land: And Joseph's brethren came, and bowed down themselves before him with their faces to the earth. And Joseph saw his brethren, and he knew them, but made himself strange unto them, and spake roughly unto them; and he said unto them, Whence come ye? And they said, From the land of Canaan to buy food. And Joseph knew his brethren, but they knew not him.
> Genesis 42:1-8

Joseph noticed that his younger brother Benjamin was not among his half brothers and he became concerned that they may have sought to harm him also in their jealousy. After questioning the brothers, he learned that Jacob was extremely protective of Benjamin because his other brother was killed and therefore was not permitted to travel with them. Doubtful of their word, Joseph put them on trial. He accused them of being spies and in order to secure their release commanded them to produce Benjamin to prove their innocence. Simeon, who was the chief instigator in Joseph's cruel treatment, was retained as a prisoner while the others returned to Canaan.

The brothers told their father about the governor of Egypt and his request to see Benjamin but Jacob refused to let him go to Egypt. Only after a period of time had elapsed and they were again faced with starvation did he relent. To console his father, Judah promised to be surety for Benjamin should anything go wrong and Jacob was comforted by his promise.

When the eleven brothers entered into Egypt, they bowed before Joseph and the dream of the eleven sheaves of wheat bowing before him came to his mind. Upon seeing his full-blood brother Benjamin among them Joseph was unable to contain himself and he departed from their presence to weep.

Still concealing his secret, Joseph sold his brothers the food provisions they re-

quired and bestowed gifts upon them, giving Benjamin a double portion of the gifts. He then tested his brothers in a severe manner. He commanded his steward to hide his silver cup which had special properties for detecting poison in Benjamin's nap-sack. When the brothers had gone out of the city they were stopped and searched by Joseph's steward who accused them of stealing the cup. Responding to the accusation, the brother's replied, "If one of us has taken your cup let him die and let the others be your servants." Upon searching each knapsack from the oldest to the youngest, the steward found the cup among Benjamin's possessions. The brothers rent their garments in anguish and returned to the city.

The brothers, in confusion and terror, felt this was a divine judgment that had come upon them for selling Joseph and lying to their father. At Joseph's demand for an explanation, Judah said, "Our great sin has found us out and we cannot clear ourselves so we shall all remain here and be your servants."

Joseph replied that only the man in whose possession the cup was found should remain as his servant and all the other brothers were free to return to their father. Judah pleaded with Joseph, appealing to him to have pity upon their aged father who would go the grave if he returned without Benjamin. Making one last appeal, he begged Joseph to make him his servant in Benjamin's place.

Joseph was convinced through this test that his brothers had undergone a character transformation. The self-confident, proud and boastful young men had become self-distrustful, humble and deeply repentant for their sin. Judah had offered to become a servant to Joseph in Benjamin's stead and the other brothers had pledged themselves to servitude with him. Joseph saw no malice or jealousy practiced towards Benjamin by his older brothers but instead a genuine brotherly, protective care. This awakened forgiveness and a new found trust in the heart of Joseph toward them.

JOSEPH REVEALS HIMSELF

Commanding his Egyptian servants to leave him alone with his brothers, Joseph revealed his true identity, saying, "I am Joseph your brother, whom ye sold into Egypt. Now therefore be not grieved, nor angry with yourselves, that ye sold me hither: for God did send me before you to preserve life. "

Seeing his brethren were troubled at his presence, Joseph sought to comfort them by the reassurance that God had overruled their malice toward him for His own purposes. Through his brothers selling him into slavery, God had been preparing a way by which many people could be preserved from the severe famine. God had also worked out His purpose of bringing Israel into Egypt by providing a refuge from the famine in the fertile plains of Goshen.

Joseph hastened his brothers to return to Canaan and bring his kindred back to Egypt. Sending them away with many well provisioned wagons, He bid them, "See that you fall not out by the way." Joseph's brother's returned to their father with the glad news that Joseph was still alive. Jacob refused to believe them at first, but after seeing the wagons, his spirit revived and he said, "It is enough; Joseph my son is yet alive: I will go and see him before I die." Finally, after twenty-two years of being separated, the father and son were reunited. Jacob lived another seventeen years of peace with his children in Egypt.

TWO LITTLE ILLUSTRATIONS FROM THIS STORY

The beautiful story of the reunion of Joseph with his father is an illustration of the reunion of Christ with His Father after thirty-three years upon this earth. They had been together for eternity and the absence had been a great suffering for the both of them. In our finite minds we can barely fathom what they both endured.

Judah's intercession on behalf of Benjamin was the very spirit of his descendant, Jesus Christ, upon the cross. He gave up His life for a guilty race, pledging Himself in the place of the sinner.

ISRAEL GIVEN THE MOST FERTILE LAND IN ALL OF EGYPT

Joseph's brethren were shepherds and herdsmen who required fertile pastures for their flocks to dwell in. Joseph had done Egypt a great service in saving the Egyptians from the famine and in recognition of that fact Pharaoh granted the kinsmen of Joseph the best of the land to dwell in. Joseph might have sought to bestow on his brothers stately offices in the palace but he knew the simple life of a shepherd would safeguard them from the idolatry and temptations of the Egyptian court.

PART 2 - IS THERE A RECORD OF JOSEPH IN EGYPT?

IMHOTEP AND JOSEPH

In the Cairo Museum there are statues of a famous historical figure called Imhotep. The similarities between Joseph and Imhotep are extraordinary which is supporting evidence that they are one and the same person. The title IM-HOTEP denotes that Joseph was a worshipper of the God "I AM".

The full list of his titles is:

> Chancellor of the King of Egypt, Doctor, First in line after the King of Upper Egypt, Administrator of the Great Palace, Hereditary nobleman, High Priest of Heliopolis, Builder, Chief Carpenter, Chief Sculptor, and Maker of Vases in Chief.
>
> Wikipedia: Imhotep

CHARACTERISTICS OF IMHOTEP IN COMMON WITH JOSEPH*

1. Minister of the king of lower Egypt (Genesis 41:41, 43)
2. Foremost under the king (Genesis 41:40)
3. Administrator of the great palace (Genesis 41:40)
4. Ruler by inheritance – adopted as son of Pharaoh (Genesis 41:44)
5. Priest in Heliopolis (Genesis 41:45)
6. Builder and architect (Genesis 41:35-36, 47-49, 41-57)
7. Discoverer of the art of building with cut stone
8. Exalted to be of godly character (Genesis 41:38)
9. Great medical skill, is compared to Greek god of healing (Genesis 50:2)
10. Was active during a period of seven years of famine followed by seven years of good harvest (Genesis 41:1-32, 47-57)
11. I need advice from God (regarding Pharaoh's dream) (Genesis 41:16)
12. Called the son of Ptah, the creator of all things (Genesis 40:8, 41:16, 25)
13. Gives Pharaoh advice (Genesis 41:1-57)
14. Comes to Pharaoh when Pharaoh is distressed (Genesis 41:8, 14)
15. Describes the tax rule (10%) to cope with the seven year long famine (Bible says 20%) (Genesis 41:34)
16. Tax law does not apply to priests (Genesis 47:26)
17. Becomes the god of healing and comes to the people as they sleep (Genesis 37:5-11, 20, 40:5-23, 40:1-36)
18. Realises when he is dying (Genesis 50:24)

* Adapted from *The Exodus Case* by Dr Lennart Moller pp.95-98

19. Has written many words of wisdom (Genesis 41:39, Psalm 105:22)
20. Dies at the age of 110 (Genesis 50:22-26)
21. Was probably not appointed and in service until Pharaoh Djoser had reigned for a time (Genesis 41:37-45)
22. Was not of royal blood but attained his position on his own merits (Genesis 37:1, 41:57)
23. Is called "Ibis", in other words, the one to whom all the ibis birds were sacrificed in Sakkara (Genesis 50:22-26)
24. Pharaoh Djoser reigned during the seven year long famine. The one who was minister of state with the status of a god was Imhotep (Genesis 41:37-45)
25. Eleven brothers

IMHOTEP MEANS: THE VOICE OF THE GOD, *IM* (I AM)

In ancient Egyptian "Imhotep" is translated to mean: "the voice (or mouth) of Im". However, there is no record of a god in Egypt called "Im". But the God of the Bible is known as, "I AM":

> God said unto Moses, I AM THAT I AM: and he said, Thus shalt thou say unto the children of Israel, I AM hath sent me unto you. Exodus 3:14

> Jesus said unto them, Verily, verily, I say unto you, Before Abraham was, I am.
> John 8:58

In the Bible, Pharaoh renamed Joseph, "Zaphenath-paneah" which has been translated by some to mean, "the God lives; the God speaks". This is very similar to Im-hotep: "the voice (or mouth) of IM". This infers that Joseph was regarded by the Egyptians as the spokesperson of God.

THE FAMINE STELA

There is a large stone on Seheil Island in Nubia which has an inscription about Pharaoh Djoser, Imhotep and the seven year famine.

1. The inscription begins with Pharaoh being in distress about his dream: "I was in distress on the Great Throne..."

   > And it came to pass in the morning that his spirit was troubled. Genesis 41:8

2. Pharaoh, troubled about his dream, asks Imhotep who the Nile god is that he may petition him about the drought. Imhotep answers: "I need the guidance of Him who presides over the fowling net..."

   > And Joseph answered Pharaoh, saying, It is not in me: God shall give Pharaoh an answer of peace. Genesis 41:16

In the Egyptian text, Imhotep is termed "the son of Ptah". Ptah was the Egyptian god known as the "creator" of everything else, including the other gods.

3. Imhotep tells Pharaoh about the Nile god and where he lives. The next part of the inscription says that the king slept and the Nile god came to him in a dream and told him there would be seven years of abundance after seven years of famine. The story is reversed to the Bible account.

IMHOTEP, THE PHYSICIAN

Imhotep is the earliest physician whose historical records survive, and although Joseph isn't mentioned as being a physician, the Bible gives one very important clue to this:

> And Joseph commanded his servants the physicians to embalm his father: and the physicians embalmed Israel. Here, the physicians are specifically stated to be under Joseph. Genesis 50:2

It is recorded in ancient Greek writings that people would visit a sanctuary of Imhotep in Memphis and would be healed in their dreams. The blessings that God brought to Egypt through Joseph were continued to be poured upon the people.

The Bible records that God spoke to Joseph through dreams and gave him the ability to interpret other people's dreams.

> And his brethren said to him, Shalt thou indeed reign over us? or shalt thou indeed have dominion over us? And they hated him yet the more for his dreams, and for his words. Genesis 37:8

> Come now therefore, and let us slay him, and cast him into some pit, and we will say, Some evil beast hath devoured him: and we shall see what will become of his dreams. Genesis 37:20

SAQQARA

Imhotep was the chief architect of Pharaoh, and built a complex at Saqqara.

12

THE IBIS GALLERIES

The Ibis Galleries are located one kilometre north-east of the Saqqara necropolis near the Dynasty III cemetery of Pharaoh Djoser and his family.

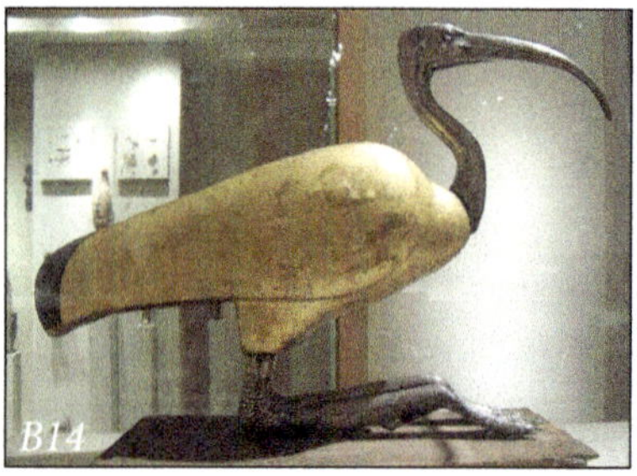

Excavators have located Imhotep's tomb not far from the Step Pyramid within a labyrinth of underground tunnels full of mummified ibis birds and bulls in separate galleries. They found inscriptions and coins showing that people went there to be healed.

Imhotep was known as the "God of Medicine," and was given the title, "Chief One of the Ibis." This connects the labyrinth with Imhotep.

In ancient Egypt the ibis birds were connected with healing. Joseph and Im-hotep were both healers, particularly in the mind through dreams.

Thousands of mummified ibis birds were brought here as tributes to Imhotep, filling the tunnels.

AN EMPTY COFFIN

The galleries connect to a pit which extends down to a funerary chamber with a second chamber full of broken stone vessels. There were also storerooms containing jars whose clay-stoppers were impressed with the seal of Djoser. This is evidence that the tomb belonged to a high-ranking official during the reign of Djoser.

Fig. B15– Empty sarcophagus in the Ibis Galleries.

In this large funerary chamber was an empty coffin with no inscriptions of whom it belonged to.

> And Joseph took an oath of the children of Israel, saying, God will surely visit you, and ye shall carry up my bones from hence. So Joseph died, being an hundred and ten years old: and they embalmed him, and he was put in a coffin in Egypt.
> Exodus 50:25-26

Joseph foresaw that the captivity of Israel in Egypt would come to an end at the termination of the prophetic period and that his people would return to Canaan. Before he died, Joseph made his brethren swear by an oath that they would carry his bones with them. We would therefore expect the tomb of Joseph in Egypt to be empty.

Ibis Gallery (1km)
Grain pits
Step Pyramid
Market place
Saqqara Complex

This mastaba tomb is different to all the other pyramid tombs in that it was oriented north instead of east. This reveals that the person in this tomb worshipped a different God.

No inscriptions were found on the walls except for an anonymous inscription by a Greek telling how he was cured through a dream.

The empty coffin and the orientation of the tomb, and its lack of inscriptions or bones, is evidence that it belonged to the Joseph of the Bible.

IS THERE EVIDENCE FOR THE FAMINE AT SAQQARA?

Saqqara is a large ancient burial ground serving as the cemetery for the ancient Egyptian capital Avaris in Memphis.

Imhotep (or Joseph) was the first to build stone tombs in honour of the king's majesty. His many titles included 'Treasurer of the King of Lower Egypt', 'Administrator of the Great Palace', and 'Imhotep the Builder, the Sculptor, the Maker of Stone Vessels'. Archaeology at Saqqara also supports that Joseph was set over the land of Egypt to lay up a fifth part of the land in the plenteous years and to administer the sale of food during the famine (Genesis 41:34-36).

THE MARKET PLACE

To the south of the Saqqara complex there is a market place which contains forty small booths from which officers sold wheat and corn. There are no foundation stones located in the booths which confirms that idols were not placed here at any time. The golden pillars resemble cobs of corn.

THE GRAIN PITS

> In the seven plenteous years the earth brought forth by handfuls. And Joseph gathered up all the food of the seven years, which were in the land of Egypt, and laid up the food in the cities: the food of the field, which was round about every city, laid he up in the same. And Joseph gathered corn as the sand of the sea, very much, until he left numbering; for it was without number.
>
> Genesis 41:47-49

The are also eleven grain pits at Saqqara which are connected by chutes with access only to the main pit. At the base of the grain-pits there are still the remains of wheat husks.

It is interesting to note that Joseph commissioned the building of eleven grain pits, which is the number of his brothers, and he filled the grain pits with life-giving produce. In a similar manner at the time of Christ's crucifixion there were only eleven faithful disciples and when Christ died He filled them with His life.

> When all the land of Egypt was famished, the people cried to Pharaoh for bread: and Pharaoh said unto all the Egyptians, Go unto Joseph; what he saith to you, do. And the famine was over all the face of the earth: And Joseph opened all the storehouses, and sold unto the Egyptians; and the famine waxed sore in the land of Egypt. Genesis 41:55

The famine ravaged Egypt. Despite the Egyptians being warned of the famine, they did not make individual preparation and were forced to sell everything in exchange for Joseph's grain supplies.

> The seven years of dearth began to come, according as Joseph had said: and the dearth was in all lands; but in all the land of Egypt there was bread. And when all the land of Egypt was famished, the people cried to Pharaoh for bread: and Pharaoh said unto all the Egyptians, Go unto Joseph; what he saith to you, do. And the famine was over all the face of the earth: And Joseph opened all the storehouses, and sold unto the Egyptians; and the famine waxed sore in the land of Egypt. And all countries came into Egypt to Joseph for to buy corn; because that the famine was so sore in all lands. Exodus 41:54-57

An inscription found in a tomb in Saqqara depicts people starving. This is evidence of a severe famine.

B23

In a tomb beside the Step Pyramid is an inscription of a high ranking official drinking from a silver cup (Genesis 44:2).

B24

ARCHAEOLOGICAL EVIDENCE OF HEBREW OCCUPATION IN GOSHEN

In the land of Goshen let them dwell. Genesis 47:5

Because Joseph's brethren were herdsmen, Pharaoh had given them the most fertile region of Egypt. God had made provision for them to grow into a great nation. In 1966 Dr Manfred Bietak of Austria discovered the remains of an Israelite village In Tell el Daba, the ancient capital city of Avaris in the north-eastern region of the Nile Delta dating to the time of Joseph.

B26

B27

This is the field excavated by Dr Manfred Bietek. Under Egyptian law agricultural fields can only be excavated when the land is not being used for crop production. This is a laborious process as once the site has been unearthed and excavated it must be covered over again for the farmers to sow and harvest crops.

On the Nile delta in Avaris they found an Asiatic dwelling dated to the Third Dynasty which is not characteristic of Egyptian architecture.

B28

B29

Fig. B30 – This is a reconstruction of the design which is typically Hebrew.

Clay cast for the signet rings of Jacob's sons

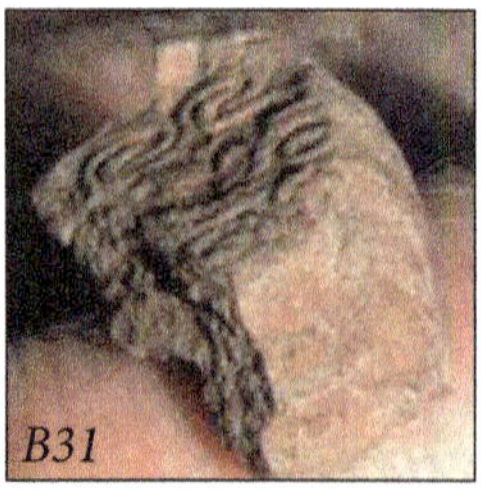

B31

In the same area of the archaeological dig they found clay casts for the signet rings of Jacob's sons. Nine seals were found during an archaeological dig at Avaris that Joseph and his men wore with the inscription "The Yakov (Jacob) Royal Ring"... It's the only time a Hebrew name has been found on an Egyptian seal.

TOMB OF BENI HASAN

> Beni Hasan is an Ancient Egyptian cemetery site. It is located approximately 20 kilometres to the south of modern-day Minya in the region known as Middle Egypt, the area between Asyut and Memphis. Wikipedia: Beni Hasan

The tomb at Beni Hasan in Middle Egypt is dated to circa 1700 B.C. This is about the time Jacob and his family entered into Egypt.

On the walls of the tomb there is a hieroglyph which records a race of Semite people in multi-coloured tunics entering into Egypt with their flocks and herds. See figure below.

The people in this hieroglyph are called "The Amo"... "God's People"... This supports the Biblical account of migration of the Semite people to Egypt.

> And he took some of his brethren, even five men, and presented them unto Pharaoh. And Pharaoh said unto his brethren, What is your occupation? And they said unto Pharaoh, Thy servants are shepherds, both we, and also our fathers. Genesis 47:1-2

B32

EVIDENCE FOR HEBREW SLAVERY IN EGYPT

> Now there arose up a new king over Egypt, which knew not Joseph... Therefore they did set over them taskmasters to afflict them with their burdens. And they built for Pharaoh treasure cities, Pithom and Raamses. Exodus 1:8-11

> And the Egyptians made the children of Israel to serve with rigor: and they made their lives bitter with hard bondage, in mortar, and in brick, and in all manner of service in the field: all their service, wherein they made them serve, was with rigor... But the more they afflicted them, the more they multiplied and grew. Exodus 1:14,12

The great Egyptian cities of Raamses and Pithom were built on the backs of Hebrew slaves.

Fig. B33 Tomb painting of slaves making mud bricks from straw and mortar.

Fig. B34 – Tomb painting of slaves with taskmasters set over them.

Fig. B35 – Mud bricks found in the Nile Delta.

Fig. B36 – Brooklyn Papyrus.

THE BROOKLYN PAPYRUS

The Brooklyn Papyrus, kept in the Brooklyn Museum in New York, records the names of seventy-nine Hebrew slaves being transferred between Egyptian owners in the 12th dynasty (figure B36). The Papyrus was found at the Abu Simbel Temple in Aswan.

B37

EVIDENCE OF SLAVERY AT ABU SIMBEL TEMPLE

Abu Simbel temple is located in Egypt, near the Nile, very close to the northern border of Sudan. At the entrance of Abu Simbel temple there are engravings on stone depicting foreign slaves. Inside the temple there is an engraving of an Egyptian task master pressing a Hebrew slave to the ground with his foot. Evidently the ancient cities of Egypt were built upon the backs of Hebrew slaves as the Bible tells us. Figure B37 is a photograph of Kerensa at Abu Simbel Temple at sunrise.

Fig. B38 – Photograph of an African slave being led in a chain of slaves with a rope tied around her neck.

Fig. B39 – Photograph of a Hebrew slave taken on the wall to the right of the fourth statue above.

THE FAMINE STELA

Seheil is an island in the Nile River in northern Nubia, which is a region of southern Egypt. The island is part of the city of Aswan and is one kilometre long and 800 metres wide. There are important archaeological hieroglyphs at this site, in particular the Famine Stela.

B40

B41

B42

B43

The Famine Stela is located at the summit of a boulder of rocks. It was discovered in 1889 by C.E. Wilbur and deciphered by various Egyptologists. It was engraved during the reign of the Ptolemy's (200 B.C.), but certain reliable clues have led Egyptologists to believe that the inscription came from an older authentic document. The Stela records that during the reign of Djoser, Egypt was afflicted with a terrible drought lasting for seven years. This Stela connects Pharaoh Djoser of the 3rd Dynasty and Imhotep with a terrible famine.

The Famine Stela reads:

> "I was in mourning on my throne. Those of the palace were in grief because Hapi had failed to come in time. In a period of seven years, grain was scant, kernels were dried up. Every man robbed, his twin children cried. The hearts of the old were needy. Temples were shut, shrines covered with dust. Everyone was in distress. I consulted one of the staff of the Ibis, the Chief lector-priest of Imhotep, son of Ptah South-of-the-Wall. He departed, he returned to me quickly, He let me know the flow of Hapi*." Famine Stela

**Hapi was the Egyptian god who flooded the Nile and made all the silt go into the fields to fertilise the soil.*

44

The first step pyramids

The Famine Stela mentions that it was in the reign of Pharaoh Djoser that the first step pyramids were built. Imhotep, as architect of Djoser's pyramid, has been honoured as the inventor of building with stone.

How the pyramids were built

The Stela also describes that the pyramids were built using limestone dissolved in a solution and poured into a mould which then set like concrete. For more information on this, visit:

> http://www.geopolymer.org/archaeology/pyramids/famine-stele-hieroglyphs-pyramids-construction

See also the following book:

> *Pyramid Illusions: A Journey to the Truth*; by Moustafa Gadalla, Bastet Publishing, Erie, PA, U.S.A.

PART 3 - MOSES THE DELIVERER IS BORN

> And the children of Israel were fruitful, and increased abundantly, and multiplied, and waxed exceeding mighty; and the land was filled with them. Now there arose up a new king over Egypt, which knew not Joseph. Exodus 1:7-8

The new Pharaoh was not ignorant of Joseph but he chose to forget what gratitude the nation owed him. Fearing that the Israelites, who were becoming mighty in number, would revolt against the Egyptians, he set task-masters over them. Despite being enslaved by the Egyptians, their number continued to grow and a death decree was issued to slay all newborn male children. It was when this decree was in full force that a son was born to the faithful Israelites Amram and his wife, Jochebed. The child was peculiarly well-natured and the parents, believing that the time was nigh when God would raise up a deliverer, determined to preserve the child.

THE FAITH OF AMRAM AND JOCHEBED

> Jochebed hid him three months and when she could no longer hide him, she took for him an ark of bulrushes, and daubed it with slime and with pitch, and put the child therein; and she laid it in the flags by the river's brink. Exodus 2:1-3

Amram and Jochebed chose for their son to be the deliverer. God rewarded their faith and gave them their hearts desire, while all the other mothers lost their children. He will do the same for us today if we will choose to do great things for Him.

His sister Miriam stood afar off, to wit what would be done to him. Exodus 2:4

The basket was guided and protected by a divine hand into Pharaoh's palace.

Pharaoh's daughter came down to the river to bathe. Having no children of her own, when she perceived the basket and opened it, she was touched with pity at the sight of the innocent baby. She resolved to adopt the child as her own. Miriam realised her opportunity had come, and springing from her hiding place among the bulrushes told the princess she knew of a nursemaid who could wean the child. Pharaoh's daughter approved of this arrangement and agreed for the baby to be weaned by a nursemaid until he was old enough to live in the palace. Moses own mother, Jochebed, was given full permission from the royal court to raise the child.

Jochebed was a praying mother who taught Moses in all the ways of God. From a young age she instilled in him that he had been especially chosen of God to be the deliverer of Israel. When Moses went to live in the palace at the age of twelve, he did not forget all that his mother had taught him. As a member of the royal household Moses became a man of intellectual greatness; skilled in combat he stood without a peer. Pharaoh sought to groom this prince of promise for the future throne but Moses was ever mindful of his great spiritual destiny.

MOSES SLAYS AN EGYPTIAN

> It came to pass in those days, when Moses was grown, that he went out unto his brethren, and looked on their burdens: and he spied an Egyptian smiting an Hebrew, one of his brethren. And he looked this way and that way, and when he saw that there was no man, he slew the Egyptian, and hid him in the sand. And when he went out the second day, behold, two men of the Hebrews strove together: and he said to him that did the wrong, Wherefore smitest thou thy fellow? And he said, Who made thee a prince and a judge over us? intendest thou to kill me, as thou killest the Egyptian? And Moses feared, and said, Surely this thing is known. Now when Pharaoh heard this thing, he sought to slay Moses. But Moses fled from the face of Pharaoh, and dwelt in the land of Midian: and he sat down by a well. Exodus 2:11-15

Moses beheld the sufferings of his people on a daily basis and he empathised with them and pitied them. He longed for the time to come when he would be able to deliver his people. When Moses slew the Egyptian he thought the people would rise and support him in a revolt. But he was greatly disappointed. Through this experience Moses quickly learned that the people were not ready to rise from their captivity to recover their liberty and that his life was now in peril. He fled from Egypt into Midian in Arabia.

MOSES LEARNS HUMILITY AND TRUST IN GOD

Moses loved God but he did not understand the simple principle of faith. He had fallen into the same error as his fathers Abraham, Isaac and Jacob. Instead of trusting wholly in God for deliverance, he thought that he must save Israel by his own hand. Real faith takes God at His word and depends upon Him to fulfil it in His own way and time.

Israel had become so resigned to their life of captivity that they did not have the faith of action to be released from it. But despite Moses' error, God still overruled and used it to accomplish His own purposes. For forty years Moses dwelt in Midian as a shepherd until the time of the promise had come. As the affliction of their slavery in Egypt intensified, the Hebrews began to cry out to God for deliverance.

LETTING GO AND LETTING GOD

Forgetting that God is the one who fulfils His own promises, Moses unnecessarily bore a tremendous burden for his people. He tried to do what only God Himself could do and the experience almost crushed him. Losing face before his own people and his adoptive royal family, Moses fled Egypt as a fugitive to a distant land and became a humble shepherd. In like manner, God does not expect us to carry the burdens which He has never asked us to bear. They are His burdens and we are to trust that He will deliver us by His own hand.

MOSES FLEES TO MIDIAN

B47

This is a picture of Constantine's Mt Sinai near St Catherine's Monastery in the Sinai Peninsula, Egypt. There is absolutely no archaeological evidence for Mt Sinai being in this region.

The Sinai Peninsula would have been an extremely unlikely place for Moses to reside as a fugitive because copper and turquoise mines were operational in the region and Egyptian military outposts were stationed round about. Moses would need to flee all regions of Egyptian control to secure his safety.

B48

Biblical references imply Midian is out of Egypt proper.

In Exodus chapter 2 it says Zipporah bare him a son, and he called his name Gershom:

> For Moses said, I have been a stranger in a strange land. Exodus 2:22

This implies Moses was no longer living in Egypt.

> Come now therefore, and I will send thee unto Pharaoh, that thou mayest bring forth my people the children of Israel out of Egypt. And Moses said unto God, Who am I, that I should go unto pharaoh, and that I should bring forth the children of Israel out of Egypt? And he said, Certainly I will be with thee; and this shall be a token unto thee, that I have sent thee: When thou hast brought forth the people out of Egypt, ye shall serve God upon this mountain.
> Exodus 3:10-12

> For this Agar is mount Sinai in Arabia, and answereth to Jerusalem which now is, and is in bondage with her children. Galatians 4:25

B49

B50

It is clear from the scriptures that the Children of Israel were to be brought out of Egypt and to the mountain of Moses in Midian (Mt Sinai).

Moses dwelt with Jethro in Midian and married his daughter Zipporah. Choosing to cast in his lot with the afflicted people of God, he fled from the palace of Pharaoh and became a humble, lowly shepherd. The desolate wilderness of Midian became the training ground for this great man of God. In personally caring for Jethro's flocks and herds he saw how Christ personally cares for His people. It was in the solitary places of the wilderness that he made His deep experience with God and wrote the books Genesis and Job.

The caves in the modern-day town of El-bad in north-west Arabia date back to the time of Abraham around 2000 B.C. but tradition has it that Jethro and Moses lived in these caves also.

WHERE DO ANCIENT SCHOLARS AND HISTORIANS LOCATE MIDIAN?

In 250 B.C. a council of seventy Jewish scholars translated the Hebrew Bible into the Greek tongue for the first time. Their translation of the Exodus account presupposed that Mt Sinai stood in the Arabian Peninsula.

- The Jewish Philosopher Philo (20 B.C. To 50 A.D.) placed the mountain east of the Sinai Peninsula and South of Palestine.
- The Apostle Paul, who was educated under the rabbi Gamaliel, located Mt Sinai in Arabia (Galatians 4:25).
- The Greek Philosopher Ptolemy (100 – 170 A.D.) located the mountain of God in Midian.
- Flavius Josephus, Jewish historian (37 – 100 A.D.), located Mt Sinai in the region of Madian.
- Sir Richard Francis Burton, explorer, ethnographer and man of letters (1821-1890), mapped and surveyed the area of Midian in Saudi Arabia. He concluded Mt Sinai to be in that region.

33 kilometres east-north-east of the Saudi Arabian town of el-bad stands Jabal Maqlua (Mt Sinai) which is located on the same mountain range as Jebel al Lawz. As a shepherd, Moses would have travelled from El-Bad in a north-easterly direction to the back side of the mountain with his herds and flocks.

> Now Moses kept the flock of Jethro his father in law, the priest of Midian: and he led the flock to the backside of the desert, and came to the mountain of God, even to Horeb. Exodus 3:1

THE BURNING BUSH

> The angel of the LORD appeared unto him in a flame of fire out of the midst of a bush: and he looked, and, behold, the bush burned with fire, and the bush was not consumed... And he said, Certainly I will be with thee; and this shall be a token unto thee, that I have sent thee: When thou hast brought forth the people out of Egypt, ye shall serve God upon this mountain. Exodus 3:1-2,12

The angel of the Lord appeared to Moses through the burning bush and commanded him to bring the Children of Israel back to that very mountain (Mt Sinai) in Saudi Arabia.

MOSES IS APPOINTED BY GOD TO DELIVER THE CHILDREN OF ISRAEL

After forty years of living the life of a meek, humble shepherd in the wilderness Moses was instructed to go before Pharaoh and demand that he let the Israelites go.

The very attribute of self-distrust that Moses had developed through his mistakes and failures in Egypt qualified him as the leader of Israel. Forty years he sojourned in the Wilderness of Arabia because of his unbelief. Over the long years God bore patiently with him until he had learned faith, trust, humility and entire dependence upon God's word.

Unbeknown to Moses, his forty year exile to Arabia was soon to be repeated. Having just graduated from the wilderness experience of unbelief himself, he was now qualified to lead God's people through the same experience. Moses had become one with his people in all their sufferings and afflictions. He had endured all their trials and temptations but to a much greater degree. In like manner, Christ partook of our humanity and experienced all our temptations and sufferings without sinning once. He is our Older Brother who understands us better than we know ourselves.

Although Moses was fearful to return to Egypt, he obeyed God and went forward. It was only after Moses set out that the Lord revealed to him all his enemies were dead. Because Moses could no longer speak the Egyptian language, God arranged for his brother Aaron to meet up with him.

MOSES IN THE COURT OF PHARAOH

Upon entering the Egyptian court, Moses and Aaron first met with the elders of their people. Moses related to the elders that God would now work for their deliverance. He demonstrated in the sight of the people the signs God performed for him at the burning bush and they received his testimony. Moses and Aaron then proceeded to the palace to deliver the message: "God has commanded that you let his people go, that they may hold a feast unto Me in the wilderness" (Exodus 5:1).

COMMENCEMENT OF THE PLAGUES

Indignant at Moses' request, and enraged by the Israelites re-observance of the Sabbath rest, Pharaoh retaliated by increasing the burden of their affliction with the command to make bricks without straw. This forced the Hebrews to go out all over the land in search of stubble to mix with the clay. Failing to meet their daily quota of bricks, they were severely punished by their Egyptian task masters.

The Hebrews began to blame Moses for their increased sufferings and in great distress Moses cried out to the Lord to deliver them. God responded: "Now shalt thou see what I will do to Pharaoh: for with a strong hand shall he let them go, and with a strong hand shall he drive them out of his land" (Exodus 6:1). Moses was again pointed back to the Covenant which God had made with Abraham, and was assured that it would be fulfilled. God had promised that at the end of four hundred years His people would be delivered from their bondage.

In the captivity of the Israelites in Egypt there is a parallel for our time also. How many of us become despondent in discouraging circumstances! We look to the hopelessness of our situation and forget that the Lord is working for our deliverance right then and there. The Children of Israel had expected God to deliver them without any test or trial of their faith but what they failed to understand was that God was going to build up their faith through the powerful miracles He was about to wrought out for them.

THE PLAGUES

1. River turned to blood

Moses and Aaron met Pharaoh at the riverside the next morning as he went down to worship his god. They repeated the message and warned him that there would be consequences for refusing to obey. Moses stretched out his rod and smote upon the water. The stream turned to blood and all the fish died. For seven days all the water in the land was turned to blood. But "the magicians of Egypt did so with their enchantments: and Pharaoh's heart was hardened, neither did he hearken unto them; as the LORD had said. And Pharaoh turned and went into his house, neither did he set his heart to this also" (Exodus 7:22-23).

2. Frogs

Moses stretched out the rod again over the waters and Egypt was overrun with a plague of frogs. The Egyptians were greatly perplexed as they regarded frogs as sacred but when they became intolerable and swarmed the palace of the Pharaoh the king was impatient to have them removed. When the set time for the removal of the plague arrived, the frogs died and their carcasses rotted and stank out the land. Yet Pharaoh "hardened his heart" (Exodus 8:15).

3. Fleas

Aaron stretched out his hand and the dust of the earth became lice all throughout Egypt. The magicians were unable to replicate the plague which demonstrated God's superiority. "Then the magicians said unto Pharaoh, This is the finger of God: and Pharaoh's heart was hardened, and he hearkened not unto them; as the LORD had said" (Exodus 8:19).

4. Flies

At a specifically stated time, another judgment of flies was inflicted upon the Egyptians filling their homes and fields with the pests. "The land was corrupted by reason of the swarm of flies" (Exodus 8:24) which were large and venomous with a painful bite. Yet Goshen was not affected.

5. Diseased cattle

At each refusal of Pharaoh to hearken to the voice of God, the severity of the plagues intensified. An infectious disease causing death was afflicted upon their sacred animals and livestock. "But of the cattle of the Children of Israel died not one" (Exodus 9:6).

6. Boils

To signify that the time of their deliverance was at hand, Moses was instructed to sprinkle the ashes of the furnace toward heaven in the sight of Pharaoh. God had shown Abraham under the figure of a smoking furnace and a burning lamp the captivity of his posterity with the promise that they would be released after four hundred years. God had stated that He would visit judgments upon their oppressors and that they would come forth with much wealth. As the ashes were sprinkled toward heaven, they produced boils on whomever they settled upon. Both man and beast were smitten with a loathsome and painful disease and the whole nation was brought to see the foolishness of trusting their magicians.

"For this cause have I raised Pharaoh up"

> For I will at this time send all my plagues upon thine heart, and upon thy servants, and upon thy people; that thou mayest know that there is none like me in all the earth. For now I will stretch out my hand, that I may smite thee and thy people with pestilence; and thou shalt be cut off from the earth. And in very deed for this cause have I raised thee up, for to show in thee my power; and that my name may be declared throughout all the earth. Exodus 9:14-16

God never purposed to destroy Pharaoh. Through the plagues he was given an opportunity to repent. Pharaoh could have left the courts of Egypt to share in the affliction of God's people but he chose to harden his heart and because of his stubborn resistance God would now proclaim His name to the world through the plagues of Egypt.

7. Hail

God again gave the command through Moses to let His people go. But Pharaoh refused. A plague of hail was threatened and Moses warned the Egyptians to bring in their livestock from the open fields. Some heeded the warning and gathered in their cattle while others despised the warning and left them in the field to perish. "And Moses stretched forth his rod toward heaven: and the LORD sent thunder and hail, and the fire ran along upon the ground; and the LORD rained hail upon the land of Egypt. So there was hail, and fire mingled with the hail, very grievous, such as there was none like it in all the land of Egypt since it became a nation. And the hail smote throughout all the land of Egypt all that was in the field, both man and beast; and the hail smote every herb of the field, and brake every tree of the field. Only in the land of Goshen, where the Children of Israel were, was there no hail." (Exodus 9:23-26).

"And Pharaoh sent, and called for Moses and Aaron, and said unto them, I have sinned this time: the LORD is righteous, and I and my people are wicked. Entreat the LORD (for it is enough) that there be no more mighty thunderings and hail... And when Pharaoh saw that the rain and the hail and the thunders were ceased, he sinned yet more, and hardened his heart... neither would he let the Children of Israel go" (Exodus 9:27-28,34-35).

8. Locusts

Moses stretched forth his rod over the land and an east wind brought a very grievous plague of locusts. There were so many locusts that the sky was darkened and every green thing was devoured. Again Pharaoh confessed his sin and begged

Moses to entreat his God to remove the plague. "And the LORD turned a mighty strong west wind, which took away the locusts, and cast them into the Red Sea; there remained not one locust in all the coasts of Egypt. But the LORD hardened Pharaoh's heart, so that he would not let the Children of Israel go" (Exodus 10:19-20). Pharaoh thought that God's long-suffering, mercy and kindness were acts of weakness which further confirmed him in his rebellion. In the face of death Pharaoh was humble but when the plagues were removed he became even more stubborn and obstinate. The mercy of God, in this sense, only hardened his heart.

9. Darkness

An even more grievous plague fell upon the land. Darkness so thick and black that it could be felt rested upon the land for three days. No one could leave their dwellings but the land of Goshen had light. God sent this plague in mercy; no lives were lost and the Egyptians had time for reflection upon their stubborn rebellion, and an opportunity to repent, if they would, before the final scourge. Pharaoh at last became fearful and summoned Moses telling him that the Israelites could leave but that they could not take their livestock with them. Moses refused the concession and replied, "There shall not an hoof be left behind" (Exodus 10:26). But Pharaoh and the priests would not let them go.

10. Death of the first born

At the final refusal of Pharaoh to relent and let the Children of Israel go, the Lord declared, "I will pass through the land of Egypt this night, and will smite all the first-born in the land of Egypt, both man and beast; and against all the gods of Egypt I will execute judgment. At midnight "there was a great cry in Egypt: for there was not a house where there was not one dead." The first-born of Egypt from the palace of Pharaoh to the firstborn of the captives in prison; and the first-born of the cattle had been smitten by the destroying angel. Shrieks and wails of horror were heard throughout the land and Pharaoh, devastated at the loss of his own son, was humbled in the dust. He "called for Moses and Aaron by night, and said, Rise up, and get you forth from among my people, both ye and the Children of Israel; and go, serve the Lord, as ye have said. Also take your flocks and your herds, as ye have said... And be gone; and bless me also" (Exodus 12:31-32).

The Passover

God gave Moses specific instructions for each family of the Children of Israel to slay a lamb without blemish and with a bunch of hyssop sprinkle its blood on the two sides of the doorframe and along the lintel at the top. At the sight of this mark, the destroying angel would not enter in and bring death into the dwelling. They were also to eat the flesh of the lamb, with unleavened bread and bitter herbs in the evening with their shoes on their feet and staff in their hand ready to leave when the moment came. It was called the Lord's Passover. By following the instructions of Moses to the letter the people were doing all that was in their power to avert the crisis. Some of the Egyptians also did likewise and were preserved.

PARALLELS BETWEEN THE 10 PLAGUES IN EGYPT & THE 7 LAST PLAGUES

At the end of the world, the Bible states there will be another outpouring of plagues similar to the plagues of Egypt (Revelation 15). The plagues are not universal but they will be the most terrible and extensive scourges ever known to man. Those who keep the commandments of God and the faith of Jesus will live and be protected through the plagues. This is called the "time of trouble such as never was" (Daniel 12:1).

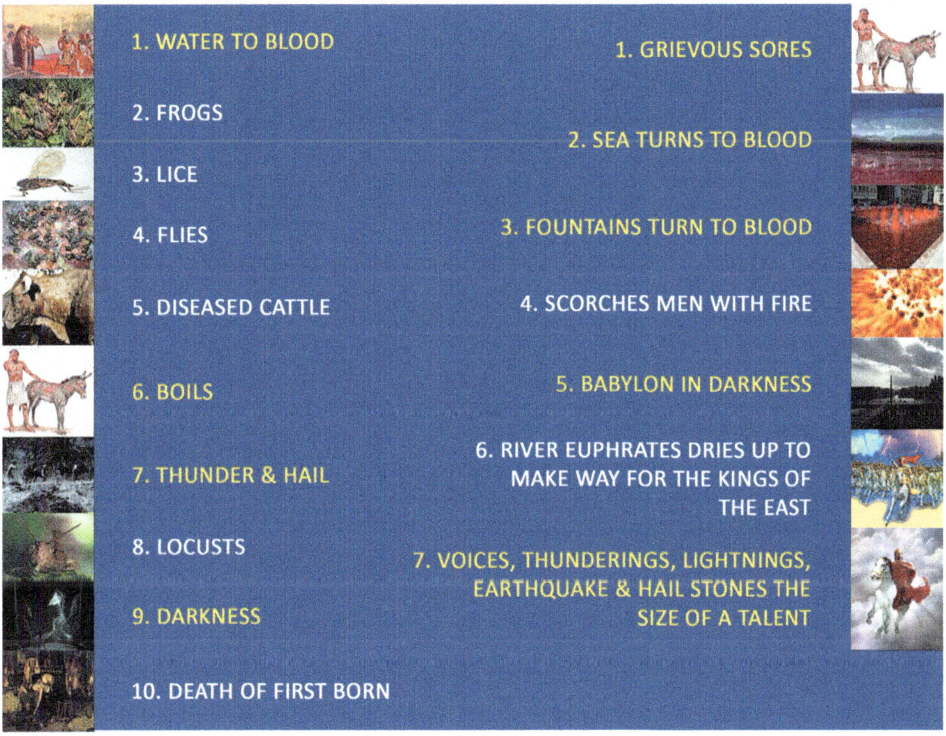

PART 4 - ARCHAEOLOGICAL EVIDENCE FOR THE PLAGUES IN EGYPT

The ten plagues of Egypt occurred approximately 3,500 years ago. This event virtually wiped out the entire economy of Egypt. The ancient Egyptians were a very proud people and are regarded by Egyptologists as notorious for embellishing their history and striking out any historical account which would cast a negative light upon them as a nation. That any record has survived describing the national devastation caused to Egypt at about the time of the Exodus is a momentous feat in itself.

AHMOSE I TEMPEST STELA

B53

The Ahmose Stela, also known as the Tempest Stela, was first unearthed in 1947, in the foundation of the third pylon at Karnak Temple, Thebes by Henri Chevalier. Between 1947 and 1951 other fragments of the Stela were found by the French Mission and a restoration of the Stela and translation of the text was published by Claude Vandersleyen (1967).

The Stela is covered with hieroglyphic inscriptions describing the Exodus. It records a great storm in Egypt like never seen before during Ahmose's reign; Egypt was enveloped in darkness; these tragedies happening because of one god that manifested His powers.

B54

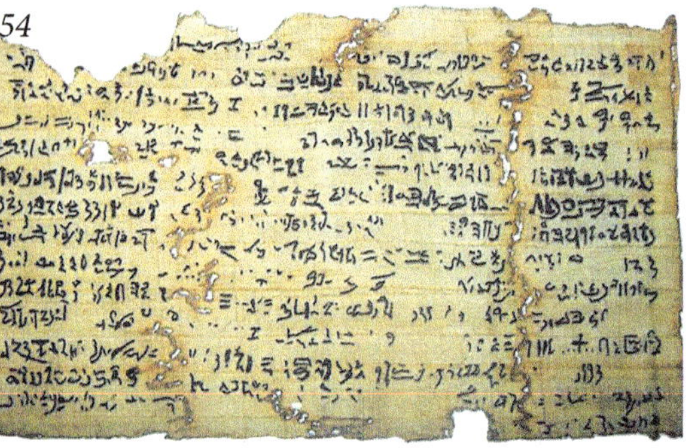

THE IPUWER PAPYRUS

In the early 19th Century a papyrus dating from around 1500 B.C., was found in Egypt. It was taken to the Leiden Museum in Holland and interpreted by A.H. Gardiner in 1909. The complete papyrus can be found in the book *Admonitions of an Egyptian from a Hieratic Papyrus in Leiden*.

The papyrus describes violent upheavals in Egypt, starvation, drought, escape of slaves (with the wealth of the Egyptians), and death throughout the land. It also records Egypt being struck by a strange hail mixed with fire and ice together exactly as the Bible account describes in Exodus 9:23-34.

The papyrus was written by an Egyptian scribe named Ipuwer and records the devastation in Egypt of the ruling class. Scribes were important people who belonged to the ruling class as administrators or military officers and their position was acquired by being a first born or in the service of an important person. The scribe refers to himself as a common man and had evidently attained this position through his own merits.

The Ipuwer Papyrus states that there was no military left In Egypt:

> "Let us go plunder; the mayor of the city goes unescorted."

Apparently there was no military, no army, no leaders, no police in Egypt so the people began looting the city for whatever they could find. In the Red Sea crossing, the Egyptian army drowned and not one of them survived. The entire Egyptian army with its officers and lower ranks that followed the people of Israel went down in the Red Sea. Of those who remained in Egypt the scribes either had no one for whom to work or, more probably the country was in complete chaos.

THE NAME OF GOD

> And in very deed for this cause have I raised thee up, for to show in thee my power; and that my name may be declared throughout all the earth. Exodus 9:16

> And he said, I will make all my goodness pass before thee, and I will proclaim the name of the LORD before thee; and will be gracious to whom I will be gracious, and will show mercy on whom I will show mercy... And the LORD descended in the cloud, and stood with him there, and proclaimed the name of the LORD. And the LORD passed by before him, and proclaimed, The LORD, The LORD God, merciful and gracious, longsuffering, and abundant in goodness and truth, Keeping mercy for thousands, forgiving iniquity and transgression and sin, and that will by no means clear the guilty; visiting the iniquity of the fathers upon the children, and upon the children's children, unto the third and to the fourth generation. Exodus 33:19, 34:5-7

The name of God is His character. His character is "merciful, gracious, longsuffering..." etc.. It is this revelation of God's character which is termed, "The Gospel". Through the manifestation of His wonders in Egypt, God's character would be revealed to the entire world.

THE NAME OF GOD WELL KNOWN

> She [Rahab] said unto the men , I know that the LORD hath given you the land, and that your terror is fallen upon us, and that all the inhabitants of the land faint because of you. For we have heard how the LORD dried up the water of the Red Sea for you, when ye came out of Egypt; and what ye did unto the two kings of the Amorites, that were on the other side Jordan, Sihon and Og, whom ye utterly destroyed. And as soon as we had heard these things, our hearts did melt, neither did there remain any more courage in any man, because of you: for the LORD your God, he is God in heaven above, and in earth beneath.
> Joshua 2:8-11

> The Lord is not slack concerning his promise, as some men count slackness; but is long-suffering to us-ward, not willing that ANY should perish, but that all should come to repentance. 2 Peter 3:9

Rahab was a heathen woman who had heard and believed in the mighty works of Jehovah that had been wrought out for the Children of Israel in Egypt and in the wilderness. She was convinced He was the one true God and by her faith of action in saving the two Israelite spies, demonstrated her allegiance to Him. Her faith was rewarded along with her family as they were spared from the destruction of Jericho.

THE WORLD WAS RIPE FOR THE GOSPEL

> But in the fourth generation they shall come hither again: for the iniquity of the Amorites is not yet full. Genesis 15:16

The wonders that God had wrought had already made Israel known around the whole earth. In the days of Abraham, the Amorites had not yet filled their cup of iniquity, but in the fourth generation their probation would cease and they would seal their destruction. God gave the Amorites and the surrounding nations time to repent. The Gospel was to be preached as a witness against them to fully justify without excuse their condemnation. The other purpose was to call out individuals such as Rahab who would take their stand on the Lord's side.

THE TEL ARMANA LETTERS

B55

The Tel Armana Letters discovered in 1907 by Norwegian Assyriologist Jorgen Alexander Knudtzon,at Tel Armana, are another important evidence for the plagues.

A letter preserved in the so-called Tel Armarna letters was sent by the widow of Pharaoh to the Hittite King Suppiluliumas and preserved by the son of the latter in an inscription.

> When the people of Misra (Egypt) learned the destruction of Amqa, they were afraid, for to make matters worse their master, Bibhuria had just died and the widowed queen of Egypt sent an ambassador to my father and wrote to him these terms:
>
> My husband is dead and I have no son. People say that you have more sons. If you send me one of your sons he will become my husband for it is repugnant to me to take one of my servants to husband.
>
> When my father learned this, he called together the council of the great: Since the most ancient times such a thing has never happened before.
>
> Tel Armana Letter; *The Exodus Case*, p.164

The queen of Egypt is appealing to the Hittite King in Canaan to send one of his sons to form a royal alliance with her through marriage. She writes that her husband and her son have suddenly died and that there are no men left from the elite class to marry. This is evidence that at a certain time in ancient Egyptian history the elite class was wiped out and that such a thing had never happened before. The Hittite king's council did not believe the queen's report and spies were sent out to investigate her claims.

TERMINATION OF THE 430 YEAR PROPHECY

> Now the sojourning of the children of Israel, who dwelt in Egypt, was four hundred and thirty years. And it came to pass at the end of the four hundred and thirty years, even the selfsame day it came to pass, that all the hosts of the LORD went out from the land of Egypt. Exodus 12:40-41

The four hundred and thirty year period commenced when Abraham departed from Haran when he was seventy-five years old. On the self-same day that the Children of Israel went out from the land of Egypt the prophecy was fulfilled.

THE ISRAELITES LEFT EGYPT WITH GREAT SUBSTANCE

> I will give this people favour in the sight of the Egyptians: and it shall come to pass, that, when ye go, ye shall not go empty: But every woman shall borrow of her neighbour, and of her that sojourneth in her house, jewels of silver, and jewels of gold, and raiment: and ye shall put them upon your sons, and upon your daughters; and ye shall spoil the Egyptians. Exodus 3:21-22

The Egyptians had come to revere the God of Israel and they feared Him. They had seen the protective hand over His people in Goshen while the rest of the land was brought to ruin. When the Children of Israel asked their taskmasters for their rightful wages, the Egyptians did not refuse their request and heaped them up with gold and silver.

PAST SINS AND FORGIVENESS

When we give our lives to Christ and come to Him in faith, the sins of our past will often times come up after us just like the Egyptians when they rose up after the Israelites to overtake them by the Red Sea. Have you ever been chased by your past sins or been troubled by them? When that happens you can say to them "Christ has taken all my sins and cast them to the bottom of the sea – they're not mine any more. I am crucified with Christ and it is no longer I that liveth but Christ that liveth in me" (Galatians 2:20).

CHRIST THEIR LEADER

> And did all drink the same spiritual drink: for they drank of that spiritual Rock that followed them: and that Rock was Christ. Neither let us tempt Christ, as some of them also tempted, and were destroyed of serpents. 1 Corinthians 10:4, 9

Throughout their sojournings in the wilderness, Jesus Christ Himself was with them in the pillar of cloud and fire. "He was their Saviour. In all their affliction He was afflicted, and the Angel of His presence saved them: in His love and in His pity He redeemed them; and He bare them, and carried them all the days of old" (Isaiah 63:8-9). When the Children of Israel were suffering for want of thirst and hunger in the wilderness, Christ was their leader and He was suffering with them. He bore long with them and loved them tenderly even though they rebelled against Him time and time again. The same compassionate Saviour who loved His people back then is the same compassionate Saviour who dwells in our hearts today.

The One who led the Israelites through the wilderness was the same that spoke the law at Sinai and who delivered the sermon on the mount of beatitudes (Matthew 5).

> Our sins make slaves of us while we are in Egypt, and when God the Holy Spirit stirs them up against us, how they beat us with cruel lashes, till our soul is worn with extreme bondage; but those very sins, by God's grace, are made the means of driving us to the Saviour. The Holy Spirit drives us to Christ, just as the Egyptians drove the people out of Egypt.
>
> The children of Israel did not go out of Egypt poorly clad; they went out with their best clothing on, and moreover, they had borrowed jewels of gold, and jewels of silver, and raiment, and they went gladly out of the land. Ah beloved that is just how a child of God comes out of Egypt.
>
> He does not come out of his bondage with his old garments of self-righteousness on: oh no; as long as he wears those he will always keep in Egypt; but he marches out with the blood & righteousness of Jesus Christ upon him, and adorned with the goodly graces of the Holy Spirit.
>
> Strangely true it is, sins do me good, said an old writer once, "because they drive me to the Saviour, and so I get good by them." Ask the humble Christian where he got his humility, and to one he will say that he got it in the furnace of deep sorrow on account of sin. See another who is tender in conscience: where did he get that jewel from? It came from Egypt. That bondage state under which thou are now labouring, thou poor way-worn child of sorrow, shall be good for thee; for when thou comest out of Egypt thou wilt steal jewels from the Egyptians; thou wilt have won pearls from the very convictions.
>
> Charles Spurgeon, Sermon: ***The Exodus***

PART 5 - THE RED SEA CROSSING

Departing from Goshen, the Israelites travelled southward through the Wilderness of the Sinai Peninsula. Crossing the vast expanse, they then headed up in a northerly direction towards the tip of the Gulf of Aqaba, when suddenly God directed Moses to turn aside into an impasse of mountains called the Wadi Watir. Approximately three weeks after departing from Goshen, the multitude with their flocks and herds poured out of the mountains onto the beach at modern-day Nuweiba.

> And the children of Israel journeyed from Rameses to Succoth, about six hundred thousand on foot that were men, beside children. And a mixed multitude went up also with them; and flocks, and herds, even very much cattle.
>
> Exodus 12:37-38

There were 600,000 Israelite men, besides women and children and there was also a large number of Egyptians who the Bible terms the "mixed multitude". The total number of people would have been around two million.

THE WADI WATIR

> For Pharaoh will say of the children of Israel, They are entangled in the land, the wilderness hath shut them in. Exodus 14:3

When the Children of Israel came to Nuweiba they were closed in by mountains called the Wadi Watir. They made their way through the mouth of the gorge and entered out onto an enormous beach. Encased by mountains the Children of Israel could not escape.

> Gulf of Aqaba: A pronounced cleft with hills rising abruptly from the shore, often over 2,000 feet. *Encyclopedia Britannica*

B57

B5

B5

B6

B6

PI-HAHIROTH

Near the mouth of the Wadi Watir lie the ruins of a Turkish fortress that has been built over the foundation of a much older Egyptian military fortress (see figures B58,B59). This is proof that Nuweiba was part of Egypt in ancient times and therefore the Children of Israel had not yet left Egypt proper.

> And the LORD spake unto Moses, saying, Speak unto the children of Israel, that they turn and encamp before Pihahiroth, between Migdol and the sea, over against Baalzephon: before it shall ye encamp by the sea. Genesis 14:1-2

On the peaks of several of the Wadis the remains of very old lookout towers have been found. Migdol may have been one of these towers.

THE ISRAELITES HEDGED IN

The Egyptians chased after the Israelites with their horses and chariots and caught up with them as the multitude poured onto the beach at Nuweiba.

> The Egyptians pursued after them, all the horses and chariots of Pharaoh, and his horsemen, and his army, and overtook them encamping by the sea, beside Pihahiroth, before Baalzephon. And when Pharaoh drew nigh, the children of Israel lifted up their eyes, and, behold, the Egyptians marched after them; and they were sore afraid: and the children of Israel cried out unto the LORD.
> Exodus 14:9-10

The Israelites were terrified because they were shut in by the mountains on either side, the sea was before them and the raging Egyptians were behind them. They accused Moses of bringing them out of Egypt to die, declaring that they would have preferred to remain in Egypt as slaves.

> And Moses said unto the people, Fear ye not, stand still, and see the salvation of the LORD, which he will shew to you to day: for the Egyptians whom ye have seen to day, ye shall see them again no more for ever. The LORD shall fight for you, and ye shall hold your peace. Exodus 14:13-14

As Moses, forty years earlier, needed to learn that he could not deliver Israel by his own hand, God was now bringing the Israelites into an experience where they could learn the same lesson. Their faith was so weak that at the same time that they cried unto the Lord they were also accusing Moses of bringing them into trouble. It was a hard lesson that God would fight their battles for them, one which they never fully learned.

That is the salvation of the Lord – He is the One who will fight to give us the victory. When we come to a realisation that without Him we can do nothing – then He is able to work out salvation for us in our lives.

Moses himself was severely tested, but not for the same reason as the people. He was not afraid and trusted that God would deliver them. But feeling the intense wrath of the Israelites and sorely disappointed by their violent murmuring, Moses pleaded with God for deliverance.

> And the LORD said unto Moses, Wherefore criest thou unto me? speak unto the children of Israel, that they go forward: But lift thou up thy rod, and stretch out thine hand over the sea, and divide it: and the children of Israel shall go on dry ground through the midst of the sea. Exodus 14:15-16

God replied, "Why are you crying to me Moses? Go and tell the Children of Israel to go forward!" He commanded Moses to tell the people that even though they felt trapped and frightened and couldn't see their way through the situation, to go forward by faith and He would open the way before them.

In our Christian walk we all meet at some point with a Red Sea experience. A problem that seems insurmountable to surpass. But even in that situation we need to move forward and trust that God is going to make an opening for us. The Bible promises we will never be tempted more than we can bear and that God will make a way of escape for us. But we must exercise faith, go forward and obey God in every particular. If the Children of Israel had not obeyed God and walked up to the Red Sea He would not have been able to work a miracle for them – so it is with our lives.

> Verily I say unto you, If ye have faith, and doubt not, ye shall not only do this which is done to the fig tree, but also if ye shall say unto this mountain, Be thou removed, and be thou cast into the sea; it shall be done. And all things, whatsoever ye shall ask in prayer, believing, ye shall receive. Matthew 21:21

This is a promise for us today. If you believe and have faith, even though it be only the size of a mustard seed, then whatever you ask in prayer, according to His will, God will remove that mountain and open the way for you. We all have mountains of difficulty in our lives; situations that seem impossible to change? But this is God's promise and all we need is to "go forward" believing that when His timing is right, He will make the way clear.

THE RED SEA CROSSING

> And the angel of God, which went before the camp of Israel, removed and went behind them; and the pillar of the cloud went from before their face, and stood behind them: And it came between the camp of the Egyptians and the camp of Israel; and it was a cloud and darkness to them, but it gave light by night to these: so that the one came not near the other all the night. And Moses stretched out his hand over the sea; and the LORD caused the sea to go back by a strong east wind all that night, and made the sea dry land, and the waters were divided. And the children of Israel went into the midst of the sea upon the dry ground: and the waters were a wall unto them on their right hand, and on their left. And the Egyptians pursued, and went in after them to

the midst of the sea, even all Pharaoh's horses, his chariots, and his horsemen. And it came to pass, that in the morning watch the LORD looked unto the host of the Egyptians through the pillar of fire and of the cloud, and troubled the host of the Egyptians, And took off their chariot wheels, that they drave them heavily: so that the Egyptians said, Let us flee from the face of Israel; for the LORD fighteth for them against the Egyptians. And the LORD said unto Moses, Stretch out thine hand over the sea, that the waters may come again upon the Egyptians, upon their chariots, and upon their horsemen. And Moses stretched forth his hand over the sea, and the sea returned to his strength when the morning appeared; and the Egyptians fled against it; and the LORD overthrew the Egyptians in the midst of the sea. And the waters returned, and covered the chariots, and the horsemen, and all the host of Pharaoh that came into the sea after them; there remained not so much as one of them. But the children of Israel walked upon dry land in the midst of the sea; and the waters were a wall unto them on their right hand, and on their left. Thus the LORD saved Israel that day out of the hand of the Egyptians; and Israel saw the Egyptians dead upon the sea shore. And Israel saw that great work which the LORD did upon the Egyptians: and the people feared the LORD, and believed the LORD, and his servant Moses. Exodus 14:19-31

B62

That night an easterly wind blew a pathway through the sea, congealing the waters on either side enabling the Children of Israel to cross over on dry ground. The Egyptians pursued the Israelites through the waters, but God troubled them with thunder and lightning and took off the wheels from their chariots. Moses stretched out his rod and the waters covered the sea destroying all the Egyptian host, including the heart-hardened Pharaoh.

B63

FAITH

This was a wonderful deliverance that God wrought for Israel but if the people had not gone forward when He had commanded them to, He never would have opened the path for them. By doing all that was in their power to do, which was merely marching down to the waters, they demonstrated their faith in God's promise, and He was able to work for them.

THE SONG OF DELIVERANCE

> And Miriam answered them, Sing ye to the LORD, for he hath triumphed gloriously; the horse and his rider hath he thrown into the sea. Exodus 15:21

The people were now free from their Egyptian captivity. Rejoicing and praising God at their new-found freedom, Moses led out in a song of victory.

> Then sang Moses and the children of Israel this song unto the LORD, and spake, saying, I will sing unto the LORD, for he hath triumphed gloriously: the horse and his rider hath he thrown into the sea. The LORD is my strength and song, and he is become my salvation: he is my God, and I will prepare him an habitation; my father's God, and I will exalt him. The LORD is a man of war: the LORD is his name. Pharaoh's chariots and his host hath he cast into the sea: his chosen captains also are drowned in the Red Sea. The depths have covered them: they sank into the bottom as a stone. Thy right hand, O LORD, is become glorious in power: thy right hand, O LORD, hath dashed in pieces the enemy. And in the greatness of thine excellency thou hast overthrown them that rose up against thee: thou sentest forth thy wrath, which consumed them as stubble. And with the blast of thy nostrils the waters were gathered together, the floods stood upright as an heap, and the depths were congealed in the heart of the sea. The enemy said, I will pursue, I will overtake, I will divide the spoil; my lust shall be satisfied upon them; I will draw my sword, my hand shall destroy them. Thou didst blow with thy wind, the sea covered them: they sank as lead in the mighty waters. Who is like unto thee, O LORD, among the gods? who is like thee, glorious in holiness, fearful in praises, doing wonders? Thou stretchedst out thy right hand, the earth swallowed them. Thou in thy mercy hast led forth the people which thou hast redeemed: thou hast guided them in thy strength unto thy holy habitation. The people shall hear, and be afraid: sorrow shall take hold on the inhabitants of Palestina. Then the dukes of Edom shall be amazed; the mighty men of Moab, trembling shall take hold upon them; all the inhabitants of Canaan shall melt away. Fear and dread shall fall upon them; by the greatness of thine arm they shall be as still as a stone; till thy people pass over, O LORD, till the people pass over, which thou hast purchased. Thou shalt bring them in, and plant them in the mountain of thine inheritance, in the place, O LORD, which thou hast made for thee to dwell in, in the Sanctuary, O Lord, which thy hands have established. The LORD shall reign for ever and ever. Exodus 15:1-18

THE SONG OF MOSES AND THE LAMB

> And I saw as it were a sea of glass mingled with fire: and them that had gotten the victory over the beast, and over his image, and over his mark, and over the number of his name, stand on the sea of glass, having the harps of God. And they sing the song of Moses the servant of God, and the song of the Lamb, saying, Great and marvellous are thy works, Lord God Almighty; just and true are thy ways, thou King of saints. Revelation 15:2-3

The Song of Moses is also the Song of the Lamb. This may be the song of our own experience if we will choose to follow God in the way He leads.

BAPTISM BY FAITH IN THE RED SEA

> Moreover, brethren, I would not that ye should be ignorant, how that all our fathers were under the cloud, and all passed through the sea; And were all baptised unto Moses in the cloud and in the sea; 1 Corinthians 10:1-2

Baptism by immersion in water represents the death of the old way of life and the entrance into a new life in Christ. This was the experience of the Children of Israel in crossing the Red Sea. Their past life of bondage was washed away, and they came out to a life of new privileges and opportunities.

GEOGRAPHY OF THE RED SEA CROSSING

At Nuweiba, at the centre of the Gulf of Aqaba (the eastern arm of the northern end of the Red Sea), there is a natural land ridge which goes to a depth of 100 metres at its deepest point. The gradient at the Red Sea crossing is not so steep as to make it impossible for carts, wagons, livestock, small children and the elderly to cross over. However, the northern and southern sides of the natural underwater land ridge slope off to much greater depths.

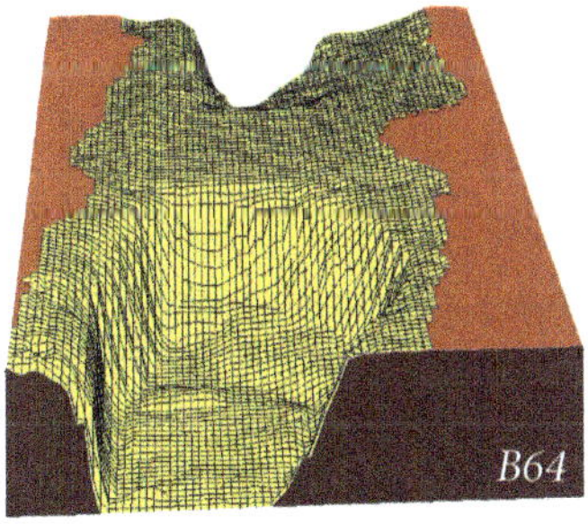

B64

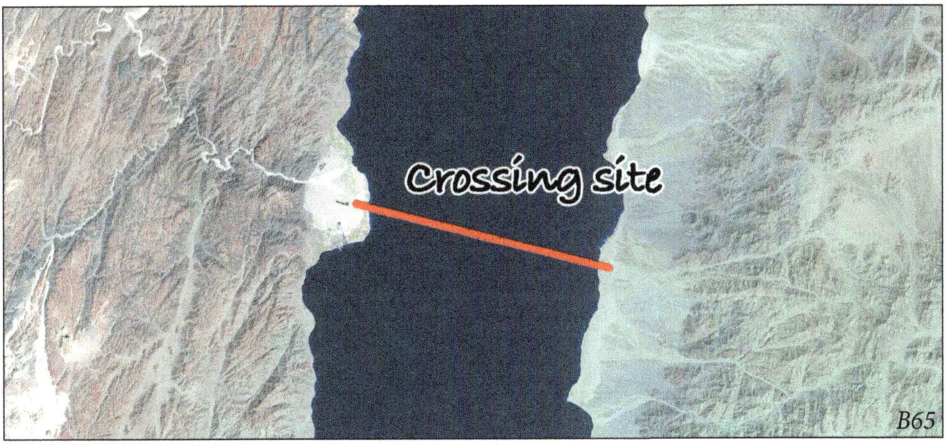

B65

ARCHAEOLOGICAL EVIDENCE FOR THE RED SEA CROSSING

Coral is a living organism which requires a solid object to grow on, such as the rock of a natural reef or a ship-wreck. The original object may decay or corrode but the coral will preserve the shape and in some instances the object itself.

The coral growths at the tip of the southern peninsular of the Gulf of Aqaba are different to the coral growths at Nuweiba. Coral does not grow in scattered clumps like it does in the area of the land bridge where the Israelites crossed. The formations of the coral growth at the Nuweiba crossing are unique to the area. It appears that there was a tragedy and the wreckage was scattered upon the sea floor. The shape of the wreckage has been preserved by the coral growth. The left image below is an example of normal coral growth and the right image is a picture of scattered coral growth at Nuweiba.

B66

B67

B68

B69

PHOTOGRAPHIC SURVEY

A photographic survey by an underwater robotic camera returned images of unnatural coral growths. Multiple objects at 90° angles, circular objects, axles, discs and wheel-like structures were found. Objects with sharp 90° angles are unnatural and this suggests that the object to which the coral has grown on was a man-made structure. Many of these objects are fused into larger masses that have the appearance of twisted wreckage.

> The LORD troubled the host of the Egyptians... and took off their chariot wheels, that they drave them heavily. Exodus 14:24-25

The coral growths indicate that the wheels were physically removed from the chariots and that the Egyptians were unable to escape before the 100 metre high walls of water crashed down upon them.

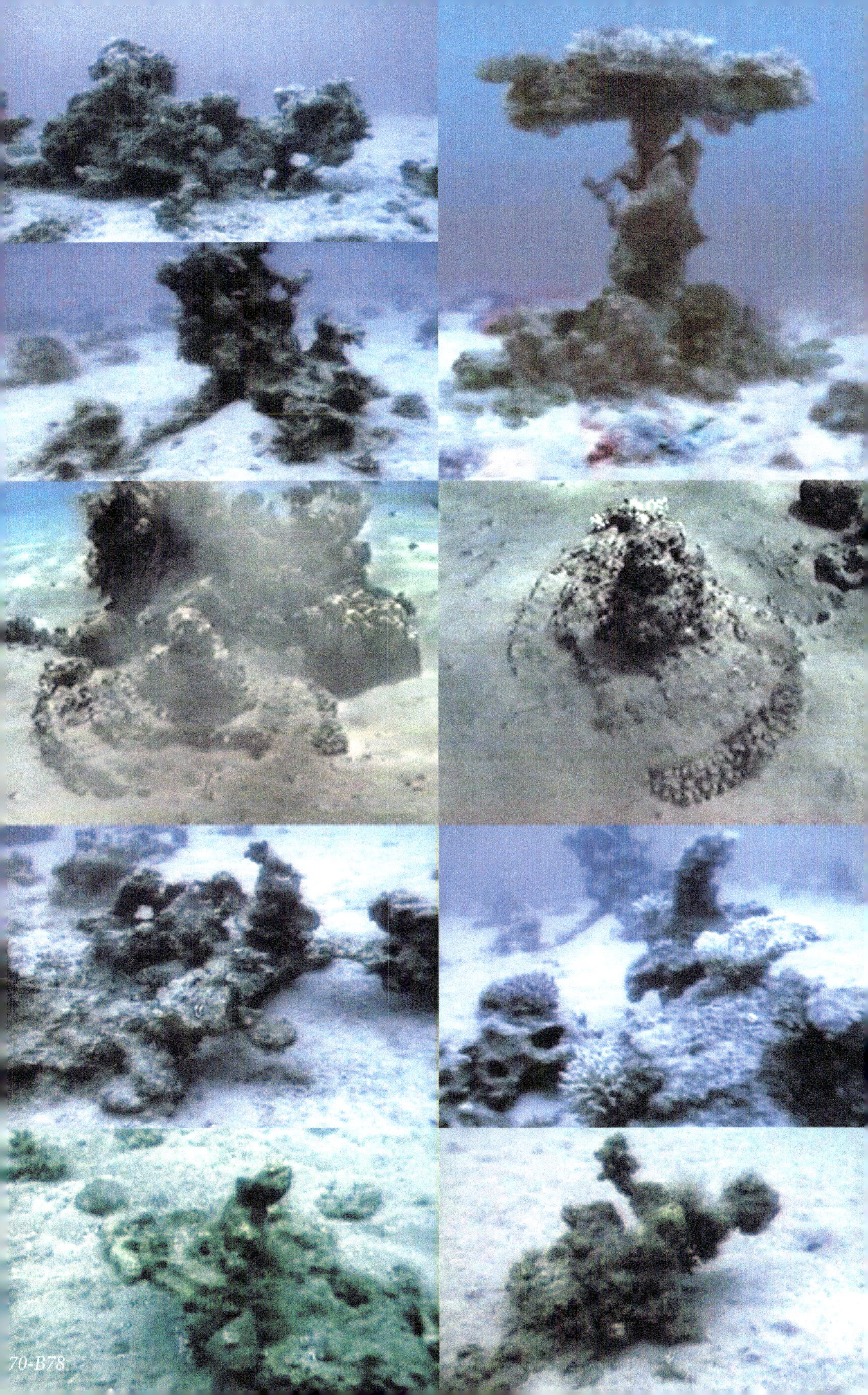
70-B78

METAL IN THE CORAL FORMATIONS

Egyptian chariots were often reinforced with bronze. To this day, evidence of metal encrusted with coral can be found on both sides of the Red Sea crossing.

Fig. B79 – Scan of a coral formation using a metal detector showing the bronze remains of a six spoke chariot wheel preserved within.

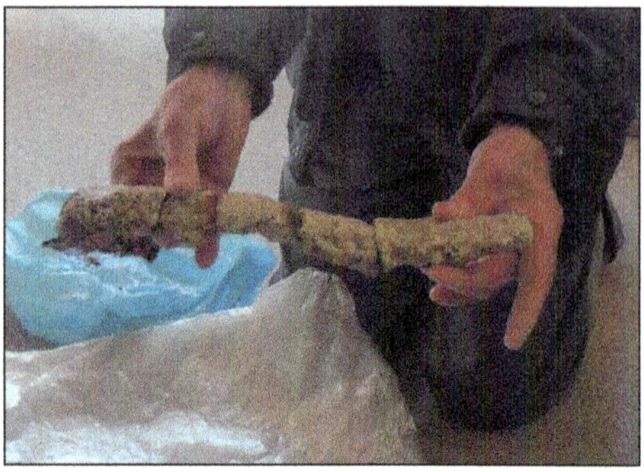

Fig. B80, B81 – Chariot spoke found on the Egyptian side of the Red Sea crossing.

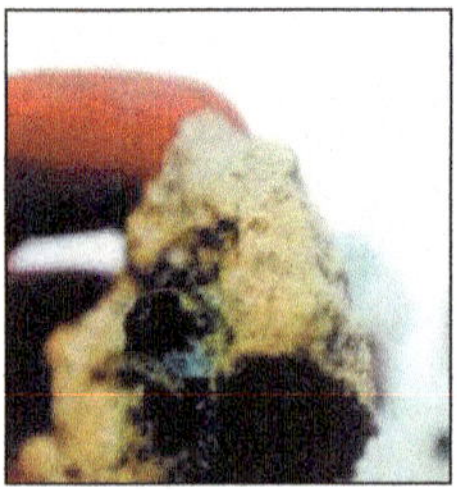

Fig. B82, B83 – Metal encrusted coral on the Arabian shore.

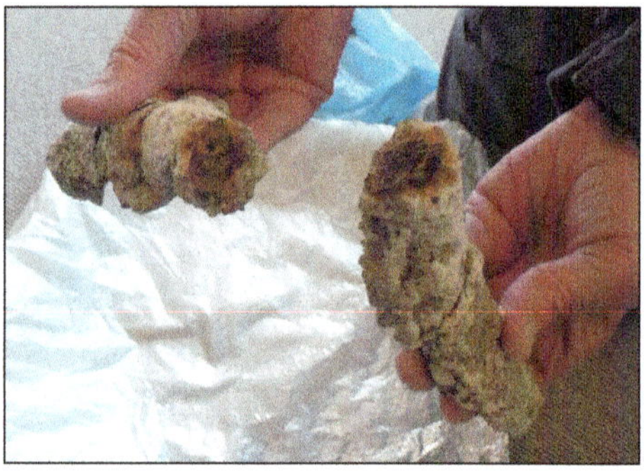

ANIMAL AND HUMAN REMAINS

The remains of a white fossilised human femur bone (figure B84,B86) and a horse's hoof which has shrunk to the size of a one dollar bill (figure B85) were also found in the sea at the crossing site. In edition to these artefacts the shattered bones of humans, horses and cattle have been found piled in heaps on the bed of the sea floor.

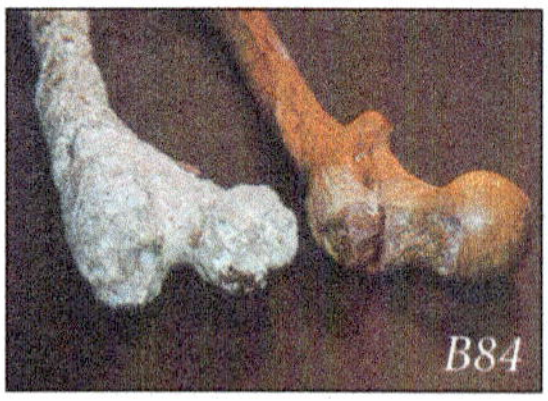

B84

B85

B86

SOLOMON'S PILLAR

> King Solomon made a navy of ships in Eziongeber, which is beside Eloth, on the shore of the Red Sea, in the land of Edom. And Hiram sent in the navy his servants, shipmen that had knowledge of the sea, with the servants of Solomon. And they came to Ophir, and fetched from thence gold, four hundred and twenty talents, and brought it to King Solomon. Exodus 9:26-28

Solomon built a port at the northern extremity at the Gulf of Aqaba, at modern day Eilat in Israel. He called the name of the place *Yam Suph* which means "in the middle" in commemoration of the Red Sea crossing taking place in the middle of the gulf of Aqaba. At his direction, two pillars were erected on either side of the Red Sea crossing in commemoration of the miraculous deliverance and as a reminder to the crew of his ships that the Lord can deliver them in great distresses.

In the early 1980's the Phoenician column in figure B1 on page 72 was found several hundred metres closer to the shore of the Nuweiba beach. In 1984, an identical column was found on the Arabian side with an inscription mentioning King Solomon, Yahweh and the crossing of the Israelites. This column was removed shortly after its discovery and a metal marker was put in its place.

PART 6 - FROM THE RED SEA TO SINAI

THE BITTER WATERS OF MARAH

> So Moses brought Israel from the Red Sea, and they went out into the wilderness of Shur; and they went three days in the wilderness, and found no water. And when they came to Marah, they could not drink of the waters of Marah, for they were bitter: therefore the name of it was called Marah. And the people murmured against Moses, saying, What shall we drink? And he cried unto the LORD; and the LORD showed him a tree, which when he had cast into the waters, the waters were made sweet: there he made for them a statute and an ordinance, and there he proved them. And said, If thou wilt diligently hearken to the voice of the LORD thy God, and wilt do that which is right in his sight, and wilt give ear to his commandments, and keep all his statutes, I will put none of these diseases upon thee, which I have brought upon the Egyptians: for I am the LORD that healeth thee. Exodus 15:23-26

Three days journey into the wilderness, the Children of Israel began to be in want of water. Arriving at the waters of Marah they were bitterly disappointed as they could not drink the bitter water. The people were ready to stone Moses even though God had so recently wrought such a mighty miracle as parting the Red Sea. God instructed Moses to take a tree and to cast it into the waters and they were made sweet. The Ten Commandments had not yet been given at Sinai but the Chil-

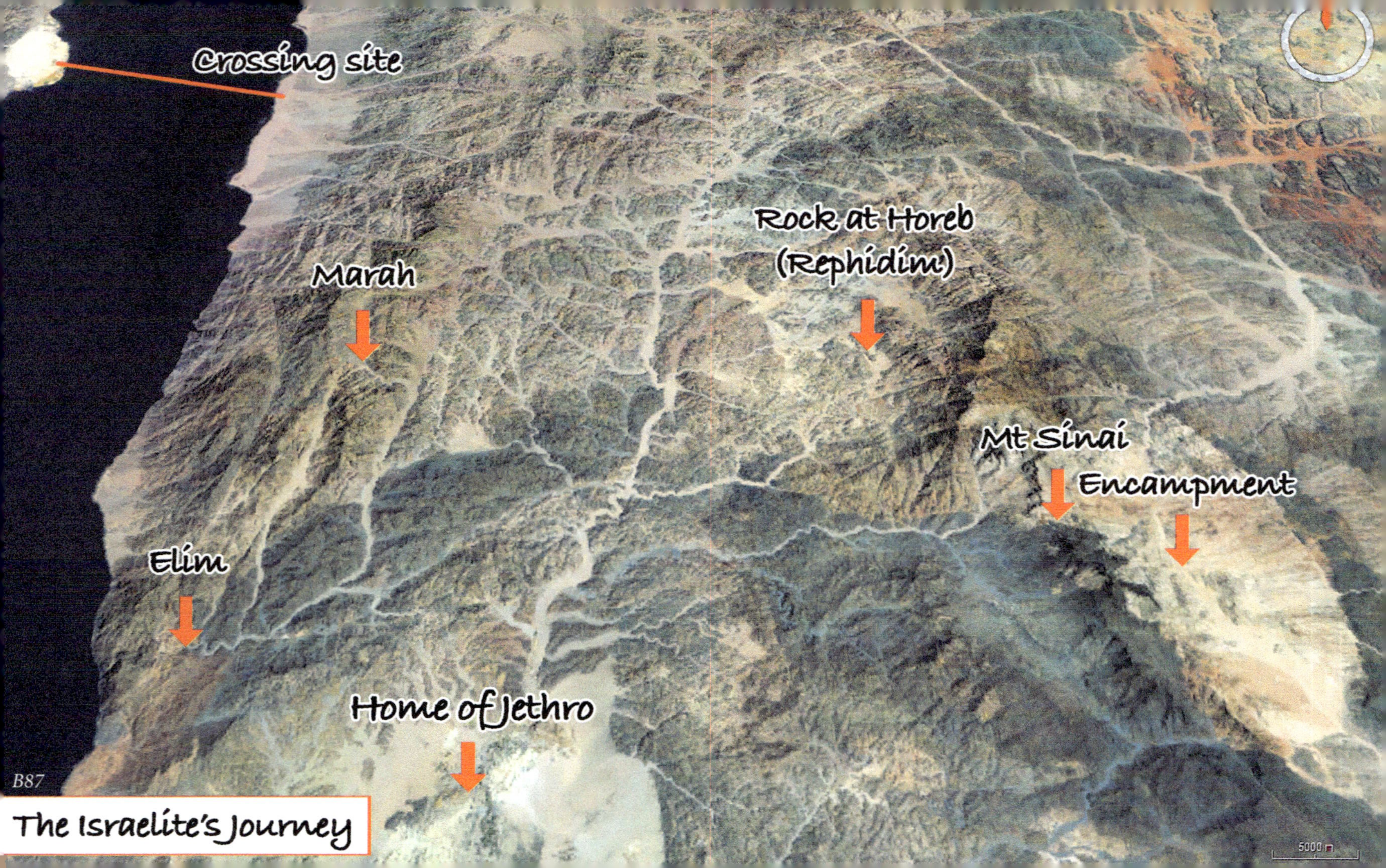

B87
The Israelite's Journey

The Israelite's Journey

dren of Israel had been taught the law of God from Abraham and God pronounced that if they would hearken to His voice, He would preserve their health.

As a shepherd, Moses had led Jethro's flocks all through the region and knew the waters at Marah would be unfit for drinking. How must he have felt when over two million tired and thirsty people were looking to him to provide for them when he saw God leading them in that direction! Yet he trusted that God would now be a faithful Shepherd to them.

The Children of Israel were tested at Marah. Destitute of food and water they could do nothing to save themselves. If God had not sweetened the water for them they all would have died of thirst. But at the last moment the Lord intervened to save them. He made the waters sweet and drinkable to sustain their life. The great lesson God was trying to teach Israel was that He would be their sufficiency and strength through all of life's circumstances.

On the brink of eternity, do we find roots of bitterness springing up in our hearts? Only God can make those bitter waters sweet. Often in the wilderness experience of our lives we start to complain and blame others for our misery or we feel as though God has forsaken us. But we must realise that it is in those very circumstances that God wants to show us that He can make the bitter waters sweet in His own timing, if we will only trust Him.

TWELVE WELLS OF ELIM

> And they came to Elim, where were twelve wells of water, and threescore and ten palm trees: and they encamped there by the waters. Exodus 15:27

The location of Elim is still populated with palm trees and the remains of twelve ancient wells can be found there.

THE WILDERNESS OF SIN

> And they took their journey from Elim, and all the congregation of the children of Israel came unto the wilderness of Sin, which is between Elim and Sinai, on the fifteenth day of the second month after their departing out of the land of Egypt. And the whole congregation of the children of Israel murmured against Moses and Aaron in the wilderness: And the children of Israel said unto them, Would to God we had died by the hand of the LORD in the land of Egypt, when we sat by the flesh pots, and when we did eat bread to the full; for ye have brought us forth into this wilderness, to kill this whole assembly with hunger.
>
> Exodus 16:1-3

The Children of Israel had only been out of Egypt for a short time when they began to murmur against Moses and Aaron in the wilderness. Although they had not yet suffered from hunger and their present wants were supplied, they feared for the future as they saw their food supplies dwindling and imagined the starvation of their children. God had promised the Israelites that if they obeyed his commandments no disease would come upon them so it was a sin for them to distrust that God would provide for their needs.

Many today look to the Israelites and their unbelief thinking that if they were in the same situation they would not have murmured and carried on like they did. But the reality is we are living in an even more degenerate and faithless age and if we were tested in the same manner our behaviour would be even worse than theirs. When we become anxious and fretful, not trusting that God will provide, we are grieving the Holy Spirit. We may find rest and peace in God, casting all our care upon Him; for He careth for us (1 Peter 5:7).

It is important for us to exercise faith in the small things of everyday life right now, so that when the great trials come we have already developed a faith strong enough to withstand the test. Building up faith is like building up muscle each day at the gym. The muscles become stronger over time.

MANNA FROM HEAVEN

> Then said the LORD unto Moses, Behold, I will rain bread from heaven for you; and the people shall go out and gather a certain rate every day, that I may prove them, whether they will walk in my law, or no. Exodus 16:4

In the Wilderness of Sin God granted the request of the Israelites and gave them quails and manna.

> It shall come to pass, that on the sixth day (Friday) they shall prepare that which they bring in; and it shall be twice as much as they gather daily... Six days ye shall gather it; but on the seventh day, which is the Sabbath, in it there shall be none. Exodus 16:5, 22

God instructed them to collect an amount of manna each day. On Friday they were instructed to collect a double portion. And on the Sabbath day (Saturday), they were commanded to rest. God used the manna as a test to see whether they would obey Him and rest on the Sabbath day. God knew if they would obey this commandment, they would keep all the other ones.

God had not yet given the Ten Commandments at Sinai but the Israelites were not ignorant of them. Their father Abraham had kept the spirit of the law written in his heart and had taught it to his posterity. The seventh-day Sabbath had been instituted in Eden "for in six days the LORD made heaven and earth, the sea, and all that in them is, and rested the seventh day: wherefore the LORD blessed the

Sabbath day, and hallowed it" (Genesis 20:11). It was a sign between God and His faithful servants throughout their generations that they would know that it is the Lord who saves them (Exodus 31:13).

A REMINDER OF DELIVERANCE

God also purposed that the Israelites would keep the Sabbath in remembrance of their deliverance from Egyptian slavery and that it was by His own mighty arm that He had brought them out (Deuteronomy 5:14-15). The Sabbath is an eternal reminder of God's mercy in delivering us from the bondage of sin.

REMEMBERING WE ARE BUT DUST

God is the potter, we are the clay. He made us out of the dust of the earth and the Sabbath hours are a time for us to reconsider how utterly dependent we are upon God. We did not make ourselves neither did we breathe life into ourselves; if it was not for God we would not be a living soul. If we did not create ourselves how can we recreate ourselves in His likeness? The reality is that we cannot save ourselves without the creative power of God.

SABBATH KEEPERS NOT SATURDAY KEEPERS

The Pharisees in the time of Christ had missed the spiritual lesson of the Sabbath and had turned it into a miserable and heavy burden. Instead of seeing God's creative and sustaining power in the day, they started to think that they themselves were holy because they kept it as an observance.

LABOURING TO CEASE FROM OUR OWN WORKS

> And on the seventh day God ended his work which he had made; and he rested on the seventh day from all his work which he had made. And God blessed the seventh day, and sanctified it: because that in it he had rested from all his work which God created and made. Genesis 2:2-3

> For he that is entered into his rest, he also hath ceased from his own works, as God did from his. Let us labour therefore to enter into that rest, lest any man fall after the same example of unbelief. Hebrews 4:10-11

> If thou turn away thy foot from the sabbath, from doing thy pleasure on my holy day; and call the sabbath a delight, the holy of the LORD, honourable; and shalt honour him, not doing thine own ways, nor finding thine own pleasure, nor speaking thine own words: Then shalt thou delight thyself in the LORD; and I will cause thee to ride upon the high places of the earth, and feed thee with the heritage of Jacob thy father: for the mouth of the LORD hath spoken it. Isaiah 58:13-14

God ceased from His own works on the seventh-day of creation. The rest that God promised the Israelites, which they never received because of unbelief, is the relief of ceasing from our own works. The Sabbath day is to be a day when we do not do our own ways, or our own pleasure, or speak our own words. It is God which is to work in us "both to will and to do of His good pleasure" (Philippians 2:13). Our works are to be God's working in us and through us, not our own. True Sabbath rest is found in letting God work out our salvation and deal with the consequences of obedience. But we cannot keep the Sabbath rest unless we have made it a habit all the other six days of the week to let go and let God.

THE BREAD FROM HEAVEN

> I am the living bread which came down from heaven: if any man eat of this bread, he shall live for ever: and the bread that I will give is my flesh, which I will give for the life of the world. The Jews therefore strove among themselves, saying, How can this man give us his flesh to eat? Then Jesus said unto them, Verily, verily, I say unto you, Except ye eat the flesh of the Son of man, and drink his blood, ye have no life in you. John 6:51-53

> It is the spirit that quickeneth; the flesh profiteth nothing: the words that I speak unto you, they are spirit, and they are life. John 6:63

B91

The Jews thought that Jesus was making a cannibalistic statement when He told them the only way they could have eternal life was to eat His flesh. It was an abominable thought to them and they were repulsed. But what He was referring to was ingesting the words that He spoke. When we eat bread, our body assimilates it and it becomes a part of us. Christ was trying to teach them that the salvation He came to bring was through believing and receiving His words. But unless His truths were received into their personal experience, they had no real life in them.

EATING OF CHRIST'S FLESH AND DRINKING OF HIS BLOOD

> Whoso eateth my flesh, and drinketh my blood, hath eternal life; and I will raise him up at the last day. For my flesh is meat indeed, and my blood is drink indeed. John 6:54-55

The Apostle Peter declared that "all flesh is as grass... that withereth... but the word of the Lord endureth forever" (1 Peter 1:24-25). Without Christ, we have no life. But if we will receive His word into our lives, we will endure forever also.

MURMURING AGAINST GOD IN THE WILDERNESS OF SIN

> Now all these things happened unto them for ensamples: and they are written for our admonition, upon whom the ends of the world are come. Wherefore let him that thinketh he standeth take heed lest he fall. 1 Corinthians 10:11-12

It was very difficult for the Children of Israel to trust God on a day to day basis for their provisions. Even though they had enough food for that day, they were in a constant state of anxiety about the future. They wanted to make long term plans to provide for themselves so they could feel secure. Many are in that situation today and forget all the wonderful things God has done for them and feel only the inconvenience and difficulty of their trials. Faith is a very difficult thing for human beings to grasp. Trusting God when everything seems to be apparently falling down around us is difficult and yet, it is in our necessities that God has the opportunity to work.

The trials we experience here on earth are to prepare us for heaven. Instead of murmuring and complaining about the difficulties of the way by which God is leading us, we need to remember all the wonderful things He has done for us in our lives and believe that if God has taken care of us in the past then He has already taken care of our future.

REPHIDIM

> In the third month, when the children of Israel were gone forth out of the land of Egypt, the same day came they into the wilderness of Sinai. For they were departed from Rephidim, and were come to the desert of Sinai, and had pitched in the wilderness; and there Israel camped before the mount. Exodus 19:1-2

The Children of Israel camped at Rephidim and complained again to Moses that there was no water to drink saying, "Wherefore is this that thou hast brought us up out of Egypt, to kill us and our children and our cattle with thirst?... and Moses cried unto the LORD, saying, What shall I do unto this people? they be almost ready to stone me" (Exodus 17:3-4). God instructed him to go to "the Rock" at Horeb and to strike it once with his rod. The fact that God instructed Moses to smite "the Rock" implies that Moses was familiar with this enormous monolith. The Rock at Horeb is a large granite boulder which stands between 18-20 metres tall and is situated upon a large mound of rocks. Towering approximately six stories high, it was a notable landmark even in the days of Moses.

THE SPLIT ROCK

> And the LORD said unto Moses, Go on before the people, and take with thee of the elders of Israel; and thy rod, wherewith thou smotest the river, take in thine hand, and go. Behold, I will stand before thee there upon the rock in Horeb; and thou shalt smite the rock, and there shall come water out of it, that the people may drink. And Moses did so in the sight of the elders of Israel. Exodus 17:5-6

Fig. B93,B94 – The split rock boulder is situated upon a natural outcropping of rocks which is several stories high. Fig. B95,B96 – Closer views of the rock showing evident water erosion. The rock is clearly visible from online satellite imagery. See page 313 for co-ordinates.

God responded to the cries of the people and instructed Moses to take the rod that was in his hand and to smite the rock in Horeb. His promise was that He would stand upon the rock and cause water to flow out from it for the people.

THE SMITTEN ROCK A SYMBOL OF CHRIST

> And did all drink the same spiritual drink: for they drank of that spiritual Rock that followed them: and that Rock was Christ. 1 Corinthians 10:4

> One of the soldiers with a spear pierced his side, and forthwith came there out blood and water. John 19:34

Moses smiting the rock at Horeb prefigured Christ being pierced in the side at Calvary and His blood being shed to cover a multitude of transgressions.

> And He (Christ) opened the rock and water flowed out. Psalm 105:41

DRINKING IN THE LIFE OF CHRIST

> Whoso eateth my flesh, and drinketh my blood, hath eternal life; and I will raise him up at the last day. For my flesh is meat indeed, And my blood is drink indeed. He that eateth my flesh, and drinketh my blood, dwelleth in me, and I in him. John 6:54-56

The temporal blessings we receive in our daily life are made possible by the life and death of Christ. He is the source of all sustenance, both spiritual and temporal. If Christ had never left the courts of heaven and come to this earth to redeem man we would not have life.

Water is necessary for life and by providing water from a flinty rock in a dry barren desert God was providing them with life. But not just any life. When the people drank from the pure water that gushed forth from the rock at Horeb they were symbolically drinking of Christ's own life.

To drink of Christ's word is, to drink of Christ Himself. The water that gushed forth from the rock at Horeb is a symbol of His blood in which is His life (Leviticus 17:11). His life becomes part of our own life when we eat of His flesh and drink His blood and it is by this means that we dwell in Him and He in us.

TOTAL SATISFACTION

> Whosoever drinketh of the water that I shall give him shall never thirst; but the water that I shall give him shall be in him a well of water springing up into everlasting life. John 4:14

The world has nothing to offer us. It only leaves us parched, unsatisfied and disappointed. But Jesus Christ offers us something far better.

They drank of that spiritual rock which is Christ. Jesus commanded Moses to smite it that the people might be sustained through His life-giving water. All through their sojournings in the wilderness Jesus was trying to reveal the plan of salvation to the people through Himself. He was trying to help them to understand through the symbolisms provided for their temporal needs that if they did not eat of His word and partake of his righteous life each day they would die spiritually. It is only through drinking in the righteous life wrought out for us in Christ that we can be eternally sustained.

They drank from that life giving water that flowed from the side of Jesus Christ. That smitten Rock of Ages that was given for the life of the world. They were baptised and they partook of the ordinance of God. They showed the Lord's death until He comes. And if they had discerned the spiritual lessons it was going to be a very short time until He would have come. They would have been the generation that would not pass till all be fulfilled; but they could not enter in because of unbelief.

THE LAST SUPPER

> Moreover, brethren, I would not that ye should be ignorant, how that all our fathers were under the cloud, and all passed through the sea; And were all baptised unto Moses in the cloud and in the sea; And did all eat the same spiritual meat; And did all drink the same spiritual drink: for they drank of that spiritual Rock that followed them: and that Rock was Christ. 1 Corinthians 10:1-6

> That the Lord Jesus the same night in which he was betrayed took bread: And when he had given thanks, he brake it, and said, Take, eat: this is my body, which is broken for you: this do in remembrance of me. After the same manner also he took the cup, when he had supped, saying, This cup is the new testament in my blood: this do ye, as oft as ye drink it, in remembrance of me. For as often as ye eat this bread, and drink this cup, ye do show the Lord's death till he come. 1 Corinthians 11:23-26

The Israelites in the wilderness were partaking of the ordinance service. If they had received the "bread from heaven" and the "water of life" by faith, they would have done so in remembrance of Christ who was their Redeemer. Their father Abraham had "rejoiced to see Christ's day" and his children were not ignorant of the Deliverer who would save them from their sins.

By partaking of the ordinances, they were to show the Lord's death till He came. Christ was the lamb slain from the foundation of the world. They were in the Gospel dispensation as much as we are today. "For unto us was the Gospel preached, as well as unto them: but the word preached did not profit them, not being mixed with faith in them that heard it" (Hebrews 4:2).

ALTAR AT REPHIDIM

Moses built an altar, and called the name of it Jehovahnissi. Exodus 17:15

The Amalekites attacked the weak and feeble of the Israelites that were straggling behind. Moses sent Joshua out to fight against them and as long as Aaron and Hur held up his arms toward God in heaven the victory was theirs.

Fig. B99 – This ancient altar is a few hundred metres from the split rock.

MOUNT SINAI (JABAL MAQLA) IN ARABIA

The true Mount Sinai is located in Arabia and the mountain range is still called "the Mountain of the Law" (Jabal Al-Lawz) to this very day. Adjacent to the mountain spans a plain extending through the valleys to the north, east and south encompassing an area that was big enough to accommodate the vast multitude.

THE LORD DESCENDED UPON THE MOUNT IN FIRE

Mount Sinai was altogether on a smoke, because the LORD descended upon it in fire: and the smoke thereof ascended as the smoke of a furnace, and the whole mount quaked greatly. Exodus 19:18

Towards the peak of the mountain, the colour of the rock changes from a light granite colour to a dark sapphire. There is a sharp, sudden contrast in the colour.

The rocks at the summit are metamorphic and unique to the area. Metamorphic rock is formed under immense pressure. The external layer of the rocks have been scorched and have a shiny external patina like sapphire stone, however the interior is pink granite.

ELIJAH AND MT SINAI

> And he arose, and did eat and drink, and went in the strength of that meat forty days and forty nights unto Horeb the mount of God. And he came thither unto a cave, and lodged there; and, behold, the word of the LORD came to him, and he said unto him, What doest thou here, Elijah? 1 Kings 19:8-9

Elijah had just witnessed a spectacular manifestation of God's power on Mt Carmel. He had trusted in God to accept his sacrificial offering on an altar which had been saturated with water. The offering was accepted by God and fire came down from heaven and devoured it. The Baal worshippers who had been mutilating themselves to win the favour of Baal stood defeated and speechless at this spectacle. In retribution for leading the nation of Israel into apostasy, Elijah slew the priests of Baal. Queen Jezebel, a devout follower of Baal was outraged by this token judgment of God and sought to take Elijah's life. Fearful for his safety Elijah fled to Mt Sinai in Arabia for refuge and hid in a cave.

Elijah's Cave is the dark cavern in the centre of figure B104 and is approximately 6 metres in height, width and depth. Figure B105 is the view from the cave and shows where the children of Israel camped and the altar of the golden calf.

Split Rock
Mt Sinai
Encampment
Israelites at Mt Sinai
1000 m

JESUS, MOSES AND ELIJAH

> And after six days Jesus taketh with him Peter, and James, and John, and leadeth them up into an high mountain apart by themselves: and he was transfigured before them. And his raiment became shining, exceeding white as snow; so as no fuller on earth can white them. And there appeared unto them Elias (Elijah) with Moses: and they were talking with Jesus. Mark 9:2-4

It is an interesting fact that all three who were in the mount of the transfiguration had all been upon Mt Sinai at some point. Moses and Elijah as intercessors for ancient Israel were able to empathise with Christ and speak words of comfort to Him before the greatest trial of His life.

PART 7 - ARCHAEOLOGY AT SINAI

EVIDENCE FOR ASIATIC OCCUPATION AT SINAI

The remains of stone circles can still be found along the route of the Israelites. At Rephidim, on the west side of Sinai, there is a large number of these circles which were most likely used to set up tents and keep the animals out.

EGYPTIAN STYLE SPEARHEADS

The book of Exodus records that the bodies of the Egyptians were washed up upon the Arabian shore of the Red Sea crossing. The Israelites collected the weapons and armoury of the dead Egyptians.

FOOT CARVINGS ON ROCKS

The Israelites carved the soles of their feet upon the rocks. God gave the Children of Israel a promise in Deuteronomy that upon condition of obedience, wherever they laid the souls of their feet they would possess the land. This land is in Arabia; the Israelites did not fulfil the conditions of the promise and thefore they did not inherit the land. This is also a spiritual promise to those who receive God's Covenant by faith, that they will possess the earth made new.

> Every place whereon the soles of your feet shall tread shall be yours: from the wilderness and Lebanon, from the river, the river Euphrates, even unto the uttermost sea shall your coast be. Deuteronomy 11:24

THE FAITH OF MOSES

Moses did not merely think of God; he saw Him. God was the constant vision before him; he never lost sight of His face. He saw Jesus as his Saviour, and he believed that the Saviour's merits would be imputed to him. This faith was to Moses no guesswork; it was a reality. This is the kind of faith we need, faith that will endure the test. Oh, how often we yield to temptation because we do not keep our eye upon Jesus!

God was real to him, ever present in his thoughts. When misunderstood, when called upon to face danger and to bear insult for Christ's sake, he endured without retaliation. Moses believed in God as one whom he needed and who would help him because of his need. God was to him a present help.

Much of the faith which we see is merely nominal; the real, trusting, persevering faith is rare. Moses realised in his own experience the promise that God will be a rewarder to those who diligently seek Him. He had respect unto the recompense of the reward. Here is another point in regard to faith which we wish to study; God will reward the man of faith and obedience. If this faith is brought into the life experience, it will enable everyone who fears and loves God to endure trials. Moses was full of confidence in God because he had appropriating faith. He needed help, and he prayed for it, grasped it by faith, and wove into his experience the belief that God cared for him. He believed that God ruled his life in particular. He saw and acknowledged God in every detail of his life and felt that he was under the eye of the All-seeing One, who weighs motives, who tries the heart. He looked to God and trusted in Him for strength to carry him uncorrupted through every form of temptation... The presence of God was sufficient to carry him through the most trying situations in which a man could be placed.

Conflict and Courage, p.85

Do you know what appropriating faith is? It means it was a faith that took God's word and applied it to *himself*. What God provided, what God had promised, Moses didn't see it as for everyone else, he didn't just see it as a blanket blessing, but he took it into his own personal experience.

Heralding the Loud Cry, p.138

GRINDING STONES

> The people went about, and gathered it (manna), and ground it in mills, or beat it in a mortar, and baked it in pans, and made cakes of it: and the taste of it was as the taste of fresh oil. Numbers 11:7-8

The above image is a collection of pottery found scattered around the encampment area. It includes a number of grinding stones which the women would have used to grind the manna to make bread and cakes.

PLAN A

MOSES RECEIVES GOD'S COVENANT TO GIVE TO THE PEOPLE

> Ye have seen what I did unto the Egyptians, and how I bare you on eagles' wings, and brought you unto myself. Now therefore, if ye will obey my voice indeed, and keep my covenant, then ye shall be a peculiar treasure unto me above all people: for all the earth is mine: And ye shall be unto me a kingdom of priests, and an holy nation. These are the words which thou shalt speak unto the children of Israel. Exodus 19:4-6

God had brought the Israelites to Mt Sinai to give them His Covenant. God reminded them of what He had done to the Egyptians and how it was He who provided their needs in the wilderness and brought them to this place. They had been completely incapable of saving themselves at the Red Sea, of sweetening the waters at Marah, of raining bread from heaven at Elim or making the water gush from the rock at Horeb. He had done all these things for them – they could not have saved themselves. Reminding them of this fact, He promises to make them a peculiar people and a holy nation. He sought to ratify the same covenant that He had made with Abraham.* Abraham had received God's Covenant simply by "believing" (Genesis 15:6), and this was all that God required of the people at Sinai.

THE PEOPLE'S RESPONSE

> And Moses came and called for the elders of the people, and laid before their faces all these words which the LORD commanded him. And all the people answered together, and said, All that the LORD hath spoken we will do. And Moses returned the words of the people unto the LORD. Exodus 19:7-8

When Moses delivered the words of God's Covenant to the people they replied, "All that the Lord hath said we will do." In their spiritual blindness, the Israelites did not realise their utter inability to make themselves holy. They had not recognised their need of God to do this for them. Instead of saying that they would do it, they should have simply said, "Amen – let it be so."

A BARRIER BECAUSE OF UNBELIEF

> And the LORD said unto Moses, Lo, I come unto thee in a thick cloud, that the people may hear when I speak with thee, and believe thee for ever. And Moses told the words of the people unto the LORD. And the LORD said unto Moses, Go unto the people, and sanctify them to day and to morrow, and let them wash their clothes, And be ready against the third day: for the third day the LORD will come down in the sight of all the people upon mount Sinai. And thou shalt set bounds unto the people round about, saying, Take heed to yourselves, that ye go not up into the mount, or touch the border of it: whosoever toucheth the mount shall be surely put to death.
>
> Exodus 19:7-12

Because the people had failed in receiving God's Covenant, they had demonstrated that they did not have faith. They did not discern that God was making them a promise but instead thought that they needed to promise Him. They had missed the point.

Abraham was declared "the friend of God" (James 2:23). The scriptures declared that because of his belief, he was accounted holy. Moses had the same faith. He had a faith that brought to him "holiness, without which no man shall see the Lord" (Hebrews 12:14). The people, lacking this faith, were excluded from the mount. Mercifully, God commanded Moses to set boundary markers around it so that no one could come into the mount, or touch it because they would die.

God never purposed to separate the people from Him, or to speak the Ten Commandments. But because of the transgression of claiming to be able to make themselves holy, He went to plan B and "added" the Ten Commandments (Deuteronomy 5:22; Galatians 3:19).

*See page 157

God's Promises to Us

I

I promise you will have no other gods before me.

II

I promise you will not make unto yourself any graven image, or any likeness of any thing that is in heaven above, or that is in the earth beneath, or that is in the water under the earth. Neither will you bow down to them, nor serve them.

III

I promise you will not take the name of the Lord your God in vain.

IV

I promise you will remember the sabbath day, to keep it holy. Six days you will labour, and do all your work: but the seventh day is the sabbath of the Lord your God: in it you will not do any work, you, nor your son, nor your daughter, your manservant, nor your maidservant, nor your cattle, nor the stranger that is within your gates: for in six days the Lord made heaven and earth, the sea, and all that in them is, and rested the seventh day: wherefore the Lord blessed the sabbath day, and hallowed it.

I promise you will love me with all your heart, all your soul, and all your mind;

Whereby are given unto us exceeding great and precious promises: that by these ye might be partakers of the divine nature, having escaped the corruption that is in the world through lust. 2 Peter 1:4

V

I promise you will honour your father and your mother.

VI

I promise you will not kill.

VII

I promise you will not commit adultery.

VIII

I promise you will not steal.

IX

I promise you will not bear false witness against your neighbour.

X

I promise you will not covet your neighbour's house, you will not covet your neighbour's wife, nor his manservant, nor his maidservant, nor his ox, nor his ass, nor any thing that is your neighbour's.

and your neighbour as yourself.

PLAN B

THE TEN COMMANDMENTS

And it came to pass on the third day in the morning, that there were thunders and lightnings, and a thick cloud upon the mount, and the voice of the trumpet exceeding loud; so that all the people that was in the camp trembled. And Moses brought forth the people out of the camp to meet with God; and they stood at the nether part of the mount. And mount Sinai was altogether on a smoke, because the LORD descended upon it in fire: and the smoke thereof ascended as the smoke of a furnace, and the whole mount quaked greatly. Exodus 19:16-18

In order to awaken the people to a sense of the awe of God and His holiness, He delivered the Ten Commandments with a terrible demonstration of His power. Thunder and lightnings electrified the atmosphere and the earth shook while the top of the mountain raged with fire. In the midst of this inferno, God spoke the Ten Commandments in an audible voice. "And when the people saw it, they removed, and stood afar off. And they said unto Moses, Speak thou with us, and we will hear: but let not God speak with us, lest we die" (Exodus 20:18-19).

TEN PRECIOUS PROMISES

Whereby are given unto us exceeding great and precious promises: that by these ye might be partakers of the divine nature, having escaped the corruption that is in the world through lust. 2 Peter 1:4

The people were so terrified that they were unable to listen to His full speech and they begged Moses to speak with them, saying, "We will hear [you]," but would not let God speak to them.

When God spoke the Ten Commandments in Exodus 20, He was repeating the same promise He had made three days before (Exodus 19:4-6). Again He was pledging that He would be the one to make them a holy nation. When God speaks, His word does not return to Him void (Isaiah 55:10-11). In the beginning God said, "Let there be light and there was light" (Genesis 1:3). He "spake and it was" (Psalm 33:9). The same creative power was in the word when He spoke at Sinai. His spoken word, if received as a promise, would have worked holiness within them. Yet the people would not hear and believe and receive. Plan B had failed.

Neither would they consider that the law came from the same rock from where the water was already flowing. And that rock was Christ (1 Corinthians 10:4).

PLAN C

THE LAW ENLARGED PRACTICALLY (THE BOOK OF THE COVENANT)

> And he said unto Moses, Come up unto the LORD, thou, and Aaron, Nadab, and Abihu, and seventy of the elders of Israel; and worship ye afar off. And Moses alone shall come near the LORD: but they shall not come nigh; neither shall the people go up with him. And Moses came and told the people all the words of the LORD, and all the judgments: and all the people answered with one voice, and said, All the words which the LORD hath said will we do. And Moses wrote all the words of the LORD, and rose up early in the morning, and builded an altar under the hill, and twelve pillars, according to the twelve tribes of Israel. And he sent young men of the children of Israel, which offered burnt offerings, and sacrificed peace offerings of oxen unto the LORD. And Moses took half of the blood, and put it in basins; and half of the blood he sprinkled on the altar. And he took the book of the covenant, and read in the audience of the people: and they said, All that the LORD hath said will we do, and be obedient. And Moses took the blood, and sprinkled it on the people, and said, Behold the blood of the covenant, which the LORD hath made with you concerning all these words. Exodus 24:1-8

The Israelites did not discern the Ten Commandments as promises. They took it as instruction that they themselves were to work out. So God met them where they were at. He invited Moses into the mount and delivered to him an enlargement of the law with all the particulars pertaining to the daily and civil life.

MAN PROMISES GOD TO KEEP HIS LAW AND STATUTES (PLAN B AND C TOGETHER)

After receiving the law audibly spoken from the mount and the minute instructions for its keeping, the people still "answered with one voice, and said, All the words which the LORD hath said will we do" (Exodus 24:3,7). Again they declared that they would make themselves holy and confirmed their covenant to God with the blood of a sacrifice.

MAN BREAKS HIS PROMISE TO GOD

The rebellion of the Israelites dancing around the golden calf resulted in God directing Moses to break the two tables of stone, thus dis-annulling their covenant that they had made with God. They had failed to keep their promise that they would be holy and keep His commandments.

THE OLD COVENANT WAS FAULTY

> But now hath he obtained a more excellent ministry, by how much also he is the mediator of a better covenant, which was established upon better promises. For if that first covenant had been faultless, then should no place have been sought for the second. Hebrews 8:6-7

The "Old Covenant" is a term used to refer to the covenant that man made with God: "All that the Lord hath said will we do." This covenant was faulty because it was based on man's worthless promises, which are like ropes of sand.

THE APOSTASY AT SINAI

After the Ten Commandments had been spoken and the Israelites had covenanted to keep all the statutes, God called Moses up into the mountain. The Israelites were accustomed to visible representations of deity and had come to see Moses as a representation of God. During the long absence of Moses, they feared that they had been abandoned by God and demanded that Aaron give them another visible representation of Him. Aaron, being weak in character, gave in to their request and fashioned a golden calf. He then set an altar before the calf and said, "These be thy gods, O Israel, which brought thee up out of the land of Egypt... Tomorrow is a feast to the LORD. And they rose up early on the morrow, and offered burnt offerings, and brought peace offerings; and the people sat down to eat and to drink, and rose up to play" (Exodus 32:4-6).

The Lord revealed to Moses the apostasy of the people and declared that He would destroy them in His anger. God was proving Moses to see if he would be a faithful father to the nation. Moses interpreted God's anger as an invitation to intercede for the people and he argued the case that if He were to destroy Israel, the surrounding nations would conclude that God had brought them into the wilderness to kill them. God gave Moses the offer to make a new nation of his own posterity, but he refused, instead identifying himself with the people. Upon returning from the mount and witnessing the licentiousness of the people as they danced naked around the golden calf, Moses, instructed by God, broke the tables of stone in righteous indignation.

> In utter discouragement and wrath because of their great sin, he [Moses] threw down the tables of stone by divine direction purposely to break them in the sight of the people, and thus signify that they had broken the covenant so recently made with God. *Signs of the Times*, May 20, 1880

After the apostasy, Moses pleaded with God on behalf of the people to spare their lives. "And Moses returned unto the LORD, and said, Oh, this people have sinned a great sin, and have made them gods of gold. Yet now, if thou wilt forgive their sin; and if not, blot me, I pray thee, out of thy book which thou hast written" (Exodis32:31-32). His interests were so identified with the people that he would rather perish with them than witness their destruction. God replied that whoever

Fig. B114-B116 – Above from left to right: bovine carvings on the altar; etched into its rock face are petroglyphs of bovine creatures, cattle and bulls.

sinned the sin would die the death. "Whosoever hath sinned against me, him will I blot out of my book" (Exodus 32:33). Judgment was speedily executed and three thousand were smitten by the sword, and this judgment was followed by a plague.

THE GOLDEN CALF

> And Aaron said, Let not the anger of my lord wax hot: thou knowest the people, that they are set on mischief. For they said unto me, Make us gods, which shall go before us: for as for this Moses, the man that brought us up out of the land of Egypt, we wot not what is become of him. And I said unto them, Whosoever hath any gold, let them break it off. So they gave it me: then I cast it into the fire, and there came out this calf. Exodus 32:22-24

Figure B113 is an enormous mound of rocks about 3 metres high and 10 metres long upon which Aaron placed the golden calf. Egyptian style petroglyphs are inscribed upon the rocks. This style of engraving is unique to this location. A few metres away is the altar Aaron built "before" the golden calf (Exodus 32:5). (See figure B117.)

In Egypt worshippers would engrave representations of their deity and worship before them. In Exodus 32:4 Aaron referred to "gods" in the plural sense.

> He received them at their hand, and fashioned it with a graving tool, after he had made it a molten calf: and they said, These be thy gods, O Israel, which brought thee up out of the land of Egypt. Exodus 32:4

When Moses came down from the mountain he would have seen the Children of Israel dancing around the golden calf which had been placed on the top of this pile.

B118

THE GRAVEYARD

> And there fell of the people that day about three thousand men. Exodus 32:28

There is a graveyard located on the periphery of the encampment at Sinai with several thousand graves marked there by erected tomb stones. The Bible gives a full explanation for the existence of a large graveyard in the middle of the wilderness.

God was calling Israel out of captivity and bondage and into His New Covenant. He had performed mighty miracles for them. They had been through the Red Sea which symbolised baptism and a new life in Jesus Christ. They had partaken of the ordinances in the Wilderness of Sin and at Rephidim. To go back to their old evil ways was now unacceptable. God was raising these people up to be a pure and holy nation of priests. If God had not put a check on the apostasy at Sinai then the heathen nations would have taunted the Israelites saying, "You worshipped false gods in the wilderness. Then we should be able to do the same." In this instance a few were punished that millions might be saved.

PLAN D

THE SANCTUARY – THE DRESS REHEARSAL

In mercy God again gave His people an opportunity to receive His Covenant by faith. The types and ceremonies of the sanctuary were object lessons to teach them that they could not save themselves. They were dependent upon the ministration of a high priest and the blood of a sacrifice. The high priest and the sacrifice typified Christ and if they had learned the lessons of the sanctuary they would have partaken of the same covenant that God made with Abraham. It was through the sacrificial system that they also could have seen Christ's day and been glad (John 8:56). When the promise of Christ was fulfilled, the sanctuary system was abolished and nailed to the cross (Colossians 2:14).

PLAN E

THE SECOND TABLES OF STONE AND THE CLEFT OF THE ROCK

The LORD said, Behold, there is a place by me, and thou shalt stand upon a rock: And it shall come to pass, while my glory passeth by, that I will put thee in a clift of the rock, and will cover thee with my hand while I pass by.

Exodus 33:21-22

And he said, The LORD is my rock, and my fortress, and my deliverer; The God of my rock; in him will I trust: he is my shield, and the horn of my salvation, my high tower, and my refuge, my saviour. 2 Samuel 22:2-3

In the solitude of the cloud-enshrouded mountain, Moses, the representative of the people, received the law a second time. Now, in a very different atmosphere, of peace and love, God placed Moses in the cleft of the rock and covered Him with His hand as He passed by. Though God's law stands unchangeable, Christ would be a Refuge and Redeemer from sin and its consequences to those who would receive Him by faith. He would hide them in Himself and impart to them His own obedient life. (Exodus 33:18-34:8.)

OF THE LAW AND THE CHRISTIAN

by John Bunyan

The law was given twice upon Mount Sinai, but the appearance of the Lord, when he gave it the second time, was wonderfully different from that of his, when at the first he delivered it to Israel.

1. When he gave it the first time, he caused his terror and severity to appear before Moses, to the shaking of his soul and the dismaying of Israel; but when he gave it the second time, he caused all his goodness to pass before Moses, to the comfort of his conscience and the bowing of his heart.

2. When he gave it the first time, it was with thunderings and lightnings, with blackness and darkness, with flame and smoke, and a tearing sound of the trumpet; but when he gave it the second time, it was with a proclamation of his name to be merciful, gracious, long- suffering, and abundant in goodness and truth, keeping mercy for thousands, forgiving iniquity, transgressions, and sins.

3. When he gave it the first time, Moses was called to go up to receive it through the fire, which made him exceedingly fear and quake: but when he went to receive it the second time, he was laid in a cleft of the rock.

4. From all which I gather, that, though as to the matter of the law, both as to its being given the first time and the second, it binds the

unbeliever under the pains of eternal damnation (if he close not with Christ by faith); yet as to the manner of its giving at these two times, I think the first doth more principally intend its force as a covenant of works, not at all respecting the Lord Jesus; but this second time not (at least in the manner of its being given) respecting such a covenant, but rather as a rule or directory to those who already are found in the clift of the rock Christ; for the saint himself, though he be without law to God, as it is considered the first or old covenant, yet even he is not without law to him as considered under grace; not without law to God, but under the law to Christ.

5. Though, therefore, it be sad with the unbeliever, because he only and wholly standeth under the law as it is given in fire, in smoke, in blackness, and darkness, and thunder; all which threaten him with eternal ruin if he fulfil not the utmost tittle thereof; yet the believer stands to the law under no such consideration, neither is he so at all to hear or regard it, for he is now removed from thence to the blessed mountain of Zion—to grace and forgiveness of sins; he is now, I say, by faith in the Lord Jesus, shrouded under so perfect and blessed a righteousness, that this thundering law of Mount Sinai cannot find the least fault or diminution therein, but rather approveth and alloweth thereof, either when or wherever it find it. This is called the righteousness of God without the law, and also said to be witnessed by both the law and the prophets; even the righteousness of God, which is by faith in Jesus Christ unto all and upon all them that believe; for there is no difference.

6. Wherefore, whenever thou who believest in Jesus, dost hear the law in its thundering and lightning fits, as if it would burn up heaven and earth, then say thou, I am freed from this law, these thunderings have nothing to do with my soul; nay, even this law, while it thus thunders and roars, it doth both allow and approve of my righteousness. I know that Hagar would sometimes be domineering and high, even in Sarah's house, and against her; but this she is not to be suffered to do, nay, though Sarah herself be barren; wherefore, serve it also as Sarah served her, and expel her out from thy house. My meaning is, when this law with its thundering threatenings doth attempt to lay hold on thy conscience, shut it out with a promise of grace; cry, The inn is taken up already; the Lord Jesus is here entertained, and here is no room for the law. Indeed, if it will be content with being my informer, and so lovingly leave off to judge me, I will be content, it shall be in my sight, I will also delight therein; but otherwise, I being now made upright without it, and that too with that righteousness which this law speaks well of and approveth, I may not, will not, cannot dare not make it my Saviour and judge, nor suffer it to set up its government in my conscience; for by so doing, I fall from grace, and Christ Jesus doth

profit me nothing.

7. Thus, therefore, the soul that is married to him that is raised up from the dead, both may and ought to deal with this law of God; yea, it doth greatly dishonour its Lord and refuse its gospel privileges, if it at any time otherwise doth, whatever it seeth or feels. "The law hath power over the wife so long as her husband liveth, but if her husband be dead she is freed from that law; so that she is no adulteress though she be married to another man." Indeed, so long as thou art alive to sin, and to thy righteousness which is of the law, so long thou hast them for thy husband, and they must reign over thee; but when once they are become dead unto thee—as they then most certainly will when thou closest with the Lord Jesus Christ—then, I say, thy former husbands have no more to meddle with thee; thou art freed from their law. Set the case: A woman be cast into prison for a debt of hundreds of pounds; if after this she marry, yea, though while she is in the jailor's hand, in the same day that she is joined to her husband, her debt is all become his; yea, and the law also that arrested and imprisoned this woman, as freely tells her, go: she is freed, saith Paul, from that; and so saith the law of this land.

The sum, then, of what hath been said is this—The Christian hath now nothing to do with the law, as it thundereth and burneth on Sinai, or as it bindeth the conscience to wrath and the displeasure of God for sin; for from its thus appearing, it is freed by faith in Christ. Yet it is to have regard thereto, and is to count it holy, just, and good; which, that it may do, it is always, whenever it seeth or regards it, to remember that he who giveth it to us "is merciful, gracious, long-suffering, and abundant in goodness and truth." John Bunyan

OPPORTUNITY AFTER OPPORTUNITY

If man had kept the law of God, as given to Adam after his fall, preserved by Noah, and observed by Abraham, there would have been no necessity for the ordinance of circumcision. And if the descendants of Abraham had kept the covenant, of which circumcision was a sign, they would never have been seduced into idolatry, nor would it have been necessary for them to suffer a life of bondage in Egypt; they would have kept God's law in mind, and there would have been no necessity for it to be proclaimed from Sinai or engraved upon the tables of stone. And had the people practiced the principles of the Ten Commandments, there would have been no need of the additional directions given to Moses. *Patriarchs and Prophets*, p.364

The Israelites were granted one opportunity after another. His original intent was that they would agree to the same covenant that God made with Abraham (Exodus 19). But when they failed to discern God's promise to them, *they pledged themselves to make themselves holy like Him*. With awful grandeur, God then showed them the majesty and might of His character to impress upon them their *complete and utter inability to attain to such a state of holiness* (Exodus 20). Yet the people again said they would do it. The Lord is long-suffering not willing that any should perish. Though the Israelites lacked faith, God did not abandon them in their failure; He adapted to their need and made every provision possible to reveal His Covenant to their dim understanding.

THE ALTAR AND TWELVE PILLARS

> Moses got up early the next morning and built an altar at the foot of the mountain and set up twelve stone pillars representing the twelve tribes of Israel.Exodus 24:4

At the base of Mt Sinai is a corral next to an altar. The animals would be led through the corral and offered as a sacrifice. The altar is made of unhewn stone just as the Bible describes.

The stone remains of pillars were also found at this site. It is proposed that at one time the stones were stacked one upon another to make a total of twelve columns, each representing one of the twelve tribes.

Fig. B119-B121 – The corral and altar at Sinai with the pillars.

PART 8 - THE LAW AND THE COVENANTS

THE ABRAHAMIC COVENANT

The covenant that God had sought to make with Israel at Sinai prior to giving the Ten Commandments was the same covenant He had made with their father Abraham.

ABRAHAM'S VISION OF JESUS

At the age of fifty five, Abraham left Ur of the Chaldees (Iraq) and went to Haran (southern Turkey) with his father. Following his father's death, God said to Abraham, "Get thee out of thy country, and from thy kindred, and from thy father's house, unto a land that I will show thee: And I will make of thee a great nation, and I will bless thee, and make thy name great; and thou shalt be a blessing: And I will bless them that bless thee, and curse him that curseth thee: and in thee shall all families of the earth be blessed" (Genesis 12:1-3). When he was separated from his nephew Lot, the last of his kindred, God fulfilled His promise to show him the land.

THE PROMISES TO ABRAHAM

- **An eternal inheritance of land**

> Get thee out of thy country, and from thy kindred, and from thy father's house, unto a land that I will show thee. Genesis 12:1

> For all the land which thou seest, to thee will I give it, and to thy seed for ever. Genesis 13:15

> I will give unto thee, and to thy seed after thee, the land wherein thou art a stranger, all the land of Canaan, for an everlasting possession. Genesis 17:8

> And the LORD said unto Abram, after that Lot was separated from him, Lift up now thine eyes, and look from the place where thou art northward, and southward, and eastward, and westward: For all the land which thou seest, to thee will I give it, and to thy seed for ever. Genesis 13:14-15

> And he gave him none inheritance in it, no, not so much as to set his foot on: yet he promised that he would give it to him for a possession, and to his seed after him, when as yet he had no child. Acts 7:5

God gave the promise of land to Abraham and His "seed" as an eternal inheritance. But Abraham, Isaac and Jacob never received the inheritance in their lifetime. God's promise did not fail. It was not the promise of merely the land of Canaan as we know it today but the promise of the resurrection of the dead to an earth made new (1 Corinthians 15:51-52; Isaiah 66:22).

An eternal inheritance can only be enjoyed by those who have everlasting life. The only way that Abraham, Isaac and Jacob could ever be resurrected from the dead to an everlasting life is by having their sins forgiven through the blood of Jesus Christ.

- **The promise of posterity**

> I will make of thee a great nation. Genesis 12:2

> And I will make thy seed as the dust of the earth: so that if a man can number the dust of the earth, then shall thy seed also be numbered. Genesis 13:16

> Thou shalt be a father of many nations. Genesis 17:4

God promised Abraham a posterity through the dead womb of Sarah. This promise, while it was fulfilled in a literal sense, more specially applies in a spiritual sense, that he would be the spiritual father of the believers in Christ of all time.

- **Promise of Christ**

> In thee shall all families of the earth be blessed. Genesis 12:3

> In thy seed shall all the nations of the earth be blessed. Genesis 22:18

> To Abraham and his seed were the promises made. And to thy seed, which is Christ. Galatians 3:16

> If ye be Christ's, then are ye Abraham's seed, and heirs according to the promise. Galatians 3:29

God pledged that the Messiah would be born through the descendants of Abraham's son, Isaac. The "seed" who would be a blessing to the whole earth was Christ. It was only those that were "in-Christ" that would receive the eternal inheritance.

THE COVENANT CONFIRMED BY A PROMISE AND AN OATH

> Wherein God, willing more abundantly to show unto the heirs of promise the immutability of his counsel, confirmed it by an oath: That by two immutable things, in which it was impossible for God to lie, we might have a strong consolation, who have fled for refuge to lay hold upon the hope set before us. Hebrews 6:17-18

CHRIST'S RETURN IN THE FOURTH GENERATION

In the fourth generation they shall come hither again: for the iniquity of the Amorites is not yet full. Genesis 15:16

And he said unto Abram, Know of a surety that thy seed shall be a stranger in a land that is not theirs, and shall serve them; and they shall afflict them four hundred years; And also that nation, whom they shall serve, will I judge: and afterward shall they come out with great substance. Genesis 15:13-14

And God spake on this wise, That his seed should sojourn in a strange land; and that they should bring them into bondage, and entreat them evil four hundred years. And the nation to whom they shall be in bondage will I judge, said God: and after that shall they come forth, and serve me in this place. Acts 7:6-7

God brought the Israelites to Mt Sinai to give them the Abrahamic Covenant and had they received it by faith, the promise of Christ, the resurrection from the dead and an everlasting inheritance on the earth made new would have been realised in their generation.

JEHOVAH-JIREH - GOD WILL PROVIDE

And being fully persuaded that, what he had promised, he was able also to perform. Romans 4:21

Abraham said, My son, God will provide himself a lamb for a burnt offering. Genesis 22:8

God had promised Abraham that he would have a child but he could not produce the child himself. He had tried to produce the promised child through Sarah's handmaid, Hagar, but only brought misery into his home. God's promise was that Sarah would give birth to the promised child. "Through faith also Sara herself received strength to conceive seed, and was delivered of a child when she was past age, because she judged him faithful who had promised" (Hebrews 11:11).

As an aged man Abraham was called of God to offer up Isaac on Mt Moriah. This was a very painful test for Abraham as Isaac was the son of his old age. On their way up the mount, Isaac, seeing only the wood for the sacrifice had asked his father "behold the fire and the wood but where is the lamb for a burnt offering?" Abraham replied, "God will provide himself a lamb for a burnt offering." Abraham built an altar at the appointed place, laid the wood in order, and bound Isaac his son upon the altar." At the moment Abraham raised the knife to slay Isaac, an angel restrained him. Seeing a ram trapped in a thicket, he offered it instead of his son. He named that place Jehovah-jireh which means "in the mount of the Lord He shall provide." It was in this place that Christ, the true sacrifice, was offered upon Calvary.

God was teaching Abraham that what He required from him only God Himself could provide. But He would never lay His requirement before Abraham without, pledging that He would fulfil it Himself.

THE GOSPEL PREACHED TO ABRAHAM AND ISRAEL

> And the scripture, foreseeing that God would justify the heathen through faith, preached before the gospel unto Abraham, saying In thee shall all nations be blessed.
> Galatians 3:8

> For unto us was the gospel preached, as well as unto them [ancient Israel]: but the word preached did not profit them, not being mixed with faith in them that heard it.
> Hebrews 4:2

Had the Israelites received the faith of their father Abraham, they would have received Christ as their only hope of salvation. The experience of having to depend totally upon God in the wilderness should have taught them their insufficiency and desperate need of a Saviour. But they never learned that God Himself would provide both that which He promised and that which He required.

STRANGERS AND PILGRIMS ON THE EARTH

> For we are strangers before thee, and sojourners, as were all our fathers.
> 1 Chronicles 29:15

> By faith Abraham, when he was called to go out into a place which he should after receive for an inheritance, obeyed; and he went out, not knowing whither he went. By faith he sojourned in the land of promise, as in a strange country, dwelling in tabernacles with Isaac and Jacob, the heirs with him of the same promise: For he looked for a city which hath foundations, whose builder and maker is God. Through faith also Sara herself received strength to conceive seed, and was delivered of a child when she was past age, because she judged him faithful who had promised. Therefore sprang there even of one, and him as good as dead, so many as the stars of the sky in multitude, and as the sand which is by the sea shore innumerable. These all died in faith, not having received the promises, but having seen them afar off, and were persuaded of them, and embraced them, and confessed that they were strangers and pilgrims on the earth. For they that say such things declare plainly that they seek a country. And truly, if they had been mindful of that country from

whence they came out, they might have had opportunity to have returned. But now they desire a better country, that is, an heavenly: wherefore God is not ashamed to be called their God: for he hath prepared for them a city.

Hebrews 11:8-16

And these all, having obtained a good report through faith, received not the promise. Hebrews 11:39

The faithful of all ages have never regarded the earth as their home. King David, at the height of his power in the nation of Israel declared, "We are strangers... and sojourners."

WHAT ISRAEL COULD HAVE BECOME

Thou shalt bring them in, and plant them in the mountain of thine inheritance, in the place, O LORD, which thou hast made for thee to dwell in, in the Sanctuary, O Lord, which thy hands have established. Exodus 15:17

Now therefore, if ye will obey my voice indeed, and keep my covenant, then ye shall be a peculiar treasure unto me above all people: for all the earth is mine: And ye shall be unto me a kingdom of priests. Exodus 19:5-6

The priest's lips should keep knowledge, and they should seek the law at his mouth: for he is the messenger of the LORD of hosts. Malachi 2:7

The Israelites would have served God as priests. They would have crossed the Jordan into Canaan. God had promised that He would drive out the inhabitants with hornets (Exodus 23:28). He did not require them to fight – He Himself would have driven the heathen from before them in His own ways. Their wives and children could have moved straight into the homes and partaken of the fruits of the fields of the heathen. Leaving them safely there, the men of Israel would have traversed the globe as "messengers of the Lord," preaching the Gospel and shortly after, the end would have come. But the Israelites as a nation never received this promise and instead became insular and self-centred, believing that they were the exclusive benefactors of the Covenant and delayed the coming of Christ.

CHRIST WILL COME WHEN THE GOSPEL IS PREACHED TO ALL THE WORLD

This gospel of the kingdom shall be preached in all the world for a witness unto all nations; and then shall the end come. Matthew 24:14

He which testifieth these things saith, Surely I come quickly. Amen. Even so, come, Lord Jesus. Revelation 22:20

> Seeing then that all these things shall be dissolved, what manner of persons ought ye to be in all holy conversation and godliness, Looking for and hasting unto the coming of the day of God, wherein the heavens being on fire shall be dissolved, and the elements shall melt with fervent heat? 2 Peter 3:11-12

Through God's miraculous manifestations in the plagues of Egypt the world was ripe for the preaching of the Gospel. God gave the Amorites and surrounding heathen nations four generations to repent of their idolatry. The Gospel was to be preached as a witness against them to fully justify without excuse their condemnation. The other purpose was also to call out the individuals such as Rahab who would take their stand on the Lord's side.

The world has now reached the same condition of iniquity as Canaan had in the fourth generation. The Gospel must be taken to the world before Christ can return. To those who reject the Gospel it's proclamation will be a witness against them.

THE TWELVE SPIES – IMMEDIATE ACTION

Twelve spies were sent into the land of Canaan to survey the land. Upon their return, ten of the spies gave an evil report stating that although the land was a good land, the giants were too big and too strong to drive out. Of the twelve spies, only two, Caleb and Joshua, gave a good report declaring that although the land was occupied, God Himself would bring them in and give it to them. The Israelites became fearful because of the evil report and doubted God's word. They were ready to stone Caleb and Joshua but the Lord intervened and pronounced judgment against Israel for its faithlessness. The people had declared, "Would God we had died in this wilderness!" (Numbers 14:2). God granted them their request and giving a year for each day of the forty day survey of Canaan, they remained in the wilderness until their carcasses fell, every one who was over the age of twenty at the rebellion, except Caleb and Joshua.

Caleb and Joshua realised the Covenant promise and they believed that God would open the way for them if they went forward in faith. Obedient to their conviction they gave the right message at the right time. Had the people responded to their call to immediate action God's promise would have been hastily fulfilled. Calebs and Joshuas are needed to give the same call today.

> Now all these things happened unto them for ensamples: and they are written for our admonition, upon whom the ends of the world are come. 1 Corinthians 10:11

All the experiences of the Children of Israel in the Wilderness were written for the benefit of those living at the end of the world. God designed that we would learn from their mistakes and not repeat them. His desire for His people is to have a child-like trust that will take Him at His word and say, "Amen. All that you have promised, I know you will do – and I will let you do it." Through the Red Sea experience God was teaching them to depend upon Him and we must learn the same lesson from our experiences in life today.

CLOSING PRAYER

Oh Lord, thou great God and Creator of the Universe, the Mighty One who ruleth over all, I exceedingly tremble and quake before my own heart. Yay, oh Lord, how love I thy law, it is my meditation all the day, but I am so scared that I shall be found seeking to perform Thy will in my own strength. Yay, Lord, though my imitation may be perfect, my copy exact, yet if it be not thee that buildeth the house, then I know that in that day it shall be burnt as stubble. And I am so afraid that this deceptive heart of mine shall cause me to glory in that which you do in me, that I will take and ascribe the honour of obedience to myself, and that my heart shall become uplifted in vanity. Truly it must needs be that I be saved from myself.

Yet I glory in thy wisdom, I glory in thy perfection and I aspire unto Thy likeness and Thou has called me to be as thyself – holy, harmless, undefiled, yet I cannot, except as thou wilt, and I believe that thou wilt. I believe oh thou Lord that thou can, yeah and will, work in me to will and do of your good pleasure, that I may have the testimony of Enoch, that I may have the inheritance of Abraham, and that I may have the righteousness of Jesus Christ. I believe that the blood of Jesus Christ cleanses me from all sin – that that life which is in the blood will purify my heart and perfect my character – and that that blood, that life, shall become as my very own, and that I may receive an inheritance among them which are sanctified by the faith that is in Jesus.

Heralding the Loud Cry, p.107

Section 3

"HE IS NOT HERE-
FOR HE IS RISEN"

CALVARY'S HIDDEN SECRET

INTRODUCTION

In the Old Testament times, the Ark of the Covenant was revered as the most sacred object within the Jewish sanctuary. It was housed in the Most Holy Place, the second compartment of the sanctuary. Once a year on the Day of Atonement the high priest of Israel would enter into the Most Holy Place and sprinkle the blood of a goat upon the mercy seat between the cherubim, to make atonement for the sins of Israel. The law of Ten Commandments, written on two tables of stone, was safely hidden in the Ark beneath the mercy seat and it was this law that required the blood of a perfect sacrifice to satisfy its claims for their transgression. This ceremony foreshadowed the New Covenant (Everlasting Covenant) of mercy and forgiveness for sins through the shedding of Christ's blood at Calvary and His ministerial work as our High Priest (Hebrews 9:11). The Bible states that "all have sinned, and come short of the glory of God"; and that "the wages of sin is death but the gift of God is eternal life through Jesus Christ our Lord" (Romans 3:23, 6:23). Every human being, apart from Christ, has transgressed the Law of God, therefore only Christ's righteous life can perfectly satisfy its claims, and this life He offers to us freely as a gift. Christ in His great love for fallen humanity had made a decree with the Father that He would be the Lamb of God slain from the foundation of the world. Just as soon as Adam sinned, Christ became the Saviour.

THE OLD COVENANT

The posterity of Abraham, the Jewish nation, was chosen of God to be the depositories of His law and to proclaim the Everlasting Gospel to the world. Initially at Mt Sinai the Children of Israel entered into the Old Covenant which was based upon their promise to keep God's Law perfectly in their own strength, without a mediator. After a period of forty days, Moses returned from the mount with the requirements of the Covenant now physically engraved upon two tables of stone, to witness the Children of Israel dancing around the golden calf. By divine direction, Moses broke the two tables of stone in righteous indignation thus signifying that the Old Covenant had been broken and dis-annulled. The Old Covenant could not have been effectual because it was a covenant based on man's pledge to God, that he would keep God's law apart from Christ. Cain's offering was of this nature – man trying to save himself through his own efforts without recognising the merits of Christ. The reality is that sinful, fallen human beings will naturally gravitate towards this covenant of self-works and try and bring it into the New Covenant wherever possible.

In the apostasy at Sinai, the ring-leaders in the rebellion were promptly dealt with and those who repented held onto the hope that God would have mercy on them. The Old Covenant had swiftly taught them that their promises to God were useless and that it was impossible for them to keep God's law in their own strength. In this sense the Old Covenant experience became their schoolmaster bringing them to Christ. They saw their sin and felt their need of a Saviour's mercy and His imparted merits to enable them to keep the law.

GOD'S EVERLASTING COVENANT

When in the mount, God told Moses that He would destroy the Children of Israel because they had broken their promise and violated His law. The terms of the Old Covenant were "obey and live or disobey and die", as with the New Covenant, except that there was no mercy for sin and no mediator in this works based covenant. Therefore as a nation the sentence pronounced upon Israel was the death penalty. But Moses, understanding that God had no desire to destroy Israel, interceded diligently for his people and persuaded God to bear with them. In answer to the prayer of Moses God gave the Children of Israel His Covenant – the Everlasting Covenant - which is also called the New Covenant. It is called the New Covenant because it was not ratified until Christ's death. This Covenant included the promise that God Himself would keep His own law as ten precious promises in the heart of man, through the imparted life of Christ received into the soul (Jeremiah 31:33, Ezekiel 11:19, 36:26).

HARD-COPY OF THE NEW COVENANT

Moses was again called into the mountain and a second copy of the Ten Commandments was given to him but not as a continuation of the original covenant man made with God. This time Moses was hid in the cleft of the rock, thus showing that Christ, the Rock of Ages, would be their surety. The tables were placed safely inside the Ark of the Covenant hidden beneath the mercy seat. These tables of stone were the hard-copy of the New Covenant. They represented that the law of God was immutable and eternal, and demanded a life of perfect obedience. But the fact that God commissioned Moses to place these two tables of stone beneath the mercy seat signified that this Covenant had a divine element to it that man could not produce himself. It was a representation of the spiritual contract, as was made with Abraham, that through faith in the impartation of Christ's obedience to us as a free gift, Christ would write His own laws upon the fleshly tables of our heart and keep them in us through His indwelling Spirit. This New Covenant, therefore, was

the promise that the perfect, righteous life of Christ, contained in His blood, would sprinkle the horns of our altars (the powers of our will) to purge our conscience (our mind) from dead works and cleanse us from all unrighteousness.

GOD'S COVENANT FORESHADOWED BY THE SANCTUARY SYSTEM

The Everlasting Covenant was foreshadowed by the sacrificial system which God gave the Israelites. Every detail of the sanctuary and its services pointed forward to Christ's life on this earth, His death at Calvary and His atoning work as our High Priest in heaven. By learning the lessons of the Covenant through the services and types of the sanctuary system the Children of Israel received the salvation that Christ had made available through His own blood. They rejoiced in the promise that they too by faith could be partakers of Christ's obedience and be resurrected from the dead at His second coming.

God went to great lengths to educate the Israelites through the symbols of the sanctuary, but as time elapsed the Israelites lost sight of Christ exemplified in the shadow and types of the New Covenant and eventually came to believe that performing the sacrifices and ceremonies themselves would save them. As we reflect back upon the history of ancient Israel we see them constantly fluctuating between the covenant of works and God's own Covenant. Losing sight of Christ in the sanctuary, their appreciation for the ceremonial law was finally diminished and they became no different to the pagans in their forms of worship. Through their persistent unbelief and hard-heartedness, God's divine protection was gradually removed and they became a prey to their enemies. The Ark of the Covenant, symbolising God's presence with the nation, was removed to a hidden location and according to Jeremiah "would not be visited any more" (Jeremiah 3:16). At the same time God promised through Jeremiah and Ezekiel that the law of God would be written in the fleshly tables of the hearts of those who embraced the Everlasting Covenant by faith in Christ.

THE ARK REMOVED

The removal of the Ark occurred in the year 586 B.C. when Jerusalem was besieged by King Nebuchadnezzar of Babylon and the treasures of the temple were carried away. All the items taken from the Hebrew sanctuary were chronicled in a book but among these treasures the Ark of the Covenant was not mentioned. God in His foresight had commanded the prophet Jeremiah just prior to the siege to secret the Ark in a cave. "And it shall come to pass, when ye be multiplied and increased in the land, in those days, saith the LORD, they shall say no more, The Ark of the covenant of the LORD: neither shall it come to mind: neither shall they remember it; neither shall they visit it; neither shall that be done any more" (Jeremiah 3:16).

THE CAPTIVITY OF ISRAEL

The Israelites lost their freedom and became captives in Babylon. They continued on with their religious forms even though the Ark had been removed from them. But there were individuals among them who remained faithful to God and kept their Covenant relationship with Him in their heart. These included notable characters such as Daniel, Shadrach, Meshach, and Abednego. Through their influence, God touched the hearts of three kings – Cyrus, Darius and Artaxerxes – to call the Jews out of captivity to rebuild their temple in Jerusalem. However, the Jews had become so comfortable in Babylon they did not want to go back. Each time the decree to rebuild the temple and the city wall was given, only a faithful remnant would heed the call and go back to Israel to take up the work. Finally, the third decree restored the civil powers in Israel.

IN SPIRIT AND IN TRUTH

Although in 586 B.C. the Ark of the Covenant had been removed from their sight, those who took hold of the Covenant promise of Christ by faith still worshipped God in Spirit and in truth. Their spiritual perceptions had learned the lessons of the symbol and their faith laid hold of the unseen realities. In fulfilment of the prophecy in Daniel 9:24 Christ came to make an end of transgressions by ratifying the New Covenant.

JOINED TO THEIR IDOLS

It was in mercy that the Lord removed the tables of stone at exactly the same time that He promised to write the law of God in their hearts. The Jews never fully realised that the Old Covenant had been dis-annulled within only a month of it being made. They looked upon the tables of stone as their fathers looked upon Mt Sinai. They never had the faith that enabled them to recognise the tables and the Ark as hard-copies of God's promises to them. They had adopted the rights and customs of the surrounding nations and therefore the tables of stone only reminded them of the condemnation of God's law. For many generations before the days of King Josiah the temple had been left in ruins and despite his vigorous attempt at reformation, the nation was too entrenched in idolatry for his reform to be enduring and the captivity could not be averted. They had turned their backs to the temple of God to worship their idols (Ezekiel 8:16); and that which was spoken of Ephraim was spoken of the nation: "Ephraim is joined to his idols: let him alone" (Hosea 4:17). God removed from them that which condemned them and they were left to make their own personal experience.

THE TABERNACLE AND ITS SERVICES

> God Himself gave to Moses the plan of that structure, with particular directions as to its size and form, the materials to be employed, and every article of furniture which it was to contain. The holy places made with hands were to be "figures of the true," "patterns of things in the heavens" (Hebrews 9:24,23)--a

miniature representation of the heavenly temple where Christ, our great High Priest, after offering His life as a sacrifice, was to minister in the sinner's behalf. God presented before Moses in the mount a view of the heavenly sanctuary, and commanded him to make all things according to the pattern shown him. All these directions were carefully recorded by Moses, who communicated them to the leaders of the people.

The building was divided into two apartments by a rich and beautiful curtain, or veil, suspended from gold-plated pillars; and a similar veil closed the entrance of the first apartment. These, like the inner covering, which formed the ceiling, were of the most gorgeous colors, blue, purple, and scarlet, beautifully arranged, while inwrought with threads of gold and silver were cherubim to represent the angelic host who are connected with the work of the heavenly sanctuary and who are ministering spirits to the people of God on earth.

The sacred tent was enclosed in an open space called the court, which was surrounded by hangings, or screens, of fine linen, suspended from pillars of brass. The entrance to this enclosure was at the eastern end. It was closed by curtains of costly material and beautiful workmanship, though inferior to those of the sanctuary. The hangings of the court being only about half as high as the walls of the tabernacle, the building could be plainly seen by the people without. In the court, and nearest the entrance, stood the brazen altar of burnt offering. Upon this altar were consumed all the sacrifices made by fire unto the Lord, and its horns were sprinkled with the atoning blood. Between the altar and the door of the tabernacle was the laver, which was also of brass, made from the mirrors that had been the freewill offering of the women of Israel. At the laver the priests were to wash their hands and their feet whenever they went into the sacred apartments, or approached the altar to offer a burnt offering unto the Lord.

C4

In the first apartment, or holy place, were the table of showbread, the candlestick, or lampstand, and the altar of incense. The table of showbread stood on the north. With its ornamental crown, it was overlaid with pure gold. On this table the priests were each Sabbath to place twelve cakes, arranged in two piles, and sprinkled with frankincense. The loaves that were removed, being accounted holy, were to be eaten by the priests. On the south was the seven-branched candlestick, with its seven lamps. Its branches were ornamented with exquisitely wrought flowers, resembling lilies, and the whole was made from one solid piece of gold. There being no windows in the tabernacle, the lamps were never all extinguished at one time, but shed their light by day and by night. Just before the veil separating the holy place from the most holy and the immediate presence of God, stood the golden altar of incense. Upon this altar the priest was to burn incense every morning and evening; its horns were touched with the blood of the sin offering, and it was sprinkled with blood upon the great Day of Atonement. The fire upon this altar was kindled by God Himself and was sacredly cherished. Day and night the holy incense diffused its fragrance throughout the sacred apartments, and without, far around the tabernacle.

Beyond the inner veil was the holy of holies, where centred the symbolic service of atonement and intercession, and which formed the connecting link between heaven and earth. In this apartment was the ark, a chest of acacia wood, overlaid within and without with gold, and having a crown of gold about the top. It was made as a depository for the tables of stone, upon which God Himself had inscribed the Ten Commandments. Hence it was called the ark of God's testament, or the ark of the covenant, since the Ten Commandments were the basis of the covenant made between God and Israel.

The cover of the sacred chest was called the mercy seat. This was wrought of one solid piece of gold, and was surmounted by golden cherubim, one standing on each end. One wing of each angel was stretched forth on high, while the other was folded over the body (see Ezekiel 1:11) in token of reverence and humility. The position of the cherubim, with their faces turned toward each other, and looking reverently downward toward the ark, represented the reverence with which the heavenly host regard the law of God and their interest in the plan of redemption.

Above the mercy seat was the Shekinah, the manifestation of the divine Presence; and from between the cherubim, God made known His will. Divine messages were sometimes communicated to the high priest by a voice from the cloud. Sometimes a light fell upon the angel at the right, to signify approval or acceptance, or a shadow or cloud rested upon the one at the left to reveal disapproval or rejection. *Patriarchs and Prophets*, pp.347-349

THE LAW HIDDEN BENEATH THE MERCY SEAT

The law of God, enshrined within the ark, was the great rule of righteousness and judgment. That law pronounced death upon the transgressor; but above the law was the mercy seat, upon which the presence of God was revealed, and from which, by virtue of the atonement, pardon was granted to the repentant sinner. Thus in the work of Christ for our redemption, symbolised by the sanctuary service, "mercy and truth are met together; righteousness and peace have kissed each other." Psalm 85:10.

The daily service consisted of the morning and evening burnt offering, the offering of sweet incense on the golden altar, and the special offerings for individual sins. And there were also offerings for sabbaths, new moons, and special feasts...

Every morning and evening a lamb of a year old was burned upon the altar, with its appropriate meat offering, thus symbolizing the daily consecration of the nation to Jehovah, and their constant dependence upon the atoning blood of Christ. God expressly directed that every offering presented for the service of the sanctuary should be "without blemish." Exodus 12:5. The priests were to examine all animals brought as a sacrifice, and were to reject every one in which a defect was discovered. Only an offering "without blemish" could be a symbol of His perfect purity who was to offer Himself as "a lamb without blemish and without spot." 1 Peter 1:19...

In the offering of incense the priest was brought more directly into the presence of God than in any other act of the daily ministration. As the inner veil of the sanctuary did not extend to the top of the building, the glory of God, which was manifested above the mercy seat, was partially visible from the first apartment. When the priest offered incense before the Lord, he looked toward the ark; and as the cloud of incense arose, the divine glory descended upon the mercy seat and filled the most holy place, and often so filled both apartments that the priest was obliged to retire to the door of the tabernacle. As in that typical service the priest looked by faith to the mercy seat which he could not see, so the people of God are now to direct their prayers to Christ, their great High Priest, who, unseen by human vision, is pleading in their behalf in the sanctuary above.

The incense, ascending with the prayers of Israel, represents the merits and intercession of Christ, His perfect righteousness, which through faith is imputed to His people, and which can alone make the worship of sinful beings acceptable to God. Before the veil of the most holy place was an altar of perpetual intercession, before the holy, an altar of continual atonement. By blood and by incense God was to be approached--symbols pointing to the great Mediator, through whom sinners may approach Jehovah, and through whom alone mercy and salvation can be granted to the repentant, believing soul...

As the priests morning and evening entered the holy place at the time of incense, the daily sacrifice was ready to be offered upon the altar in the court without. This was a time of intense interest to the worshipers who assembled at the tabernacle. Before entering into the presence of God through the ministration of the priest, they were to engage in earnest searching of heart and confession of sin. They united in silent prayer, with their faces toward the holy place. Thus their petitions ascended with the cloud of incense, while faith laid hold upon the merits of the promised Saviour prefigured by the atoning sacrifice...

The showbread was kept ever before the Lord as a perpetual offering. Thus it was a part of the daily sacrifice. It was called showbread, or "bread of the presence," because it was ever before the face of the Lord. It was an acknowledgment of man's dependence upon God for both temporal and spiritual food, and that it is received only through the mediation of Christ. God had fed Israel in the wilderness with bread from heaven, and they were still dependent upon

His bounty, both for temporal food and spiritual blessings. Both the manna and the showbread pointed to Christ, the living Bread, who is ever in the presence of God for us. He Himself said, "I am the living Bread which came down from heaven." John 6:48-51...

The most important part of the daily ministration was the service performed in behalf of individuals. The repentant sinner brought his offering to the door of the tabernacle, and, placing his hand upon the victim's head, confessed his sins, thus in figure transferring them from himself to the innocent sacrifice. By his own hand the animal was then slain, and the blood was carried by the priest into the holy place and sprinkled before the veil, behind which was the ark containing the law that the sinner had transgressed. By this ceremony the sin was, through the blood, transferred in figure to the sanctuary. In some cases the blood was not taken into the holy place; but the flesh was then to be eaten by the priest, as Moses directed the sons of Aaron, saying, "God hath given it you to bear the iniquity of the congregation." Leviticus 10:17. Both ceremonies alike symbolised the transfer of the sin from the penitent to the sanctuary.

Such was the work that went on day by day throughout the year. The sins of Israel being thus transferred to the sanctuary, the holy places were defiled, and a special work became necessary for the removal of the sins. God commanded that an atonement be made for each of the sacred apartments, as for the altar, to "cleanse it, and hallow it from the uncleanness of the children of Israel." Leviticus 16:19.

Once a year, on the great Day of Atonement, the priest entered the most holy place for the cleansing of the sanctuary. The work there performed completed the yearly round of ministration.

On the Day of Atonement two kids of the goats were brought to the door of the tabernacle, and lots were cast upon them, "one lot for the Lord, and the other lot for the scapegoat." The goat upon which the first lot fell was to be slain as a sin offering for the people. And the priest was to bring his blood within the veil, and sprinkle it upon the mercy seat. "And he shall make an atonement for the holy place, because of the uncleanness of the children of Israel, and because of their transgression in all their sins; and so shall he do for the tabernacle of the congregation, that remaineth among them in the midst of their uncleanness."

"And Aaron shall lay both his hands upon the head of the live goat, and confess over him all the iniquities of the children of Israel, and all their transgressions in all their sins, putting them upon the head of the goat, and shall send him away by the hand of a fit man into the wilderness: and the goat shall bear upon him all their iniquities into a land not inhabited." Not until the goat had been thus sent away did the people regard themselves as freed from the burden of their sins. Every man was to afflict his soul while the work of atonement was going forward. All business was laid aside, and the whole congregation of Israel spent the day in solemn humiliation before God, with prayer, fasting, and deep searching of heart.

Important truths concerning the atonement were taught the people by this yearly service. In the sin offerings presented during the year, a substitute had been accepted in the sinner's stead; but the blood of the victim had not made full atonement for the sin. It had only provided a means by which the sin was transferred to the sanctuary. By the offering of blood, the sinner acknowledged the authority of the law, confessed the guilt of his transgression, and expressed his faith in Him who was to take away the sin of the world; but he was not entirely released from the condemnation of the law. On the Day of Atonement the high priest, having taken an offering for the congregation, went into the most holy place with the blood and sprinkled it upon the mercy seat, above the tables of the law. Thus the claims of the law, which demanded the life of the sinner, were satisfied. Then in his character of mediator the priest took the sins upon himself, and, leaving the sanctuary, he bore with him the burden of Israel's guilt. At the door of the tabernacle he laid his hands upon the head of the scapegoat and confessed over him "all the iniquities of the children of Israel, and all their transgressions in all their sins, putting them upon the head of the goat." And as the goat bearing these sins was sent away, they were, with him, regarded as forever separated from the people. Such was the service performed "unto the example and shadow of heavenly things." Hebrews 8:5....

The blood of Christ, while it was to release the repentant sinner from the condemnation of the law, was not to cancel the sin; it would stand on record in the sanctuary until the final atonement; so in the type the blood of the sin offering removed the sin from the penitent, but it rested in the sanctuary until the Day of Atonement.

In the great day of final award, the dead are to be "judged out of those things which were written in the books, according to their works." Revelation 20:12. Then by virtue of the atoning blood of Christ, the sins of all the truly penitent will be blotted from the books of heaven. Thus the sanctuary will be freed, or cleansed, from the record of sin. In the type, this great work of atonement, or blotting out of sins, was represented by the services of the Day of Atonement--the cleansing of the earthly sanctuary, which was accomplished by the removal, by virtue of the blood of the sin offering, of the sins by which it had been polluted.

As in the final atonement the sins of the truly penitent are to be blotted from the records of heaven, no more to be remembered or come into mind, so in the type they were borne away into the wilderness, forever separated from the congregation.

Since Satan is the originator of sin, the direct instigator of all the sins that caused the death of the Son of God, justice demands that Satan shall suffer the final punishment. Christ's work for the redemption of men and the purification of the universe from sin will be closed by the removal of sin from the heavenly sanctuary and the placing of these sins upon Satan, who will bear the final penalty. So in the typical service, the yearly round of ministration closed with the purification of the sanctuary, and the confessing of the sins on the head of

> the scapegoat.
>
> Thus in the ministration of the tabernacle, and of the temple that afterward took its place, the people were taught each day the great truths relative to Christ's death and ministration, and once each year their minds were carried forward to the closing events of the great controversy between Christ and Satan, the final purification of the universe from sin and sinners.
>
> *Ibid.*, pp. 349-358

RIGHTEOUSNESS BY FAITH

> For if, when we were enemies, we were reconciled to God by the death of his Son, much more, being reconciled, we shall be saved by his life. Romans 5:10

While Christ's death brings us to the point of justification where our past sins are forgiven, it is actually through partaking of Christ's righteous life that we gain complete victory over sin and become saved.

PART 1 – ARCHAEOLOGY AT MT MORIAH

Mount Moriah is a very special place because it was on this very mount that Abraham offered up Isaac. Through this great test of faith, Abraham came to understand that one day God would offer up His only begotten Son as a sacrifice for the sins of the world upon this very same site.

Christ was meant to be offered upon the Temple Mount, but just as God had removed the Ark of the Covenant from the people because they failed to discern the New Covenant, Christ was crucified without the old city because they failed to discern the very man of the Covenant Himself. Christ being offered up without the city walls signified the Gospel would now be committed to the Gentiles as the Jews had failed in their high calling to proclaim the Gospel to the world.

THE CITY OF DAVID AND JERUSALEM

Towards the end of his life, King David went against God's counsel and sought to number the people of Israel. Because of this act, God's protection was withdrawn and the land was afflicted with a terrible plague. As the destroying angel drew close to the city, it halted above the threshing floor of Ornan. In order to make restitution, at the prophet Gad's direction, David ran out of his city and purchased the threshing floor of Ornan and sacrificed upon it; and the plague was stayed.

Jebus was the original name of the City of David. After his inauguration, David conquered the well-fortified city and established his headquarters there. Not far from its walls was the very place where Abraham offered his son Isaac upon the altar. It was this same spot in which the threshing floor of Ornan had later been built. And it was this same place where Solomon in later years, built the "House of God".

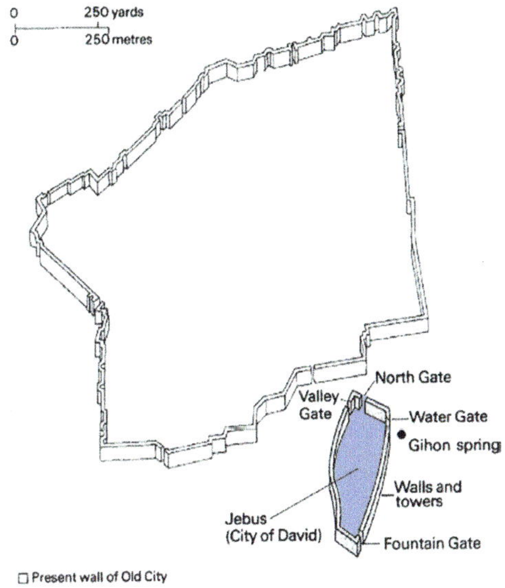

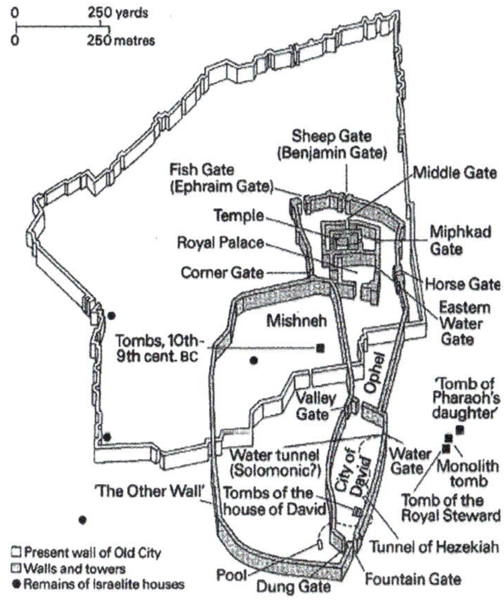

Fig. C5 – The city of David can be seen at the bottom right corner. King David was in his city when he made the agreement with Ornan to buy his threshing floor which was at the time outside of the temple site in the city of Jerusalem. Fig. C6 – Old Jerusalem.

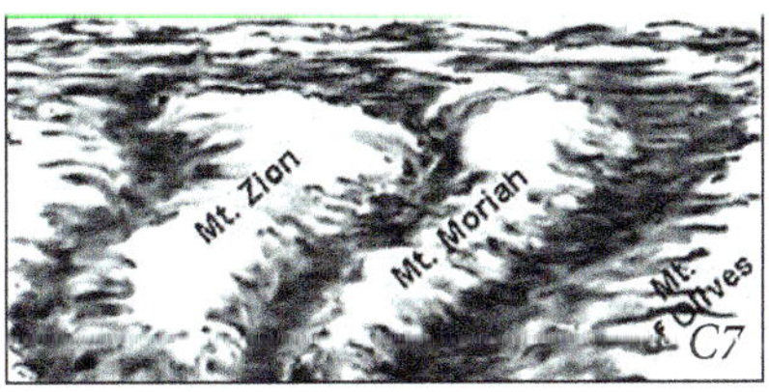

The city of Jerusalem is built upon three mountains which signify the three persons of the Godhead. Mount Zion represents the mountain of God, Mt Moriah the mountain of Christ and the Mount of Olives the mountain of the Holy Spirit.

King Solomon's Temple was destroyed by the Babylonian forces in 586 B.C. and rebuilt by the returned captives. In approximately 18 B.C. it was completely rebuilt by King Herod. This temple was also destroyed in 70 A.D., and the area is now occupied by the Dome of the Rock.

Fig. C8 – Dome of the Rock with Mt of Olives behind it.

THE DOME OF THE ROCK

The Dome of the Rock is one of the wonders of the World. It was built by the Muslims in 691 A.D. and its design and octagonal shape was influenced by Byzantine architecture. The nearby Al-Aqsa Mosque which is within the same precinct is the third most important site in the Islamic religion. Being the original site of Solomon's temple, the land is heavily contested by the Jews.

THE OLD CITY STREETS

Meandering down the old city streets, one feels as if transported back in time two thousand years. Arab merchants hustle and bustle as they try to sell their wares. Catholic and Armenian Pilgrims chant hymns and prayers as they trace the *Via Della Rosa* to the Stations of the Cross. Jewish men march single eyed to the Wailing Wall to supplicate their prayers. There is such a richness and diversity of culture in this tiny old city.

Fig. C10-C13 – Top left: spice rack at a market in the Old City at Jerusalem (top right). Bottom left: shopping mall close to Damascus Gate entrance. Bottom right: busy street life.

C15

THE DAMASCUS GATE

On the left side of the entrance to the Damascus Gate, twenty feet below current ground level, is another gate which is of similar level to the gate through which Christ would have been led out to Calvary. Jerusalem has been destroyed and rebuilt a number of times which has elevated the foundation of the present day city.

Where Jesus also, that He might sanctify the people with His own blood, suffered without the gate. Hebrews 13:12

THE CALVARY ESCARPMENT

> The place where Jesus was crucified was nigh to the city. John 19:20

To the north of the Damascus Gate the limestone Calvary escarpment where Christ was crucified can still be seen. The escarpment was formerly a quarry where stones were cut out for King Solomon's Temple. Before the quarry existed there was a gradual incline to the summit of a hill. At the top of the hill there is a Muslim graveyard but Christ was not crucified at this site.

GOLGOTHA

> And when they were come unto a place called Golgotha, that is to say, a place of a skull. Matthew 27:33

In Matthew 27:33 it says Jesus carried His cross to "a place of a skull". There is no place nigh to the old city of Jerusalem other than the Calvary escarpment which resembles the place of a skull. Upon exiting the northern gate of the old city Christ would have taken His final steps in the direction of the Skull Face. The place where Jesus gave up His life for the sins of the world is now the location of a bus port.

Fig. C17 – photo of the Skull Face taken in the late 1800's. Fig. C18 – Bus port built next to the Skull Face. Fig. C19 – Kerensa at the Skull Face viewing platform in the Garden Tomb.

Garden Tomb
Damascus Gate
Dome of the Rock
Gethsemane
MOUNT OF OLIVES
MUSLIM QUARTER
CHRISTIAN QUARTER
OLD CITY
JEWISH QUARTER
ARMENIAN QUARTER
JERUSALEM
(ירושלים)
MUSRARA
Saint Louis French Hospital
Yeusefiya Cemetery
Rockefeller Garden
Mamilla Cemetery
Independence Park
Armenian Cemetery
Bikur Cholim
Chaldan 6
Shchem
King David
60

Fig. C23 – The Calvary escarpment in the late 1800's showing the Skull Face centre-left; Jeremiah's Grotto centre-right; the boundary wall of the Garden Tomb far left and the main highway fore-front.

Fig. C24 – View from above the Calvary escarpment. You can see the bus port to the left at the base of the cliff, the Garden Tomb in the centre and the Muslim graveyard on the top of the hill. Jeremiah's Grotto is to the lower left.

JEREMIAH'S GROTTO

> Then took they Jeremiah, and cast him into the dungeon of Malchiah the son of Hammelech, that was in the court of the prison: and they let down Jeremiah with cords. And in the dungeon there was no water, but mire: so Jeremiah sunk in the mire. Jeremiah 38:6

The ancient site of Jeremiah's Grotto is located just east of the Skull Face. The Bible records that Jeremiah was thrown into this pit and therefore he suffered very closely to his Saviour. They were connected in their sufferings at the Calvary Escarpment. In ancient Israel, when prisoners were on trial, it was customary to throw them into a dark pit naked as a form of torture.

There is a tradition that Christ was also thrown into a miry pit in-between His trials.

> Thou hast laid me in the lowest pit, in darkness, in the deeps. Psalm 88:6

> You brought me up also out of an horrible pit, out of the miry clay, and set my feet upon a rock, and established my goings. Psalm 40:2

The prophet of God faithfully gave the warning to King Zedekiah and the princes of Judah that they were not to resist the armies of Nebuchadnezzar but to submit to the captivity. His refusal to speak smooth words angered the princes and Jeremiah's voice was silenced by imprisonment. Although the king had compassion and removed him to the court of the prison with daily provision he eventually submitted to the princes and they lowered him into the "dungeon of Malchiah".

Fig. C25 Christ lowered into the pit - Church of St Peter in Gallicantu.

THE TRIAL OF JESUS

The Church of Saint Peter in Gallicantu, located on the eastern slope of Mt Zion, is believed to be the house of Annas the high priest, where Christ was put on pre-trial and lowered into a pit for several hours in the night. The pit is still preserved in the basement of the church.

Fig. C26 – Church of St Peter, Gallicantu

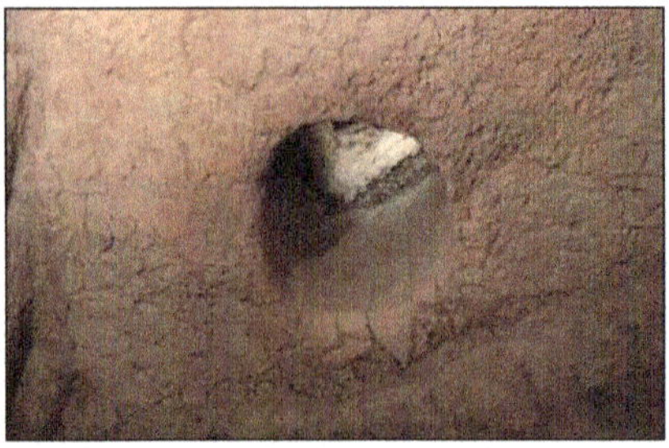

Fig. C27,C28 – Left: The hole through which Christ was lowered. Right: Looking up from the pit.

CHRIST SUFFERS WITH US TOO

Throughout all His sufferings, God was still with Jesus and He promised to hold His hand. He will do the same for us. He holds our hand in the most trying of circumstances.

> For I the LORD thy God will hold thy right hand, saying unto thee, fear not; I will help thee. Isaiah 41:13

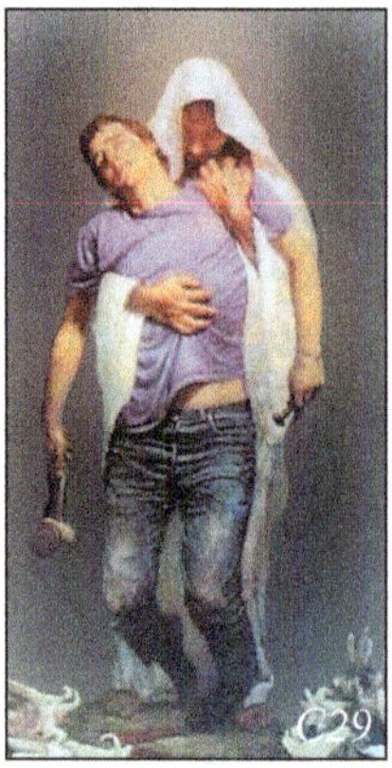

Have you ever been in a pit in your life that you cannot get out of? When that happens Jesus doesn't just stand on the side of the pit and call down to us; He comes into that horrible miry pit with us, into that hopeless situation, whatever it is. He puts His arm around us and together we ascend the rope that the Father has thrown down to us. Jesus is a very intimate friend and He knows our sufferings more than we ourselves know them. He came into the pit of human suffering when He became fashioned as a man and took upon himself our very own nature.

When Jesus lived upon this earth He was always looking for ways to help sinners. He met them according to their needs. Christ never spoke a word of condemnation. He just wanted to help them and restore them into the beautiful creatures He always intended them to be. Christ had restorative power to comfort a broken-heart and to heal those afflicted with terrible illnesses.

GETHSEMANE

> He went a little farther, and fell on his face, and prayed, saying, O my Father, if it be possible, let this cup pass from me: nevertheless not as I will, but as thou wilt. Matthew 26:39

Before Christ's trial and crucifixion He entered the Garden of Gethsemane with three of His disciples – Peter, James and John. Urging them to pray for Him and for themselves He went a short distance from them and fell upon His face. As the Father began to lay the heavy burden of our guilt upon Christ in Gethsemane, His humanity shrank from it. An angel was sent by God to encourage and strengthen Christ at this time for the trial which lay ahead of Him.

THE SACRIFICIAL LAMB

Under the Levitical system, the Father of each family was the priest of the home. At the Passover, a lamb without physical blemish would be selected from among their flocks and would live in the home with the family for a time. This innocent lamb would become a household pet and it would joyfully play with the children and follow its master wherever he went. At the time of the Passover sacrifice, the father would lead the lamb to the sanctuary, lay his hands upon its head and confess the sins of his family. This signified that the guilt for the sins of the family had been transferred to the lamb.

In like manner, our Heavenly Father is the Father and priest of the human family. Christ, His innocent precious Son, the joy of His life who had been constantly by His side for eternity, was now to become the sacrifice for the guilty human race. In Gethsemane the Father began to press the weight and sin of the world upon His beloved Son. Christ's humanity shrank from this experience but He did not resist. The pressure of the sin being laid upon Him was so great that it made Him feel completely shut out from the Father's presence. This separation pained Christ's heart for He had always been with the Father. As Christ wept tears of agony and at times fainted under the weight of the sin pressed upon Him, God sent an angel to strengthen His Son in the Garden and to assure Him that He loved Him more than ever, and that many souls would be brought to the kingdom through His supreme sacrifice. The angel's words encouraged Him for the great trial which lay ahead.

CHRIST'S HARDEST TEMPTATION

When Christ was tempted not to drink the bitter cup in Gethsemane what He was really saying was "Father, I am tempted not to die for the sins of my people, their sins are too great, and I know I will have to suffer the penalty for all of their sins." The reality is that Christ was tempted in the Garden of Gethsemane to give up on you and me. Could you imagine where we would be now if He hadn't passed the test? The humanity of Christ was the same as ours. He shrank from the thought of being blamed for every sin in the entire world just we would shrink from it. But Christ was filled with the Spirit and He did the will of the Father regardless of how He felt. Will we do the same? The Apostle Paul writes in Galatians 2:20, "I am crucified with Christ: nevertheless I live; yet not I, but Christ liveth in me: and the life which I now live in the flesh I live by the faith of the Son of God, who loved me, and gave himself for me." Are we crucified with Christ? Would we do the will of God even though we don't feel like doing it? If Christ reigns in our heart supremely, we will exercise the faith that Christ Himself exercised in trusting and obeying the will of the Father.

C30

THE GARDEN OF GETHSEMANE

The Garden of Gethsemane is located at the base of the Mount of Olives. In the photo above it is just to the left of the gold dome which is the Church of Mary Magdalene. The photo was taken from the east side of the Temple Mount. Jesus often retreated with His disciples to this peaceful garden just outside the city walls.

The olive trees in the garden have been grafted from much older trees that existed in the time of Christ (figure C31 and C32). In this place, He pleaded with the Father.

C31

C32

CONSIDERING CHRIST

At times we become so overwhelmed with our own problems and perplexities that we forget Christ is one with us in all our afflictions. Consider that if we are one with Christ, He is feeling as we are feeling, and suffering when we suffer. If we really believed this, we would not wallow in our own self-pity. We would also be very careful not to hurt our Friend by making wrong decisions in life and bringing the consequences of our sins upon Him. Kerensa in figure C32 (above) and in figure C34 (right).

Fig. C33 – Jewish men praying by the Wailing Wall. There is a small section to the right of the wall where the Jewish women pray.

THE WAILING WALL

The Wailing Wall has great significance to the Jewish people because it is the only remaining wall from the third temple. The Jews still dream of building another temple on the site of the Dome of the Rock but the Bible says this will never happen. When Christ died at Calvary, the Levitical priesthood came to an end and Christ ascended up to heaven to start His ministration as the true high priest in the heavenly tabernacle, not made with hands (Hebrews 9:11).

> Now of the things which we have spoken this is the sum: We have such an high priest, who is set on the right hand of the throne of the Majesty in the heavens; A minister of the sanctuary, and of the true tabernacle, which the Lord pitched, and not man. Hebrews 8:1-2

> For Christ is not entered into the holy places made with hands, which are the figures of the true; but into heaven itself, now to appear in the presence of God for us. Hebrews 9:24

C34

THE GARDEN TOMB

The Garden Tomb is located on a side street off Nebulus Road (Shchem). There is a little arrow pointing down the lane way to the entrance.

The garden is fortified by buildings and a natural limestone escarpment which insulate the garden from the noise of the hustle and bustle outside. The perfect peace of Christ's Sabbath rest in the tomb still pervades the atmosphere. The tomb in which the body of Christ was laid is to the left as you enter into the garden.

Today the Garden Tomb is landscaped beautifully to capture the essence of what it might have been like when Christ was crucified and buried there in 31 A.D.

C35

C3

C3

C38

C

CHRIST'S TOMB WAS IN A GARDEN NEARBY

Now in the place where he was crucified there was a garden; and in the garden a new sepulchre wherein was never yet man laid. There laid they Jesus therefore because of the Jews' preparation day; for the sepulchre was nigh at hand.

John 19:41-42

The Bible records that the newly built sepulchre of Joseph of Arimathaea was in a garden close to the crucifixion site.

ANCIENT WINE-PRESS

I have trodden the wine-press alone; and of the people there was none with me:

Isaiah 63:3

Located in front of the entrance to the Garden Tomb is an ancient wine-press which would have been used for pressing grapes. This suggests that this area was used as a vineyard at one time. We remember that Christ likened His experience in Gethsemane and Calvary to the wine-press. The sins which were laid upon Christ in Gethsemane caused Him to sweat drops of blood. The Roman soldiers pressed the crown of thorns deep into Christ's brow and blood poured down His temples. This signified the weight of sin pressing heavier and heavier upon His soul.

C40

THE PRAYER OF CHRIST TO THE FATHER AS HE BORE OUR GUILT

For innumerable evils have compassed me about: mine iniquities have taken hold upon me, so that I am not able to look up; they are more than the hairs of mine head: therefore my heart faileth me... My prayer is unto thee, O LORD, in an acceptable time: O God, in the multitude of thy mercy hear me, in the truth of thy salvation.

Psalm 40:12, 69:13

THE FATHER'S RESPONSE TO HIS SON'S PRAYER

Thus saith the LORD, In an acceptable time have I heard thee, and in a day of salvation have I helped thee: and I will preserve thee, and give thee for a covenant of the people, to establish the earth, to cause to inherit the desolate heritages. Isaiah 49:8

When our first parents were expelled from the Garden of Eden, God cursed the land with thistles and briers. When the crown of thorns pressed into Christ's brow He took upon Himself the curse that was placed upon the world.

Jesus likens His experience in the garden to the wine-press (Isaiah 63:3). He went through an agonising, excruciating process of carrying all the world's sins as His own and bearing it all alone. When He took our sin upon Himself He felt totally cut off from the Father but it wasn't His sin that He was carrying. It was our sin that He paid the consequences for. Do we feel totally alone and cut off from the Father when we have sinned against Him so that our head is so heavy we can't even lift it up to pray? Despite His ordeal God loved His Son – in fact He loved Him even more for giving His life to save you and me.

When we feel sinful, that is the very time we must go to the Father and ask for forgiveness. He will be faithful to hear us and to forgive us. He will not leave us alone in our sin and suffering.

> If we confess our sins, he is faithful and just to forgive us our sins, and to cleanse us from all unrighteousness. 1 John 1:9

> Let us therefore come boldly unto the throne of grace, that we may obtain mercy, and find grace to help in time of need. Hebrews 4:16

> For in that he himself hath suffered being tempted, he is able to succour them that are tempted. Hebrews 2:18

> There hath no temptation taken you but such as is common to man: but God is faithful, who will not suffer you to be tempted above that ye are able; but will with the temptation also make a way to escape, that ye may be able to bear it.
>
> 1 Corinthian 10:13

WATER CISTERN

The water cistern located in the Garden Tomb is the third largest in Jerusalem and holds one million litres of water. If a garden existed there in the time of Christ then a water cistern would certainly have been required to sustain it. The water cistern in the Garden Tomb is ancient and dates back to the days of Abraham, however during the Roman occupation the walls of the cistern were re-plastered.

Fig. C41 – Inside the cistern.

THE TOMB OF CHRIST

> There laid they Jesus therefore because of the Jews' preparation day; for the sepulchre was nigh at hand. John 19:41-42

This scripture tells us that the tomb Jesus was buried in was close to the Skull Face (Golgotha). The tomb of Jesus is 100 metres from the Skull Face and the crucifixion site falls between these two sites.

When Christ died Joseph of Arimathaea begged the body of Jesus from Pontius Pilate. Joseph then carried the body to the tomb which was 60 metres from the crucifixion site.

Under Jewish law only a relative had the right to claim the body of the deceased. In the case of a convicted criminal not even a relative could be granted the body. This affirms that Joseph of Arimathaea was not only a family member but a highly influential member of the Sanhedrin. Jewish rulers and Pilate had purposed to give Jesus a burial of shame but God overruled and gave His Son the burial of a King.

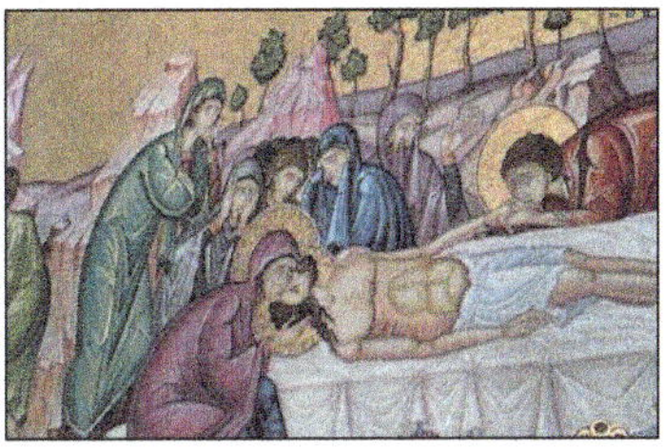

> He made his grave with the wicked, and with the rich in his death; because he had done no violence, neither was any deceit in his mouth.
> Isaiah 53:9

Fig. C42-C45 – Tiled murals telling the story of the crucifixion at the Church of the Holy Sepulchre. Top to bottom: Nicodemus, Joseph of Arimathaea, women weeping over Jesus at the Garden Tomb, placing the body of Jesus in the sepulchre.

C46

C4

Brief History

As early as 1842, a German Theologian named Otto Thenius proposed the idea that the outcropping of rock known today as “Skull Hill” could possibly be significant in the identification of the site of the crucifixion. Several years later In 1867 the tomb of Christ was unearthed. General Charles Gordon, an influential man from Britain, began to publish his theory that this was the place of Christ’s burial causing people to seriously look into his claims. Charlotte Hussey and Louisa Hope followed his ideas and thought that the place ought to be preserved. In September 22, 1892 a notice was placed in the London Times asking people to donate the funds necessary to purchase the site (then offered for sale by a German family). The Garden Tomb Association was formally established in 1893 and the purchase of the property was bought about in 1894. Since its establishment, the Garden Tomb has been visited by many Christians of all denominations around the world.

Foot washing basin

A shallow basin for foot washing has been chiselled into the stone very close to the entrance to the tomb and it is believed early Christians worshipped at this site. Foot washing signified Christ washing and cleansing the life from sin.

Fig. C48 – Foot washing basin just outside the tomb.

Engraved cross

Notice to the right hand side of the picture a large cross has been chiselled into the wall of the tomb. This suggests it was revered by Christians who later worshipped there.

Fig. C49 – Cross engraved at the far right of the tomb.
Fig.C50 – The engraving has been indicated.

51

52

Low entrance to the tomb

Then arose Peter, and ran unto the sepulchre; and stooping down, he beheld the linen clothes laid by themselves, and departed, wondering in himself at that which was come to pass.

Luke 24:12

The tomb fits this small detail given in the Bible.

Inside the tomb

When the even was come, there came a rich man of Arimathaea, named Joseph, who also himself was Jesus' disciple: He went to Pilate, and begged the body of Jesus. Then Pilate commanded the body to be delivered. And when Joseph had taken the body, he wrapped it in a clean linen cloth, And laid it in his own new tomb, which he had hewn out in the rock: and he rolled a great stone to the door of the sepulchre, and departed. And there was Mary Magdalene, and the other Mary, sitting over against the sepulchre. Matthew 27:56-61

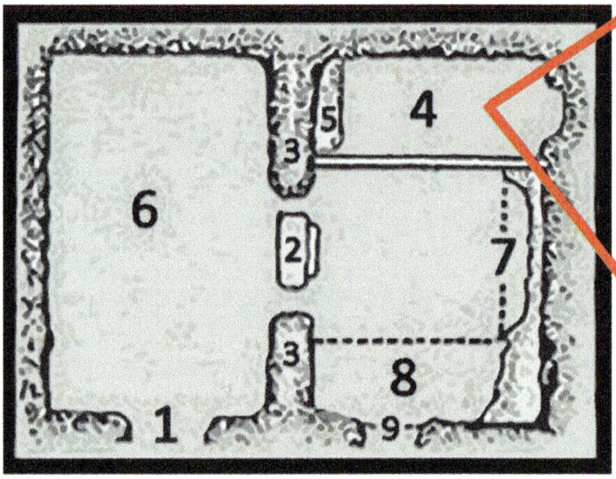

Fig. C54 – Layout of the inside of the chamber.

Section 6 is where the women would have come in weeping with Joseph of Arimathaea, Nicodemus and some of the disciples.

Section 4 on the diagram is where the body of Jesus was laid. An incision was made in the tomb for the feet of Jesus. Originally the tomb was made for a shorter man. Based on the length of section 4 we can know that Joseph of Arimathaea was about 5 foot 8 inches in height but at the last moment he had the tomb extended to 5 foot 11 inches for the body of Jesus. In their haste to prepare the tomb before the opening of the Sabbath the masons only had time to extend the bottom of the wall in the area of the feet. This is evidence that this tomb was initially intended for someone else but was used for Christ at the last moment.

In section 7 Joseph of Arimathaea and Nicodemus would have embalmed the body of Jesus and wrapped it in an expensive linen cloth.

55

56

Section 8 would have been intended for Joseph of Arimathaea's wife but the tomb was never used again after the burial of Jesus.

The Gospel of Mark records that when Mary Magdalene came into the tomb she saw one angel sitting on the right side. There are two shelves on the right side of the tomb where the angel could have sat.

Christ walks forth from the tomb

It was in this chamber that Christ arose from the dead victorious. And this is His promise to every believer – complete victory over sin and death through receiving His imparted life and the resurrection from the grave at His second coming.

> For if, when we were enemies, we were reconciled to God by the death of his Son, much more, being reconciled, we shall be saved by His life. Romans 5:10

In His death, Jesus rested on the Sabbath day, the rest day He had instituted at the creation. (Genesis 2:2.) When He arose from the dead, He walked through the door of the tomb clothed in His new immortal body and stepped out in victory.

The sign on the door reads, "He is not here for He is risen." This is our hope and glory. By abiding in Christ and He in us one day we will rise to a new life also.

Fig. C60 – Looking out from the tomb.

C61

The sealing stone

Now the next day, that followed the day of the preparation, the chief priests and Pharisees came together unto Pilate, Saying, Sir, we remember that that deceiver said, while he was yet alive, After three days I will rise again. Command therefore that the sepulchre be made sure until the third day, lest his disciples come by night, and steal him away, and say unto the people, He is risen from the dead: so the last error shall be worse than the first. Pilate said unto them, Ye have a watch: go your way, make it as sure as ye can. So they went, and made the sepulchre sure, sealing the stone, and setting a watch.

Matthew 27:62-66

Fearing Christ's prophetic words of His resurrection would actually come true, the Jewish leaders asked Pilate to secure the tomb. At their request he sent soldiers to guard the tomb and seal the stone making it secure.

Fig. C62 – Artistic depiction.

Stone groove

At the base of the exterior rock face of Christ's tomb there is a grooved trough two feet wide. This is where the sealing stone would have been rolled into position and secured.

Iron peg

> Behold, there was a great earthquake: for the angel of the Lord descended from heaven, and came and rolled back the stone from the door, and sat upon it. His countenance was like lightning, and his raiment white as snow: And for fear of him the keepers did shake, and became as dead men. Matthew 28:2-4

The remains of a lead and iron peg can still be seen on the left side of the wall. The peg is lead on the inside and iron on the outside which was typical in Herodian times. An iron and lead peg would have been placed either side of the entrance and attached to a metal chain keeping the stone locked in position. This is further evidence that Christ was buried in this chamber and that the Romans secured it. No similar markings are found at other tombs.

Fig. C64,C65 – The iron peg can be seen 1 metre to the left of the entrance. Inset is a close-up. Approximately two metres to the right of the door there is a hole where the second metal peg was located. The rock face is cracked from the tomb to past the hole.

C66

When Christ arose from the dead there was an earthquake. The angel struck the chain loose and rolled away the stone. In figure C65 the iron remains of the peg appear to have been fused with the lead.

The Tomb Stone

In a Byzantine monastery at Mt Nebo the sealing stone to the tomb has been located (see figure C66). It is the perfect size and in sample testing has proven to be cut from the same rock as the Garden Tomb. Figure C63 of the tomb shows a stone stopper in the trough which would have prevented the stone from rolling.

THE PROMISE OF THE RESURRECTION OF THE DEAD AT HIS SECOND COMING

> In a moment, in the twinkling of an eye, at the last trump: for the trumpet shall sound, and the dead shall be raised incorruptible, and we shall be changed. For this corruptible must put on incorruption, and this mortal must put on immortality. So when this corruptible shall have put on incorruption, and this mortal shall have put on immortality, then shall be brought to pass the saying that is written, Death is swallowed up in victory. 1 Corinthians 15:52-54

C67

> The Lord himself shall descend from heaven with a shout, with the voice of the archangel, and with the trump of God: and the dead in Christ shall rise first: Then we which are alive and remain shall be caught up together with them in the clouds, to meet the Lord in the air: and so shall we ever be with the Lord. 1 Thessalonians 4:16

> He hath appointed a day, in the which he will judge the world in righteousness by that man whom he hath ordained; whereof he hath given assurance unto all men, in that he hath raised him from the dead. Acts 17:31

Fig. C68 – A map of the garden.

CRUCIFIXION SITE

To the east of the Garden Tomb, there is a chapel with a red roof. A few metres to the east of the chapel, in the direction of the Skull Face, is a flight of stairs leading up to a smaller area beside the escarpment with benches for seating. It was upon this site that Christ was crucified and can be identified by two cut outs in the rock face. In the time of Christ the ground level was approximately 2-3 metres lower than the existing platform.

Fig. C69,C70 – Red chapel located just down the stairs from the crucifixion site.

Opposite page:
Fig. C71 – Top left: view of the crucifixion site from the Skull Face viewing platform looking east to west.
Fig. C72 – Top right: looking south from the cut-outs.
Fig. C73 – Middle left: looking west to east from the cut-outs.
Fig. C74 – Middle right: looking north at the cut-outs.
Fig. C75 – Bottom: the crucifixion site.

THE MESSIANIC PROPHECIES FORETELLING CHRIST'S CRUCIFIXION

For dogs have compassed me: the assembly of the wicked have enclosed me: they pierced my hands and my feet. I may tell all my bones: they look and stare upon me. They part my garments among them, and cast lots upon my vesture. But be not thou far from me, O LORD: O my strength, haste thee to help me. Deliver my soul from the sword; my darling from the power of the dog. Save me from the lion's mouth: for thou hast heard me from the horns of the unicorns. I will declare thy name unto my brethren: in the midst of the congregation will I praise thee. Psalm 22:16-22

For he shall grow up before him as a tender plant, and as a root out of a dry ground: he hath no form nor comeliness; and when we shall see him, there is no beauty that we should desire him. He is despised and rejected of men; a man of sorrows, and acquainted with grief: and we hid as it were our faces from him; he was despised, and we esteemed him not. Surely he hath borne our griefs, and carried our sorrows: yet we did esteem him stricken, smitten of God, and afflicted. But he was wounded for our transgressions, he was bruised for our iniquities: the chastisement of our peace was upon him; and with his stripes we are healed. All we like sheep have gone astray; we have turned every one to his own way; and the LORD hath laid on him the iniquity of us all. He was oppressed, and he was afflicted, yet he opened not his mouth: he is brought as a lamb to the slaughter, and as a sheep before her shearers is dumb, so he openeth not his mouth. He was taken from prison and from judgment: and who shall declare his generation? for he was cut off out of the land of the living: for the transgression of my people was he stricken. And he made his grave with the wicked, and with the rich in his death; because he had done no violence, neither was any deceit in his mouth. Yet it pleased the LORD to bruise him; he hath put [him] to grief: when thou shalt make his soul an offering for sin, he shall see his seed, he shall prolong his days, and the pleasure of the LORD shall prosper in his hand. He shall see of the travail of his soul, and shall be satisfied: by his knowledge shall my righteous servant justify many; for he shall bear their iniquities. Therefore will I divide him a portion with the great, and he shall divide the spoil with the strong; because he hath poured out his soul unto death: and he was numbered with the transgressors; and he bare the sin of many, and made intercession for the transgressors. Isaiah 53:2-12

Fig. C76 – Extract from the Dead Sea Scrolls. Fig. C77 – Qumran. Fig. C78 – Shrine of the Book, Israel Museum.

THE DEAD SEA SCROLLS

The discovery of the Dead Sea Scrolls in 1947 is arguably the most important and greatest archaeological find of the century. Housed in the Israel Museum, the scrolls are the oldest copies of the Hebrew Bible found to date and describe the life, times and beliefs of the Dead Sea Sect. These ancient manuscripts were discovered over a period of nine years (from 1947 to 1956) in eleven caves on the north-west shores of the Dead Sea near Khirbet Qumran. The scrolls, dating from the 3rd century B.C. to the 1st century A.D., were written on parchment and papyrus and found mostly in fragments.

The Isaiah Scroll is one of the original seven scrolls found and is the largest and best preserved of all of the biblical scrolls. And, it is the only one that was discovered in its entirety – 54 columns containing all 66 chapters. The scroll dates from around 100 B.C. and as such is 1,000 years older than the oldest Hebrew biblical manuscript, The Aleppo Codex. During the period of excavation, fragments of approximately 950 different scrolls were found.

The Shrine of the Book at the Israel Museum houses a facsimile of the Isaiah Scroll in a specially designed hall resembling the tops of the clay jars that the scrolls were discovered in. This impressive exhibit allows the visitors to see the 2.60 metre long scroll. To add to the spectacular vision of the lengthy scroll, a small original fragment is also on display.

Death by crucifixion had not been invented in the time of King David, yet Psalm chapter 22 foretold in detail the manner in which Christ would die. The Dead Sea Scrolls are an important evidence confirming the validity of the Bible account.

THE VEIL TORN IN TWO

The moment Christ died there was an earthquake and the rocks rent asunder (Matthew 27:51). At that very moment the evening sacrifice in the temple that was about to be sacrificed escaped and the veil of the curtain was ripped in two from the top to the bottom. This signified four things; firstly that the Father's heart was broken in two when He witnessed the death of His Son. Secondly, Christ's heart was broken because of the separation He felt from His Father. Thirdly the veil represented Christ's flesh being ripped as the sin bearer of the world. And fourthly the veil of unbelief had now been removed through the ratification of the New Covenant.

At the moment the temple curtain was ripped in two, it was seen that there was no Ark of the Covenant in the Most Holy Place. God was publicly declaring that the old sacrificial system was no longer required because His Son had fulfilled all the shadows and types of the Sanctuary Service.

> Jesus, when he had cried again with a loud voice, yielded up the ghost. And, behold, the veil of the temple was rent in twain from the top to the bottom; and the earth did quake, and the rocks rent. Matthew 27:50-51

The veil in the temple was ripped from the top to the bottom by the divine hand of the Father in righteous indignation at witnessing the death of His only begotten Son. The veil was approximately sixty feet high and four inches thick, therefore a human being could not have done this.

MT SINAI AND CALVARY

In the prayer of Habakkuk we are shown how Calvary was perfectly outplayed at Mt Sinai.

> O LORD, revive thy work in the midst of the years, in the midst of the years make known; in wrath remember mercy. God came from Teman, and the Holy One from mount Paran. Selah. His glory covered the heavens, and the earth was full of his praise. And his brightness was as the light; he had horns coming out of his hand (margin: bright beams out of His side): and there was the hiding of his power. Before him went the pestilence (plagues of Egypt), and burning coals went forth at his feet (burning peak of Mt Sinai). He stood, and measured the earth: he beheld, and drove asunder the nations; and the everlasting mountains were scattered, the perpetual hills did bow: his ways are everlasting. I saw the tents of Cushan in affliction: and the curtains of the land of Midian did tremble. Habakkuk 3:1-7

The prophet Habakkuk uses similar language and imagery to describe Mt Sinai and Calvary. Christ's ministry solely to the Jews, the wrath and mercy experienced at Calvary, Christ's pierced side, the earthquake, the veil or temple curtain being ripped in two, are all vividly portrayed in these few verses. The manifestations of God on both occasions were to direct the minds of the people to Christ as their Saviour.

THE ROCKS RENT WHEN CHRIST DIED

> Jesus, when he had cried again with a loud voice, yielded up the ghost. And, behold, the veil of the temple was rent in twain from the top to the bottom; and the earth did quake, and the rocks rent. Matthew 27:50-51

> Now when the centurion, and they that were with him, watching Jesus, saw the earthquake, and those things that were done, they feared greatly, saying, Truly this was the Son of God. Matthew 27:54

Fig. C80,C81 – Earthquake crack filled in with cement to the right of the cut-outs. The crack runs from the top of the Calvary escarpment to deep in the earth.

There are historical accounts of the earthquake at Christ's death as having been felt as far away as Europe and parts of Africa. At the crucifixion site this earthquake caused a foot wide crack extending all the way from the top to the bottom of the Calvary escarpment. The crack at the bottom has been filled with cement by the caretakers of the garden.

Fig. C82 – The cut-outs at Calvary.

Fig. C83 – Cut-out in Greece.

THE PLACING OF THE SIGN

In the time of Christ it was common to place large signs next to criminals who were being crucified so that the people could read what their crime had been.

> Pilate wrote a title, and put it on the cross. And the writing was, JESUS OF NAZARETH THE KING OF THE JEWS. This title then read many of the Jews: for the place where Jesus was crucified was nigh to the city: and it was written in Hebrew, and Greek, and Latin. Then said the chief priests of the Jews to Pilate, Write not, The King of the Jews; but that he said, I am King of the Jews. Pilate answered, What I have written I have written. John 19:19-22

The three inscriptions inscribed in Hebrew, Greek and Latin above the cross were actually a prophecy of Jesus as being the king of the Jews. This saying angered the Jewish leaders who requested Pilate to take down the signs – but he refused.

> The superscription of his accusation was written over, the king of the Jews.
>
> Mark 15:26

In the Gospel of John it says the signs were "put on" the cross and in the Gospel of Mark it says the signs were "put over" the cross. The Greek word "epi" can mean on or over. The cut-outs in the Calvary escarpment tell us that the signs were "placed over" the cross.

JESUS CHRIST WAS CRUCIFIED ON A CROWDED HIGHWAY

Most people have come to believe that the cross was high up on a hill because that is how the picture books show it. But we know from historical accounts that it was not on a hill – it was next to a crowded highway. The people passing by would need to have been close enough to read the accusation of the crime on the signs.

> Whenever we crucify criminals very crowded highways are chosen, so that many may see it, and many may be moved by fear of it; because all punishment does not pertain to revenge so much as to example.
>
> Quintillian, *Declarations*, 90 A.D.

As the people passed by Jesus they railed on Him, wagging their heads. If He were on a hill, they could not have passed by Him.

> They that passed by railed on him, wagging their heads, and saying, Ah, thou that destroyest the temple, and buildest it in three days, save thyself, and come down from the cross. Mark 15:29-30

CALVARY WAS A CONSPICUOUS PLACE

> Altars (Hebrew: mizbe'ah, "a place of slaughter or sacrifice") in the Hebrew Bible were typically made of earth (Exodus 20:24) or unwrought stone (20:25). Altars were generally erected in conspicuous places (Genesis 22:9; Ezekiel 6:3; 2 Kings 23:12; 16:4; 23:8). Wikipedia: Altars

"IS IT NOTHING TO YOU?"

> Is it nothing to you, all ye that pass by? behold, and see if there be any sorrow like unto my sorrow, which is done unto me, wherewith the LORD hath afflicted me in the day of his fierce anger. Lamentations 1:12

The book of Lamentations describes what Jesus was feeling upon that cross in those hours of suffering and humiliation. He said, "Is it nothing to you all you that pass by. Is it nothing to you that I am carrying the blame for all your sins, all your sorrows, all your sicknesses, all your infirmities? Am I dying in vain?" His heart was breaking from the sense of being separated from His Father. But there were a few glimmerings of hope that all would be worthwhile. Simon of Cyrene carried His cross; the thief gave his heart to Christ at the eleventh hour; and the testimony of the centurion who bowed his head and said, "Surely this was the son of God."

These words are spoken to you and me today also.

CALVARY

> And when they were come to the place, which is called Calvary, there they crucified him, and the malefactors, one on the right hand, and the other on the left. Luke 23:33

See figure C89, a diagram giving a depiction of the cross-holes.

> Thou mayest not sacrifice the passover within any of thy gates, which the LORD thy God giveth thee: But at the place which the LORD thy God shall CHOOSE to place his name in, there thou shalt sacrifice the passover at even, at the going down of the sun, at the season that thou camest forth out of Egypt.
> Deuteronomy 16:5-6

God chose Calvary as the place where His Son was to die. Two thousand years before on the same mountain God chose the place of sacrifice for Abraham to offer up his son Isaac and placed His name there (Jehoveh-Jireh).

> And Abraham called the name of that place Jehovahjireh. As it is said to this day in the mount of Jehovah it shall be provided. Genesis 22:14 ASV

The name *Jehovahjireh* means "the Lord will provide" (Bible margin).

CHRIST SACRIFICED ACCORDING TO THE SANCTUARY SYSTEM

> He shall kill it on the side of the altar northward before the LORD: and the priests, Aaron's sons, shall sprinkle his blood round about upon the altar. Leviticus 1:11

The spot where Abraham offered up His son Isaac on Mount Moriah was also the place where King David sacrificed to stay the plague. It was revered as holy ground and during King Solomon's reign the Jewish temple was built upon it. The sanctuary faced east to west and the sacrifices were offered on the northern side of the altar in the outer court. Had the Jews accepted Christ as the anti-typical lamb His life would have been offered up for the sins of the world in the outer-court of the temple. But in fulfilment of His rejection, as typified by the red heifer, He was sacrificed outside of the city, north of the temple.

CROSS HOLE

During an excavation of the crucifixion site in 1979 by Ron Wyatt, three cross holes were found sealed with square stone plugs approximately ten feet below the current day ground level. Another cross hole with a stone plug was found closer to the cliff at a slightly higher elevation. After the crucifixion the soldiers would have removed the cross and put the stone plug back in the cross hole to stop debris falling into the hole.

One of the cross hole plugs retrieved was found to have two finger niches either side with which to pull it up. Under that plug there was found to be a square post hole going down 23 ½ inches deep into the rock. The stone plug was 13 inches by 14 inches.

Shortly after Christ died a Roman soldier was commanded to pierce Him in the side with a spear to make sure He was dead. By offering up His spotless life Christ ratified the New Covenant.

Fig. C84 – Stone plug sealing the cross hole of one of the thieves.

> For all have sinned, and come short of the glory of God; Being justified freely by his grace through the redemption that is in Christ Jesus: Whom God hath set forth to be a propitiation through faith in his blood, to declare his righteousness for the remission of sins that are past, through the forbearance of God; To declare, I say, at this time his righteousness: that he might be just, and the justifier of him which believeth in Jesus. Romans 3:23-26

THE FOUNDATION OF AN OLD CHURCH

Although crucifixion was continued for a time after the death of Jesus, that particular site was never used by the Romans again for crucifixion. The scene of Calvary was so terrifying to the Jews and Romans that the site was abandoned. The earthquake scene is only briefly spoken of in the Bible but a letter written by the wife of Pontius Pilate reveals that the whole city was in a panic. It was an immense earthquake; people were thrown and tossed about. Dead bodies were hurled out of the graves. The thick darkness covered the land for three hours and many people thought the end had come.

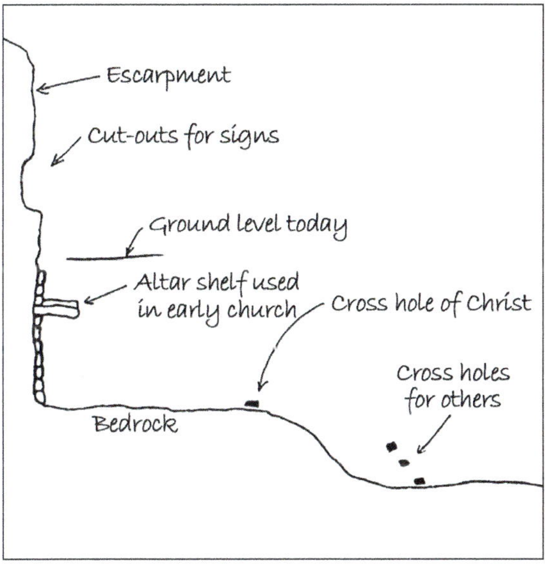

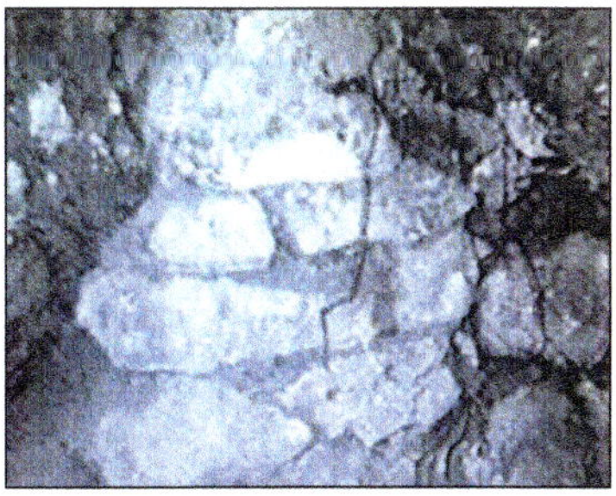

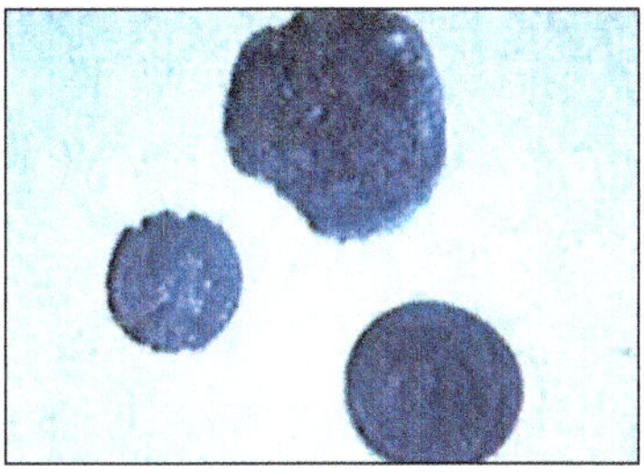

Fig. C89 – Diagram: Under the Calvary escarpment.

Fig. C86 – Top right: an altar stone that was found protruding out of the escarpment wall below the cut-outs.

Fig.C87 – Centre-right: the foundation of a stone wall approximately 10 feet below the ground which was built around the crucifixion site.

Fig. C88 – Right: Coins were also found dated to Tiberius Caesar who was the reigning emperor when Christ died.

PART 2 - THE HIDDEN SECRET

The Bible says, "We were reconciled to God by the death of his Son," but then it says, "*much more*, being reconciled, we shall be saved by his life." While the death of Christ on the cross and the shedding of His blood is a crucial component of our salvation, it is not the all encompassing means of our salvation. The scripture in Romans 5:10 makes it clear that we are "saved by His life". But what does this mean in real terms? How are we saved by the Saviour's life? The following pages will explain the prophecies about Christ and then reveal the hidden secret of our salvation in a plain and simple way.

CHRIST'S MINISTRY AND SACRIFICE FORETOLD IN BIBLE PROPHECY

> The spirit of the Lord GOD is upon me; because the LORD hath anointed me to preach good tidings unto the meek; he hath sent me to bind up the broken-hearted, to proclaim liberty to the captives, and the opening of the prison to them that are bound; Isaiah 61:1

> And he came to Nazareth, where he had been brought up: and, as his custom was, he went into the synagogue on the sabbath day, and stood up for to read. And there was delivered unto him the book of the prophet Esaias. And when he had opened the book, he found the place where it was written, The Spirit of the Lord is upon me, because he hath anointed me to preach the gospel to the poor; he hath sent me to heal the brokenhearted, to preach deliverance to the captives, and recovering of sight to the blind, to set at liberty them that are bruised, To preach the acceptable year of the Lord. Luke 4:16-19

Had the Jews studied into the above prophecy they would have recognised Christ as their Saviour. When Christ entered the synagogue and read from chapter sixty-one in the book of Isaiah He was reading of Himself and publicly announcing that the fulness of time had come. At the commencement of the sixty-ninth week Christ would now impart a new element of life and power to restore and uplift mankind from His degraded condition.

THE "SEVENTY WEEKS" PROPHECY

> Seventy weeks are determined upon thy people and upon thy holy city, to finish the transgression, and to make an end of sins, and to make reconciliation for iniquity, and to bring in everlasting righteousness, and to seal up the vision and prophecy, and to anoint the most Holy. Daniel 9:24

In Daniel 9:24 the future ministry and sacrifice of Christ was prophesied. At a definite future point in time Christ was to:

- finish the transgression
- make an end of sins
- make reconciliation for iniquity
- bring in everlasting righteousness
- seal up the vision and prophecy
- be anointed by the Holy Spirit

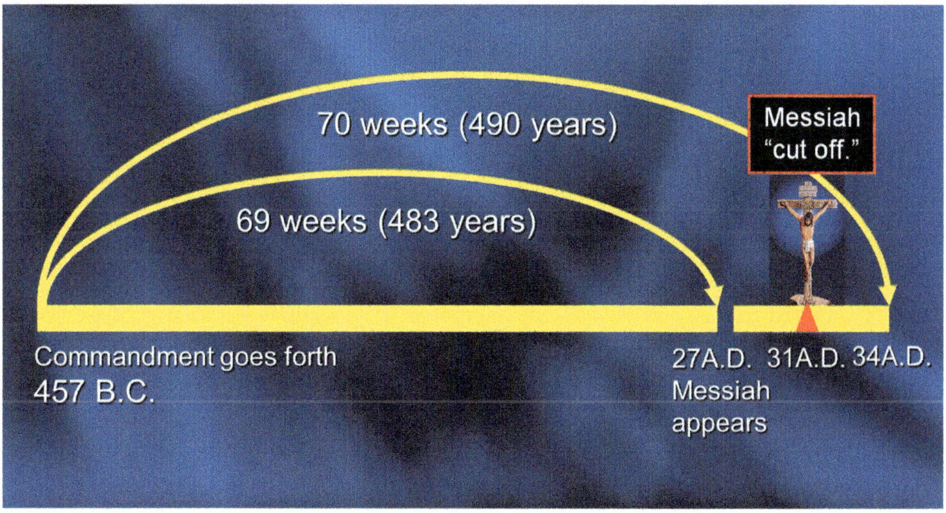

At the end of the "69 weeks" Christ commenced His public ministry in 27 A.D.. Three and a half years later He was crucified in 31 A.D (in the middle of the prophetic week). The Gospel was then proclaimed exclusively to the Jews for another three and half years until 34 A.D. (the close of the prophetic week) at which time Stephen was stoned and the Gospel went out to the Gentiles.

The burden of Christ's preaching was, "The time is fulfilled, and the kingdom of God is at hand; repent ye, and believe the gospel." Thus the gospel message, as given by the Saviour Himself, was based on the prophecies. The "time" which He declared to be fulfilled was the period made known by the angel Gabriel to Daniel. "Seventy weeks," said the angel, "are determined upon thy people and upon thy holy city, to finish the transgression, and to make an end of sins, and to make reconciliation for iniquity, and to bring in everlasting righteousness, and to seal up the vision and prophecy, and to anoint the most holy." Daniel 9:24. A day in prophecy stands for a year. See Numbers 14:34; Ezekiel 4:6. The seventy weeks, or four hundred and ninety days, represent four hundred and ninety years. A starting point for this period is given: "Know therefore and understand, that from the going forth of the commandment to restore and to build Jerusalem unto the Messiah the Prince shall be seven weeks, and threescore and two weeks," sixty-nine weeks, or four hundred and eighty-three years. Daniel 9:25. The commandment to restore and build Jerusalem, as completed by the decree of Artaxerxes Longimanus (see Ezra 6:14; 7:1, 9, margin), went into effect in the autumn of B. C. 457. From this time four hundred and eighty-three years extend to the autumn of A. D. 27. According to the prophecy, this period was to reach to the Messiah, the Anointed One. In A. D. 27, Jesus at His baptism received the anointing of the Holy Spirit, and soon afterward began His ministry. Then the message was proclaimed. "The time is fulfilled."

The Desire of Ages, p.233

A DAY FOR A YEAR PRINCIPLE IN BIBLE PROPHECY

> After the number of the days in which ye searched the land, even forty days, each day for a year, shall ye bear your iniquities, even forty years, and ye shall know my breach of promise. Numbers 14:34

> And when thou hast accomplished them, lie again on thy right side, and thou shalt bear the iniquity of the house of Judah forty days: I have appointed thee each day for a year. Ezekiel 4:6

In the Bible there is a very important rule which is used to decode prophecy and it is called the day for a year principle. The foundation for this principle is found in Numbers 14:34 and Ezekiel 4:6. In these verses we are told that when a day is spoken of in prophecy it actually means one year. Employing this principle correctly we substitute the word "day" for the word "year" – only when decoding prophecy – so we can do the calculations correctly.

THE "ONE WEEK" PROPHECY

> He shall confirm the covenant with many for one week: and in the midst of the week he shall cause the sacrifice and the oblation to cease. Daniel 9:27

> Then, said the angel, "He shall confirm the covenant with many for one week [seven years]." For seven years after the Saviour entered on His ministry, the gospel was to be preached especially to the Jews; for three and a half years by Christ Himself; and afterward by the apostles. "In the midst of the week He shall cause the sacrifice and the oblation to cease." Daniel 9:27. In the spring of A. D. 31, Christ the true sacrifice was offered on Calvary. Then the veil of the temple was rent in twain, showing that the sacredness and significance of the sacrificial service had departed. The time had come for the earthly sacrifice and oblation to cease.
>
> The one week – seven years – ended in A. D. 34. Then by the stoning of Stephen the Jews finally sealed their rejection of the gospel; the disciples who were scattered abroad by persecution "went everywhere preaching the word" (Acts 8:4); and shortly after, Saul the persecutor was converted, and became Paul, the apostle to the Gentiles.
>
> The time of Christ's coming, His anointing by the Holy Spirit, His death, and the giving of the gospel to the Gentiles, were definitely pointed out. It was the privilege of the Jewish people to understand these prophecies, and to recognise their fulfilment in the mission of Jesus. Christ urged upon His disciples the importance of prophetic study. *The Desire of Ages*, pp.233-234

In 31 A.D. Christ was crucified in the "midst of the week" (in the middle of the seven years) and then the Jews were given another three and a half years of spiritual privilege.

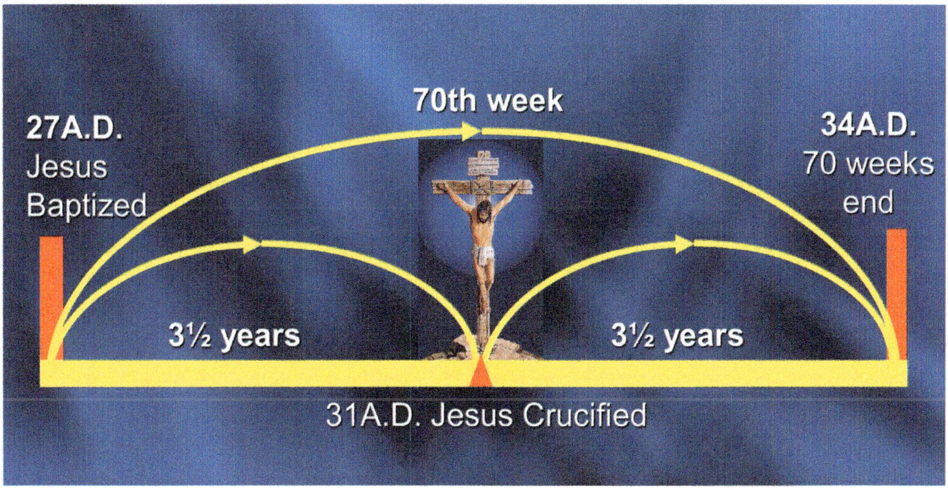

REVIVING THE EVERLASTING COVENANT

> O LORD, I have heard thy speech, and was afraid: O LORD, revive thy work in the midst of the years, in the midst of the years make known; in wrath remember mercy. Habakkuk 3:2

At His crucifixion Christ did away with the ceremonial system to revive the primitive faith of the fathers which had been lost sight of. He was bringing their attention back to the Everlasting Covenant.

THE GOSPEL GOING TO THE GENTILES

> And they stoned Stephen, calling upon God, and saying, Lord Jesus, receive my spirit. Acts 7:59

When the Jews failed to recognise Christ as the fulfilment of the sacrificial system, the prophecy of Daniel 9:24-27 was fulfilled and the Gospel went out to the heathen nations. The Jewish nation had rejected the privilege of being the light of the world. In 34 A.D. the deacon Stephen was stoned for testifying that Christ was the one upon whom all their hopes centred. The persecution of Christ's disciples was so severe in Jerusalem that they were forced to flee for their lives. God permitted this persecution to scatter them that they might preach the Gospel to the Gentiles. God came to Peter in a dream instructing Him that He was to no longer be exclusive with the truth and that salvation was for all.

PETER'S DREAM

> On the morrow, as they went on their journey, and drew nigh unto the city, Peter went up upon the housetop to pray about the sixth hour: And he became very hungry, and would have eaten: but while they made ready, he fell into a

trance, And saw heaven opened, and a certain vessel descending unto him, as it had been a great sheet knit at the four corners, and let down to the earth: Wherein were all manner of fourfooted beasts of the earth, and wild beasts, and creeping things, and fowls of the air. And there came a voice to him, Rise, Peter; kill, and eat. But Peter said, Not so, Lord; for I have never eaten any thing that is common or unclean. And the voice spake unto him again the second time, What God hath cleansed, that call not thou common. This was done thrice: and the vessel was received up again into heaven. Acts 10:9-16

In Peter's vision God used the symbol of calling the unclean, clean, to represent that the Gospel was now to go to the world. In the Old Testament God had declared certain animals to be unclean and they were not to be eaten (Leviticus 11). This vision is not to be interpreted literally as giving full permission to eat that which God has declared to be unclean, but to establish that the Gospel must be proclaimed to every nation without prejudice.

This was foretold in the 70 week prophecy of Daniel 9:24 as in 34 A.D. the Gospel went out to the Gentiles.

THE BLOTTING OUT OF ORDINANCES

Blotting out the handwriting of ordinances that was against us, which was contrary to us, and took it out of the way, nailing it to his cross; Colossians 2:14

The book of Exodus reveals that two laws were given to Moses at Mount Sinai: there was the moral law (the Ten Commandments) given on tables of stone and placed in the Ark and the Law of Moses which was written in a book and placed in the side of the Ark.

The Law of Moses contained the ceremonial laws for the sanctuary service, special feast days and laws to govern the nation of Israel. The Ten Commandments (the moral law) were engraved with God's own finger and the Law of Moses was written with ink on animal skins. It was the ceremonial law, (the Law of Moses) which foreshadowed the work of Christ that was nailed to the cross. Type met anti-type in the death of Christ at Calvary. When Christ died, the animal sacrifices of the sanctuary were no longer required because in Christ these symbolisms met their fulfilment.

The language of "blotting out" in Colossians 2:14 would not be used in reference to something that was set in stone. Engravings on stone cannot be blotted out. The Rosetta stone in Egypt, for example, was engraved thousands of years ago, and the writing on it is just as clear now as it was back then. Writing on stone has an enduring quality about it. The "blotting out" would be used in reference to something written with ink.

The law that was blotted out was the ceremonial law (the sanctuary law). It consisted of instructions and regulations pertaining to the sacrifices and services of the tabernacle, which pointed forward to the Lamb of God, the divine sacrifice. This sanctuary system had been important in that it was intended to direct the minds of the people to the New Covenant of mercy. But when Christ offered up His life on the cross, the shadow met its fulfilment and the laws pertaining to the sanctuary were "nailed to the cross".

In the law of Moses there is more instruction given apart from the ceremonial laws. The Feast days for example are "a shadow of things to come." While a number of the feasts met their fulfilment in Christ there are still some that signify future events. Also contained in the law of Moses were social and judicial laws which were a practical enlargement of the Ten Commandments.

NOT JUDGING OTHERS

> Let no man therefore judge you in meat (in keeping the special eating and drinking requirements of the feast days), or in drink, or in respect of an holyday (keeping special Jewish feast days), or of the new moon (Feast of Trumpets), or of the Sabbath days (High days – feast days which fall on the Saturday sabbath): Which are a shadow of things to come; but the body is of Christ.
>
> Colossians 2:16-17

There were those in Apostle Paul's day, as in our day, who continued to keep the Jewish feasts. In respect to these persons, the Apostle Paul advised that there was to be no judgment upon them. All have liberty to choose to keep them or not, however the New Testament does not make them binding. Those who decide to keep them must be careful not to lose sight of what they signify, as the Jews did.

THE TEN COMMANDMENTS NOT NAILED TO THE CROSS

> For whosoever shall keep the whole law, and yet offend in one point, he is guilty of all. For he that said, Do not commit adultery, said also, Do not kill. Now if thou commit no adultery, yet if thou kill, thou art become a transgressor of the law. So speak ye, and so do, as they that shall be judged by the law of liberty.
>
> James 2:10-12

The Ten Commandments have not been done away with. Rather than a bondage, it is the "law of liberty" to those who keep it in the Spirit of Christ. The law in Christ's time was perverted and it has been perverted today. Those who endeavour to find salvation through the law make it a bondage to themselves and an abhorrence to others. But when they understand it as they should, there will be liberty.

THE NEW WAY

> By a new and living way, which he hath consecrated for us, through the veil, that is to say, his flesh; And having an high priest over the house of God;
>
> Hebrews 10:20-21

It was not the hand of the priest that rent from top to bottom the gorgeous veil that divided the holy from the Most Holy Place, but the hand of God. When Christ cried out, "It is finished," He was announcing the opening of a new and living way for all. The veil being rent was the removal of the system of accessing God via the priest. Now God would be accessed through the humanity of Christ.

> Seeing then that we have a great high priest, that is passed into the heavens, Jesus the Son of God, let us hold fast our profession. For we have not an high priest which cannot be touched with the feeling of our infirmities; but was in all points tempted like as we are, yet without sin. Let us therefore come boldly unto the throne of grace, that we may obtain mercy, and find grace to help in time of need. Hebrews 4:14-16

Christ did not take His sinful human flesh back to heaven with Him but He did take our humanity. The word "flesh" in the above scripture is referring to His human nature. By His spotless life, His suffering and His death He was earning the right to advocate for man in the Father's presence. Without becoming a partaker of our humanity, Christ could not have understood our temptations and sorrows.

Christ appeased the wrath of the law by His death. He then took His blood, in which was His life (Leviticus 17:11), back to heaven. The penalty had been paid on earth but the sins recorded in the books of heaven now needed to be dealt with. Christ would plead with the Father before the law saying, "The penalty has already been paid, I died the death. This person deserves to live because here is a perfect life. My blood! My blood! My life! My life! In the place of this sin look upon my perfect life instead."

CHRIST OUR ADVOCATE IN THE HOLY PLACE

> I will bear the indignation of the LORD, because I have sinned against him, until he plead my cause, and execute judgment for me: he will bring me forth to the light, and I shall behold his righteousness. Micah 7:9

The reality is that none of us have a perfect life to offer God – we have all transgressed the law of God and fallen short of His character; therefore according to Romans 6:23 we all deserve to die an eternal death. But Christ in His love for humanity took upon Himself the punishment for our sin at Calvary that through faith in Him we would accept the gift of His life.

If we sin, we have a merciful high priest in Jesus who is faithful and just to forgive our sins when we confess and forsake them. Christ is our advocate who will plead our cause to the Father. He will plead with Him not to look upon our filthy garments stained by sin but to look at His perfect life.

> He says, "I have taken the sinner's place. Look not upon this wayward child, but look on me. Look not upon his filthy garments, but look on my righteousness."
> *Thoughts from the Mount of Blessing*, p.9

THE DAY OF ATONEMENT

The book of Leviticus describes the sanctuary services that were performed by the Hebrews. Each day of the year a lamb would be slain as the morning and evening sacrifice for the sins of Israel. The people would confess their sins over the lamb; the lamb would be slain by the priest and then the blood of the lamb would be sprinkled in the Holy Place (the first compartment of the Hebrew Sanctuary). The Holy Place became polluted and filthy with the sins of the people, every sin being transferred there and it could not be cleansed out until the Day of Atonement.

Once a year on the Day of Atonement the sanctuary would be cleansed. Two goats would be selected: the Lord's goat and the scapegoat. The Lord's goat would be slain and offered up as a sin offering for the people. The high priest was the only person permitted to officiate in this ceremony. He would take the blood of the goat, enter into the Most Holy Place and sprinkle the blood upon the mercy seat. This blood represented the life of Christ – it was only the perfect, righteous life of Christ contained in the blood that could atone for the broken law.

After the high priest had offered the blood of the goat upon the mercy seat to make atonement for the broken law of God, He then left the Most Holy Place. On his way out of the sanctuary he sprinkled the items of furniture in the Holy Place with the blood of the goat symbolising that the sins in the Holy Place had been transferred to himself. He then left the sanctuary and transferred the blame for all the sins of Israel – in token being carried by himself – upon the head of the scapegoat. A strong man was then selected from among the people to lead the scapegoat into the wilderness, signifying that the guilt of the sins of Israel had been removed from them forever.

THE 2300 DAYS

> And he said unto me, Unto two thousand and three hundred days; then shall the sanctuary be cleansed.
> Daniel 8:14

The 2300 days had been found to begin when the commandment of Artaxerxes for the restoration and building of Jerusalem went into effect, in the autumn of 457 B.C. Taking this as the starting point, there was perfect harmony in the application of all the events foretold in the explanation of that period in Daniel 9:25-27. Sixty-nine weeks, the first 483 of the 2300 years, were to reach to the Messiah, the Anointed One; and Christ's baptism and anointing by the Holy Spirit, A.D. 27, exactly fulfilled the specification. In the midst of the seventieth week, Messiah was to be cut off. Three and a half years after His baptism, Christ was crucified, in the spring of A.D. 31. The seventy weeks, or 490 years, were to pertain especially to the Jews. At the expiration of this period the nation sealed its rejection of Christ by the persecution of His disciples, and the apostles turned to the Gentiles, A.D. 34. The first 490 years of the 2300 having then ended, 1810 years would remain. From A.D. 34, 1810 years extend to 1844. "Then," said the angel, "shall the sanctuary be cleansed." All the preceding specifications of the prophecy had been unquestionably fulfilled at the time appointed. *The Great Controversy*, p.410

THE INVESTIGATIVE JUDGMENT

For eighteen centuries this work of ministration continued in the first apartment of the sanctuary. The blood of Christ, pleaded in behalf of penitent believers, secured their pardon and acceptance with the Father, yet their sins still remained upon the books of record. As in the typical service there was a work of atonement at the close of the year, so before Christ's work for the redemption of men is completed there is a work of atonement for the removal of sin from the sanctuary. This is the service which began when the 2300 days ended. At that time, as foretold by Daniel the prophet, our High Priest entered the most holy, to perform the last division of His solemn work – to cleanse the sanctuary.

As anciently the sins of the people were by faith placed upon the sin offering and through its blood transferred, in figure, to the earthly sanctuary, so in the new covenant the sins of the repentant are by faith placed upon Christ and transferred, in fact, to the heavenly sanctuary. And as the typical cleansing of the earthly was accomplished by the removal of the sins by which it had been polluted, so the actual cleansing of the heavenly is to be accomplished by the removal, or blotting out, of the sins which are there recorded. But before this can be accomplished, there must be an examination of the books of record to determine who, through repentance of sin and faith in Christ, are entitled to the benefits of His atonement. The cleansing of the sanctuary therefore involves a work of investigation--a work of judgment. This work must be performed prior to the coming of Christ to redeem His people; for when He comes, His reward is with Him to give to every man according to his works. Revelation 22:12. *Ibid.*, p.421

CHRIST OUR ADVOCATE IN THE MOST HOLY PLACE

The high priest in the Old Testament sanctuary was a representation of Jesus and His ministerial work in the heavenly sanctuary.

Christ being come an high priest of good things to come, by a greater and more perfect tabernacle, not made with hands, that is to say, not of this building; Neither by the blood of goats and calves, but by his own blood he entered in ONCE into the holy place, having obtained eternal redemption for us. For if the blood of bulls and of goats, and the ashes of an heifer sprinkling the unclean, sanctifieth to the purifying of the flesh: How much more shall the blood of Christ, who through the eternal Spirit offered himself without spot to God, purge your conscience from dead works to serve the living God? Hebrews 9:11-14

Christ is now in the heavenly sanctuary doing the very same work that the high priest did on the Day of Atonement. All our sins are recorded in the books of heaven. Before the Father, He presents our case. As our sins come up before the judgment, He stands before the bar as our defence. Having been in the very situation Himself, knowing the inward workings of our wicked and deceitful heart, and tracing from cause to effect, He pours out His supplications on our behalf. He pleads with the Father to have mercy upon us and to forgive the transgression. He points the Father to Calvary, to His wounded side, to the wounds in His hands. He had paid the price. He had died the death. Would this not appease the wrath of the law? Indeed. Presenting Himself before the bar, He points to His own perfect life filled with complete submission to the will of the Father, beseeching that the Father would not look upon the sinner, but upon Himself.

THE MOST HOLY PLACE A SYMBOL OF OUR MIND

> What? know ye not that your body is the temple of the Holy Ghost which is in you, which ye have of God, and ye are not your own? 1 Corinthians 6:19

> How much more shall the blood of Christ, who through the eternal Spirit offered himself without spot to God, purge your conscience from dead works to serve the living God? Hebrews 9:14

The Most Holy Place and its furniture is a symbol of our mind. The scriptures state that our bodies are a temple for the Holy Ghost. Therefore we are a living representation of the sanctuary in heaven and Christ is cleansing and blotting sin from our mind as we confess and forsake it.

A TIME OF DEEP HEART SEARCHING

The Day of Atonement in the Hebrew sanctuary was a day of investigative judgment. If any unconfessed sins remained in the camp, God's blessing would not be received. The people were dependent upon God for their daily provision; if the blessing failed to come, the rain would be withheld and the sun would scorch the land, or their enemies would be at their gates. It was a fearful day for a father and mother with their children who earnestly sought God's approbation.

This ceremony has a spiritual application for our time also. As the nearness of Christ's coming approaches, He is looking to see the hearts of His people. Do they care for and acknowledge His blessings which daily surround them yet they have taken for granted? Are they serious about putting sin out of their lives? Are they thirsting for His salvation?

CHRIST FINISHES HIS MINISTRATION

> He that is unjust, let him be unjust still: and he which is filthy, let him be filthy still: and he that is righteous, let him be righteous still: and he that is holy, let him be holy still. And, behold, I come quickly; and my reward is with me, to give every man according as his work shall be. Revelation 22:11-12

Since 1844 A.D. (the termination of the 2300 day prophecy in Daniel 8:14) Christ has been judging the cases of all those who have made a Christian profession, from Adam right through to the present age. However, in order for the sum of the reward to be given every man according to His works, that judgment must come to a decided close.

SAVED FROM OUR SINS NOT IN OUR SINS

> And she shall bring forth a son, and thou shalt call his name JESUS: for he shall save his people from their sins. Matthew 1:21

The Bible says that Christ will subdue all our iniquities (Micah 7:19) and that He will save us *from* our sins – not *in* our sins. After forgiving Mary Magdalene's sins, Christ instructed her to "go and sin no more" (John 8:10-11). If He had not made it possible for her to do so, He would not have given her that command.

CUT OFF FROM GOD BY CHERISHED SIN

> For whatsoever soul it be that shall not be afflicted in that same day, he shall be cut off from among his people. Leviticus 23:29

Any Israelite who would not confess and forsake their sins on the Day of Atonement would be cut off from among God's people. If we are not having victory over sin in our lives through the influence of the Holy Spirit we will be adding sins to the books of heaven at the same time as Christ is trying to remove them. We should be earnestly seeking to examine our hearts to confess any known sins and forsake them in His strength or else His atoning ministry in the sanctuary above is in vain.

While God bears long with us and offers pardon for sin, we cannot go on wilfully sinning against Him. When Christ ceases His intercession, any sins remaining upon the books or newly added will condemn us.

GOD'S GRACE MORE ABOUNDING

> Where sin abounded, grace did much more abound. Romans 5:20

At times we may have a terrible battle on our hands because of our past life and the tremendous hold our sins have on us. But God has promised that where sin abounds grace much more abounds. The grace of God is far more powerful than any sin that has a grip on you, therefore God's grace will always be sufficient. If we really believe this, we will not be afraid of entering into the combat with our own carnal heart.

THE APOSTLE PAUL'S EXPERIENCE

> Though I might also have confidence in the flesh. If any other man thinketh that he hath whereof he might trust in the flesh, I more: Circumcised the eighth day, of the stock of Israel, of the tribe of Benjamin, an Hebrew of the Hebrews; as touching the law, a Pharisee; Concerning zeal, persecuting the church; touching the righteousness which is in the law, blameless.
>
> Philippians 3:4-6

Saul of Tarsus was a zealous Jew who believed he kept the law to the letter. He honestly believed himself to be a righteous man despite persecuting the early Christian church and thinking he was doing God a favour. One day on the road to Damascus he had a personal encounter with Jesus Christ and for the first time saw himself as he really was – a sinner. The blazing glory of Christ blinded him for a time, but the eyes of his understanding were opened and within a few days, his faith laid hold of a crucified and risen Saviour.

Apostle Paul was a man of like passions as we ourselves. He had a wretched human body with sinful tendencies just like us. Although he realised the Covenant promise of God in his own life, he was never free from temptation. His old self would be constantly urging itself upon him, seeking for his attention. It was a daily struggle for even this man of great faith; but he looked to Christ and Him crucified with the old Saul of Tarsus. All that he could do was summarised in the words:

> I die daily. 1 Corinthians 15:31

A LIVING EXAMPLE

> I therefore so run, not as uncertainly; so fight I, not as one that beateth the air: But I keep under my body, and bring it into subjection: lest that by any means, when I have preached to others, I myself should be a castaway.
>
> 1 Corinthians 9:26-27

> The apostle declares that he did not run in the Christian race uncertainly, that is, indifferently, willing to be left behind; neither did he fight as the pugilist (boxer) practices prior to the fray, beating the air with empty blows, having no opponent. But as, when in actual conflict, he contends for the mastery, overcomes his antagonist by repeated and well-directed blows, beats him to the ground, and holds him there till he acknowledges himself conquered, so did the apostle fight against the temptations of Satan and the evil propensities of the carnal nature. *The Life of Paul*, p.167

Apostle Paul had been a hypocrite in his past life, and now he shunned all false appearances. His life was devoted to the salvation of souls and in all things he sought to be a living demonstration of the truths he taught. He was a true minister of God who practiced the very thing that he preached.

THE FATHER'S LOVE FOR HUMANITY

> Therefore doth my Father love me, because I lay down my life, that I might take it again. John 10:17

The Father could not bear the thought of spending the rest of eternity without you and me. And when His Son pledged to give His life for us, the Father was so appreciative of it, that He now loves His Son even more.

> And lo a voice from heaven, saying, This is my beloved Son, in whom I am well pleased. Matthew 3:17

The Father says to His Son, "I am well pleased because you are bringing my children back to me through your unselfish, untiring, self-sacrificing love."

CHRIST'S LOVE FOR THE SINNER

> When the Pharisees saw it, they said unto his disciples, Why eateth your Master with publicans and sinners? Matthew 9:11

The self-righteous Pharisees murmured among themselves because Jesus ate with sinners.

> When Jesus heard that, he said unto them, They that be whole need not a physician, but they that are sick. Matthew 9:12

The Pharisees may have looked all holy on the outside but Jesus knew what was in their hearts. He knew that they were secretly plotting to kill Him. They were hypocrites and Jesus told them so on several occasions. But despite their hypocrisy Jesus still longed to save them.

Mary Magdalene and Levi Matthew, the tax collector, on the other hand, both knew they were sinners, so when Jesus came along they said in brutal honesty,

"Yes Lord, I'm a sinner. That's what I am without you. I need your righteousness because mine is pathetic." What a difference!

> But go ye and learn what that meaneth, I will have mercy, and not sacrifice: for I am not come to call the righteous, but sinners to repentance. Matthew 9:13

Jesus says to the Pharisees, "Go and think about what this means: I will have mercy and not sacrifice." The Pharisees were performing their animal sacrifices thinking that would make them righteous; the true Lamb of God was standing right in front of them.

When Mary Magdalene was caught in the act of adultery and the Pharisees had brought her to Jesus for her condemnation, His response was: "He that is without sin among you, let him first cast a stone at her" (John 8:7). Then He proceeded to write all their secret sins in the sand. They were exposed before the people and with guilt stricken hearts, from the greatest to the least, they walked away.

> When Jesus had lifted up himself, and saw none but the woman, he said unto her, Woman, where are those thine accusers? Hath no man condemned thee? She said, No man, Lord. And Jesus said unto her, Neither do I condemn thee: go, and sin no more. John 8:10-11

Christ did not condemn Mary Magdalene and neither did He condemn the Pharisees. Christ came to show us the Father, – that He is not some terrible tyrant waiting to hurl thunderbolts at us. Christ did not live His own life. The love and compassion He manifested was the love and compassion of the Father in heaven.

THE PRODIGAL SON

In the parable of the prodigal son, a young man received an inheritance from his father and then departed into a foreign country and squandered it all on harlots. When all the inheritance was wasted, he lived with a citizen who sent him out to feed the pigs. This young man had reached the bottom of the pit. He had made a complete mess of his life. How many of us feel like that at times? But one day he "came to himself" – he realised his foolishness in squandering away his inheritance and decided to return to his father to beg him to employ him as a servant.

> But when he was yet a great way off, his father saw him, and had compassion, and ran, and fell on his neck, and kissed him. And the son said unto him, Father, I have sinned against heaven, and in thy sight, and am no more worthy to be called thy son. But the father said to his servants, Bring forth the best robe, and put it on him; and put a ring on his hand, and shoes on his feet: And bring hither the fatted calf, and kill it; and let us eat, and be merry: For this my

> son was dead, and is alive again; he was lost, and is found. And they began to be merry. Luke 15:18-24

This story represents the love of the Father in heaven for us. Every day the father of the prodigal son would watch out for him. His heart was yearning for His son to come home again. Then one day the Father sees his son a long way off and he runs over to him and has compassion on him and kisses him. The father does not even give his son time to beg employment because he considers him still being worthy as his son. The prodigal acknowledges his unworthiness and that he had been a disappointment to his father. But the father doesn't hold any grudges against him and He tells one of the servants to bring the best robe and to put that robe upon his son. Then the father kills the fatted calf for the son. This is the attitude of our Father in heaven. He is constantly waiting with arms open wide for us to return to Him. He doesn't hold our past against us; and even if we stink like swine, He will hold us tight in His arms.

THE JEALOUS OLDER BROTHER

> Now his elder son was in the field: and as he came and drew nigh to the house, he heard music and dancing. And he called one of the servants, and asked what these things meant. And he said unto him, Thy brother is come; and thy father hath killed the fatted calf, because he hath received him safe and sound. And he was angry, and would not go in: therefore came his father out, and entreated him. And he answering said to his father, Lo, these many years do I serve thee, neither transgressed I at any time thy commandment: and yet thou never gavest me a kid, that I might make merry with my friends: But as soon as this thy son was come, which hath devoured thy living with harlots, thou hast killed for him the fatted calf. And he said unto him, Son, thou art ever with me, and all that I have is thine. It was meet that we should make merry, and be glad: for this thy brother was dead, and is alive again; and was lost, and is found. Luke 15:28-32

The elder brother was like the Pharisees who looked upon the publicans and harlots as being too sinful for the favour of God. They did not understand why Jesus was giving His blessing to sinners. They considered themselves as the worthy ones. There are many professed Christians today who look down upon those around them who are struggling with sin, and often failing in that struggle. Their attitude is one of, "Come not near unto me for I am holier than thou." They fear they will be polluted by the atmosphere of sinners. But Christ showed us that the Father's love is impartial. All who will cry to Him for help – no matter what their condition – He will hear, and save.

The fatted calf in the parable represents Christ being slain to justify the repentant sinner. But because the Pharisees did not recognise their need of Christ's atonement, His sacrifice was of no benefit to them.

> Then drew near unto Him all the publicans and sinners for to hear him. And the Pharisees and scribes murmured, saying, this man receiveth sinners, and eateth with them. Luke 15:1-2

Jesus said, "The publicans and the harlots go into the kingdom before you" (Math 21:31). And "many that are first shall be last; and the last first" (Mark 10:31).

> He longs to come in contact with those who are laden with sins who are *permeated* through and through with sins, in order that this holiness, finding an entrance, shall consume the sin, and save the soul. That is Christ's holiness.
> *General Conference Bulletin*, 1895, p.312

DON'T WAIT UNTIL YOU FEEL BETTER

> Come now, and let us reason together, saith the LORD: though your sins be as scarlet, they shall be as white as snow; though they be red like crimson, they shall be as wool Isaiah 1:18

> If you see your sinfulness, do not wait to make yourself better. How many there are who think they are not good enough to come to Christ. Do you expect to become better through your own efforts? "Can the Ethiopian change his skin, or the leopard his spots? then may ye also do good, that are accustomed to do evil." Jeremiah 13:23. There is help for us only in God. We must not wait for stronger persuasions, for better opportunities, or for holier tempers. We can do nothing of ourselves. We must come to Christ just as we are. *Steps to Christ*, p.31

During Christ's ministry it was the sinners and outcasts who responded to His love because they felt their great need of Him. It doesn't matter how terrible a sinner you may have been in the past. Consider Mary Magdalene the harlot, the two men possessed by demons and the thief on the cross. We can come to Christ just as we are, in our worst situation and He will forgive and *forget* our past.

The rabbis and the Jewish leaders on the other hand thought they were alright. They didn't feel their need of Christ's righteousness because they thought their own righteousness was good enough. And therefore Christ said, "Your sin remaineth" (John 9:41).

A NEW LIFE PREPARED FOR US

> LORD, thou wilt ordain peace for us: for thou also hast wrought all our works in us. Isaiah 26:12

What Christ has done for us we can never do for ourselves. There is nothing we can do to earn or merit our own salvation. We cannot go out and earn "brownie points" to gain our way to heaven – nothing we can do will avail – it is all through Christ.

THE LAW DEMANDS A PERFECT LIFE

> But we are all as an unclean thing, and all our righteousnesses are as filthy rags; and we all do fade as a leaf; and our iniquities, like the wind, have taken us away. Isaiah 64:6 (margin: righteous acts)

The law requires nothing short of God's perfection. Because all have sinned and come short of the glory of God (Romans 3:23), the law will not accept our obedience no matter how perfectly we try to obey it. If it is not God Himself doing the works the law cannot be satisfied. It requires the right-doing of God Himself and Christ was sent to bring this to us.

CHRIST'S LIFE WAS FULL OF THE FATHER'S WORKING

> I can of mine own self do nothing: as I hear, I judge: and my judgment is just; because I seek not mine own will, but the will of the Father which hath sent me. John 5:30

> Believest thou not that I am in the Father, and the Father in me? the words that I speak unto you I speak not of myself: but the Father that dwelleth in me, he doeth the works. John 14:10

Christ did not do His own works or speak His own words. He had emptied Himself and was filled with the Father. "I can of mine own self do nothing... The Father that dwelleth in me, He doeth the works". When Christ calmed the stormy billows of Galilee, it was not by His own power. That power He had laid down. All His miracles were performed by the Father Himself – Christ continually yielding to His Father's working. He was completely dependent upon God, no less than we are.

CHRIST BRINGS THE FATHER TO US THROUGH HIMSELF

When we accept Christ, He brings God to us through Himself. Christ's life upon this earth was all about revealing the character of the Father and when we receive Christ's life, we receive of the Father's life in all its holiness. One day in heaven, we will discover Christ's own character, but on this earth His role was to reveal the Father.

CHRIST BROUGHT US GOD'S RIGHT-DOING

> For what the law could not do, in that it was weak through the flesh, God sending his own Son in the likeness of sinful flesh, and for sin, condemned sin in the flesh: That the righteousness of the law might be fulfilled in us, who walk not after the flesh, but after the Spirit. Romans 8:3-4

God could not change His law to meet man in his fallen condition. As the law reveals who God is, it can never be altered. Therefore God had to enable man in his fallen condition to meet the requirements of the law. By sending His own Son to become at one with us, He brought His own right-doing within our reach. Christ was one with us and when the Father worked His will in Him, the Father was working His will in us. What God did for Him, He did for us; what God worked in Him, He worked in us. Therefore if we will only accept this precious gift, and yield ourselves to the Holy Spirit, our life will be filled with the right-doing of God.

THE WORK OF THE HOLY SPIRIT

> Howbeit when he, the Spirit of truth, is come, he will guide you into all truth: for he shall not speak of himself; but whatsoever he shall hear, that shall he speak: and he will show you things to come. He shall glorify me: for he shall receive of mine, and shall show it unto you. All things that the Father hath are mine: therefore said I, that he shall take of mine, and shall show it unto you.
>
> John 16:13-15

It is the Holy Spirit who identifies sin in our lives and invites us to engage in the work of its removal. He shows us the perfect life that Christ lived on our behalf, and as we receive the Spirit into our hearts, He imparts to us that life.

A NEW LIFE FOR EVERY INDIVIDUAL

> I am crucified with Christ: nevertheless I live; yet not I, but Christ liveth in me: and the life which I now live in the flesh I live by the faith of the Son of God, who loved me, and gave himself for me. Galatians 2:20

When the life of Christ is imparted to us as a gift we do not lose our individuality. We all have different lives with a unique set of circumstances and experiences. We all have different trials, we make different mistakes and gain different victories. In order for us to stand justified before the law, Christ had to work out a perfect life for every single individual on this planet. Therefore every person has a perfect life, and that life is as it would have been had we never sinned.

JESUS WAS IN ALL POINTS LIKE US

> Forasmuch then as the children are partakers of flesh and blood, he also himself likewise took part of the same; that through death he might destroy him that had the power of death, that is, the devil; And deliver them who through fear of death were all their lifetime subject to bondage. Verily he took not on him the nature of angels; but he took on him the seed of Abraham. Wherefore in all things it behoved him to be made like unto his brethren, that he might be a merciful and faithful high priest in things pertaining to God, to make reconciliation for the sins of the people. For in that he himself hath suffered being tempted, he is able to succour them that are tempted. Hebrews 2:14-18

> For we have not an high priest which cannot be touched with the feeling of our infirmities; but was in all points tempted like as we are, yet without sin. Let us therefore come boldly unto the throne of grace, that we may obtain mercy, and find grace to help in time of need. Hebrews 4:15-16

Christ took part of the same flesh and blood as ourselves. He was made like us in all things so that He would be able to experience our trials and temptations and be with us when we endure them. His experience in warring with the sinful, carnal nature was no different to our own, except that He never sinned. Despite having plunged into the deep miry pit of human suffering and misery – our fallen human nature with all its clamourings to sin and its associated consequences – not for one moment did He cherish a sinful thought in His mind. Even though He was tried to the uttermost, He resisted sin until death – even unto the cruel, inhumane and shameful death upon the cross.

He knows the power of sin. He knows the strong pull of temptation. He understands our experiences and struggles to overcome our inherited and cultivated tendencies to evil. He knows how hard it is to do what is right. To use the old phrase, He knows "where the shoe pinches", because He Himself has worn the shoes and walked in them. And because He knows all this, He is our faithful high priest who makes intercession for us.

GOD'S ATONEMENT WITH MAN

> For such an high priest became us, who is holy, harmless, undefiled, separate from sinners, and made higher than the heavens. Hebrews 7:26

When Christ became one with humanity it was not just in a general sense but in a personal and individual sense - Jesus became "me". There are several examples in the Bible to show that Christ became as the individual himself:

- A sojourner to Abraham – Abraham was a sojourner and Christ appeared to him as a sojourner to confirm the Covenant that Sarah was to have the promised child. (Genesis 18.)
- A wrestler to Jacob – Jacob was a wrestler and Christ came to him at the river Jabbok as a wrestler. Jacob thought He was an enemy until dawn when Christ touched his thigh and miraculously dislocated it. Jacob realised that the wrestler was the Lord Himself and wept upon his neck saying, "I will not let thee go unless thou bless me" (Genesis 32:24). Christ changed Jacob's name to Israel – he had power with God and prevailed. Christ was demonstrating to Jacob He had become at one with him and His strength and skill were equal to his own, therefore the fight had been equal until dawn. (Genesis 32.)
- Captain of the Host to Joshua – Joshua was captain of the Lord's host and Jesus appeared to Joshua as captain of the Lord's host. (Joshua 5:14.)
- Meshach, Shadrach & Abednego in the fiery furnace - Christ appeared as the fourth man identical to them in their experience. (Daniel 3.)

Faith therefore must be purely taught: namely, that by faith thou art so entirely and nearly joined unto Christ, that he and thou are made as it were one person; so that thou mayst boldly say: I am now one with Christ, that is to say, Christ's righteousness, victory and life are mine. And again, Christ may say: I am that sinner, that is, his sins, death etc. are mine, because he is united and joined unto me, and I unto him. For by faith we are so joined together, that we are become one flesh and one bone, as Ephesians 5:30.

Martin Luther, *Commentary on Galatians*

The Lord did also lead me into the mystery of union with the Son of God; that I was joined to Him, that I was flesh of His flesh, and bone of His bone; ... for if He and I were one, then His righteousness was mine, His merits mine, His victory also mine. Now could I see myself in heaven and earth at once: in heaven by my Christ, by my head, by my righteousness and life, though on earth by my body or person.

John Bunyan, *Grace Abounding to the Chief of Sinners*

By divine decree, there existed such an union between Christ and his people, that all Christ did his people did: and all Christ has performed, his people did perform in him, for they were in his loins when he descended to the tomb, and in his loins they have ascended up on high; with him they entered into bliss; and with him they sit in heavenly places.

Charles Spurgeon, *Christ in the Covenant*

CHRIST WAS OURSELVES

For we have not an high priest which cannot be touched with the feeling of our infirmities; but was in all points tempted like as we are, yet without sin.

Hebrews 4:15

Christ could not be tempted in all points like us, unless He was in all points like us. Likewise, He could not feel as we feel unless He was where we are, and as we are. His perfect life can only stand in the place of mine if His life is my own life. Every individual is faced with trials and temptations that are peculiar to that person's experience. No two lives are the same. To meet the claims that the law has upon every individual, Christ's perfection must meet each life in every particular.

A CHRIST IN THE PAST TOO DISTANT

The life Jesus lived 2000 years ago is a powerful example of a perfect life; but it is not personal enough for the temptations we struggle with in the 21st century. Even if Jesus Christ was here, today, on the other side of the room, it would still not be close enough. We need a Saviour who is right here, right now, who knows what we are going through because He is going through it as one with us individually, personally.

TEMPTATION IS NOT SIN

> But every man is tempted, when he is drawn away of his own lust, and enticed. Then when lust hath conceived, it bringeth forth sin: and sin, when it is finished, bringeth forth death. James 1:14-15

> For what the law could not do, in that it was weak through the flesh, God sending his own Son in the likeness of sinful flesh, and for sin, condemned sin in the flesh. Romans 8:3

It is not a sin to be tempted to sin. It is when we cherish the thought and then act upon the impulse that it becomes actual transgression. As one with ourselves, Christ can be tempted in exactly the same way we are at exactly the same time, yet choose to repulse the sinful thought. By doing so He is working out a perfect life that will stand in the place of our failure if we yield to that temptation. But if we have accepted His life as our own, then we will not sin because as He overcomes, we will overcome with Him.

CHRIST FELT THE GUILT OF OUR SIN AS THOUGH IT WERE HIS OWN

> About the ninth hour Jesus cried with a loud voice, saying, My God, my God, why hast thou forsaken me? Matthew 27:46

> Behold, the LORD'S hand is not shortened, that it cannot save; neither his ear heavy, that it cannot hear: But your iniquities have separated between you and your God, and your sins have hid his face from you, that he will not hear.
> Isaiah 59:1-2

Although Christ never sinned, He took our failures upon Himself and experiences with us the sense of guilt for sin. That is why He could not even lift His head upon the cross - the guilt of our sin became His own.

TAKE MY YOKE

> Take my yoke upon you, and learn of me; for I am meek and lowly in heart: and ye shall find rest unto your souls. For my yoke is easy, and my burden is light.
> Matthew 11:29-30

> Those who accept the one principle of making the service and honour of God supreme will find perplexities vanish, and a plain path before their feet.
> *The Desire of Ages*, p.330

We have the assurance that Christ has already fought the battle for us. And if we will engage in the conflict, we are fighting in a war that has already been won. All we need to do is continue to submit our will to God's will and ways, and the victory will be ours.

> There is nothing Christ dislikes more than for his people to make a show-thing of him and not to use him. He loves to be worked. He is a great labourer; he always was for His Father, and now He loves to be a great labourer for His brethren. The more burdens you put on His shoulders the better He will love you. Cast your burden on Him. You will never know the sympathy of Christ's heart and the love of His soul so well as when you have heaved a very mountain of trouble from yourself to His shoulders, and have found that He does not stagger under the weight. Are your troubles like huge mountains of snow upon your spirit? Bid them rumble like an avalanche upon the shoulders of the Almighty Christ. He can bear them all away, and carry them into the depths of the sea. Do use thy Master, for this very purpose He was put into the covenant, that thou mightest use Him whenever thou needest Him. Charles Spurgeon, *Christ in the Covenant*

BELIEVING IS NOT EASY

> Because I tell you the truth, ye believe me not. John 8:45

> He that undertakes to believe sets upon the hardest task that ever was proposed to man; not because the things imposed upon us are unreasonable or unaccountable, but because the heart of man, the more true anything is, the more it sticks and stumbles thereat; and, says Christ, "Because I tell you the truth, ye believe me not" (John 8:45). Hence believing is called labouring, (Heb 4:11); and it is the sorest labour, at times that any man can take in hand, because assaulted with the greatest oppositions; but believe thou must, be the labour never so hard. John Bunyan, *The Work of Christ as Advocate*

Nothing Christ said was unreasonable or unaccountable, the problem is that the heart of man sticks and stumbles when it hears the truth and it wants to resist it. For those who want to depend upon outward evidences, believing God and taking Him at His word is very difficult. It is for this reason that we need to trust God in our daily experiences to build faith. It should be a simple thing to believe God and take Him at His word but the reality is it is not something that comes to us naturally – we have to work at believing.

ADAM "KNEW" EVE

> Therefore shall a man leave his father and his mother, and shall cleave unto his wife: and they shall be one flesh. Genesis 2:24

> And Adam knew Eve his wife; and she conceived, and bare Cain, and said, I have gotten a man from the LORD. Genesis 4:1

> God Himself gave Adam a companion. He provided "an help meet for him"--a helper corresponding to him--one who was fitted to be his companion, and

> who could be one with him in love and sympathy. Eve was created from a rib taken from the side of Adam, signifying that she was not to control him as the head, nor to be trampled under his feet as an inferior, but to stand by his side as an equal, to be loved and protected by him. A part of man, bone of his bone, and flesh of his flesh, she was his second self, showing the close union and the affectionate attachment that should exist in this relation. "For no man ever yet hated his own flesh; but nourisheth and cherisheth it." Ephesians 5:29. "Therefore shall a man leave his father and his mother, and shall cleave unto his wife; and they shall be one." *Patriarchs and Prophets*, p.46

The intimate relationship between Adam and Eve is a symbol of us being brought into a oneness (at-one-ment) with Christ. Yet it does not perfectly illustrate the total unity between Christ and the believer.

WHAT IT MEANS TO "KNOW" JESUS

> Now when I passed by thee, and looked upon thee, behold, thy time was the time of love; and I spread my skirt over thee, and covered thy nakedness: yea, I sware unto thee, and entered into a covenant with thee, saith the Lord GOD, and thou becamest mine. Ezekiel 16:8

> I will betroth thee unto me for ever; yea, I will betroth thee unto me in righteousness. Hosea 2:19-20

The Bible uses the word "to know" or "knew" in the sense of a marriage consummation. In the text above, we see how God uses the union of the male and the female on the evening of their marriage to demonstrate His Covenant union with us through Christ becoming ourselves. In the marriage union, personal individuality is not lost, but the two lives are blended harmoniously into the one where each one becomes a counterpart of the other or, in a sense, a second self. They are now entering into a relationship of interdependence. In our union with Christ, Christ does not cease to be Christ, and we do not cease to be ourselves and become Christ. Yet the two are as one – this is the "mystery among the Gentiles; which is Christ in you, the hope of glory" (Colossians 1:27).

"I NEVER KNEW YOU"

> Many will say to me in that day, Lord, Lord, have we not prophesied in thy name? and in thy name have cast out devils? and in thy name done many wonderful works? And then will I profess unto them, I never knew you: depart from me, ye that work iniquity. Matthew 7:22, 23

To those who never enter into an intimate relationship with Christ, He says, "I never knew you" because they never became one with Him.

If they had become one with Christ they would not boast "*we*" have done all these wonderful works in your name. With a heart of thanksgiving they would have said instead, "Lord, *you* have wrought all these wonderful works in us because we have lived *your* life and you are our source of life."

THE NECESSITY OF FAITH

> Whatsoever is not of faith is sin. Romans 14:23

It doesn't matter how right we do something, if we do it of ourselves, it is not good enough. The law demands the right-doing of God, therefore we must have a faith that will bring it to us. This is why the scriptures declare, "whatsoever is not of faith is sin."

ONLY ONE FAITH THAT SAVES

> One Lord, one faith, one baptism. Ephesians 4:5

> Faith is not something that comes from ourselves with which we believe upon Him, but it is that something with which He believed--the faith which He exercised, which He brings to us, and which becomes ours and works in us--the gift of God. That is what the word means, "Here are they that keep the commandments of God and the faith of Jesus." They keep the faith of Jesus because it is that divine faith which Jesus exercised Himself.
>
> *General Conference Bulletin*, 1895, p.270

THE FAITH OF JESUS

> But now the righteousness of God without the law is manifested, being witnessed by the law and the prophets; Even the righteousness of God which is by faith of Jesus Christ unto all and upon all them that believe: for there is no difference: Romans 3:21-22

> Here is the patience of the saints: here are they that keep the commandments of God, and the faith of Jesus. Revelation 14:12

It is only through the impartation of Christ's obedient life that we are able to keep the law of God. Christ came to this earth to show us how to live a perfect life, and as He wrought out that perfect life, He was working out a perfect life for us also. His faith brought to Him the obedience of the Father, and as He had become ourselves, His faith brought to *us* the obedience of the Father. To every soul who places His trust in God's word, God will respond to that trust and dwell with Him just as He did with Christ.

EMMANUEL, GOD WITH US – NOT GOD WITH HIM

> Behold, a virgin shall be with child, and shall bring forth a son, and they shall call his name Emmanuel, which being interpreted is, God with us. Matthew 1:23

> God dwelt with Him and He was ourselves. Therefore His name is Emmanuel, God with us. Not God with Him. God was with Him before the world was; He could have remained there and not come here at all and still God could have remained with Him and His name could have been God with Him. He could have come into this world as He was in heaven and His name could still have been God with Him. But that never could have been God with us. But what we needed was God with us. God with Him does not help us, unless He is we. *Ibid.*

CHRIST'S VICTORY IS OUR VICTORY

> I will put my trust in him. Hebrews 2:13

> When He [Christ] stood where we are, He said, "I will put my trust in Him" [the Father] and that trust was never disappointed. In response to that trust the Father dwelt in Him and with Him and kept Him from sinning. Who was He? We. And thus the Lord Jesus has brought to every man in this world divine faith. That is the faith of the Lord Jesus. That is saving faith. *Ibid.*

When the Father dwelt in Christ and kept Him from sinning, He was keeping us from sinning because Christ was ourselves. What God worked in Him, He was working in us. Christ's faith laid hold of this reality. He knew that His victory was our victory. If we have the faith of Jesus, we will believe that when Christ overcame, we overcame in Him and that the victory is already ours.

> And Christ having taken our human nature in all things in the flesh and so having become ourselves, when we read of Him and the Father's dealings with Him, we are reading of ourselves and of the Father's dealings with us. What God did to Him was to us; what God did for Him was for us. *Ibid.* p.299

CHRIST CONQUERED BY THE WORD

> He answered and said, It is written, Man shall not live by bread alone, but by every word that proceedeth out of the mouth of God. Matthew 4:4

Christ overcame Satan in the wilderness of temptation by the power of the word. To every temptation, He replied with, "It is written." It was by the Word that the Father worked in Christ. The same word is our source of life.

THE WORD WORKS

> So shall my word be that goeth forth out of my mouth: it shall not return unto me void, but it shall accomplish that which I please, and it shall prosper in the thing whereto I sent it. Isaiah 55:11

God said, "Let there be light, and there was light"(Genesis 1:3). He "commanded" the light to shine out of the darkness (2 Corinthians 4:6). God's word produces the very thing itself. When He speaks, the very words themselves will have the effect He purposes. This is why, God cannot lie (Titus 1:2).

THE FATHER WORKED IN CHRIST THROUGH THE WORD

Search the scriptures; for in them ye think ye have eternal life: and they are they which testify of me. John 5:39

But that the world may know that I love the Father; and as the Father gave me commandment, even so I do. Arise, let us go hence. John 14:31

"Jesus Christ understood the power of the word. And He submitted Himself to its influence. In the Old Testament, the Father showed Him what He was doing. To the believers in the upper room after His resurrection, Christ "said unto them, These are the words which I spake unto you, while I was yet with you, that all things must be fulfilled, which were written in the law of Moses, and in the prophets, and in the psalms, concerning me" (Luke 24:44). In the law of Moses, in the Prophets, and in the Psalms, the Father had showed His Son what it was that He would work within Him and at what time. To the two heart-broken disciples on the road to Emmaus, "beginning at Moses and all the prophets, he expounded unto them in all the scriptures the things concerning himself." (Luke 24:27.) The entire Old Testament was the revelation of the life that the Father would live in His own Son when He sent Him here to this earth. And as Christ studied that word with a heart receptive to its influence, when the fullness of time was come, the Father wrought through His word...

"Christ received the word of God as speaking of Himself personally. And day by day, the Father unfolded to Him His will, like turning from page to page. From that which He realised at the first Passover in Jerusalem – that His life would be given for the sins of the world – through to riding on the colt at His triumphal entrance, and then Gethsemane and Calvary, each moment of His life was a submission to the wonderful working of the word of God as He took it and applied it to Himself personally."

A Life that Measures with the Life of God, pp.24, 28

THE PROMISES FULFILLED

The LORD is my shepherd; I shall not want. He maketh me to lie down in green pastures: he leadeth me beside the still waters. He restoreth my soul: he leadeth me in the paths of righteousness for his name's sake. Yea, though I walk through the valley of the shadow of death, I will fear no evil: for thou art with me; thy rod and thy staff they comfort me. Thou preparest a table before me in the presence of mine enemies: thou anointest my head with oil; my cup runneth over. Surely goodness and mercy shall follow me all the days of my life: and I will dwell in the house of the LORD for ever. Psalms 23

> Taking these words... as being themselves the salvation of God which comes to us, they themselves will work in us the salvation of God itself. That is where Christ got it. When He put Himself where we are, where did He get salvation? He did not save Himself. That was the taunt, "He saved others; Himself He cannot save... Let Him now come down from the cross and we will believe on Him." He could have done it. But if He had saved Himself, it would have ruined us. We would have been lost if He had saved Himself. O, but He saves us! Then what saved Him? This word of salvation saved Him when He was ourselves, and it saves us when we are in Him. He leads me in the paths of righteousness for His name's sake – me, me! And this in order that every one on the earth can say in him, "He leadeth me."
>
> "Yea, though I walk through the valley of the shadow of death." Where was He in the twenty-second Psalm? On the cross, facing death. The twenty-third Psalm comes right in there, in proper order, you see, as He steps into the dark valley. "Though I walk through the valley of the shadow of death, I will fear no evil: for thou art with me; thy rod and thy staff they comfort me." Who? Christ and in Him ourselves, and we know it because God did it once for us in Him. And in Him it is done still for us. *General Conference Bulletin*, 1895, p.301

HOW WE HAVE THE FAITH OF JESUS

In order for us to have the faith of Jesus, we need to have a faith that believes that Christ's faith brought to Him *as us* the power of God which worked in Him the victory.

The only way that we can ever have His faith is by believing that He became "me". His faith brought to Him as "me" the perfect obedience of the Father. We must believe that the power of God that was working in Him, was working also in "me". Therefore His victory was "my" victory in all the small and great trials of life

Christ was as a vessel and God filled the vessel with all of humanity and as He poured His blessing into that vessel, He was pouring it upon all humanity. What Christ received, I also received.

CHRIST IS OUR SUCCESS

> LORD, thou wilt ordain peace for us: for thou also hast wrought all our works in us. Isaiah 26:12

We must be constantly reaching out to Jesus with all our might – crying, "Jesus, I can't do it, please help me to get the victory." A cry like that He will never turn away from, but we must have a faith that will *let* Him work His own right-doing in us.

God is saddened when He sees us trying to keep the law in our own strength. He has made a wonderful provision at an infinite cost, and all that we need to do is to receive the Gift. He rejoices to see the righteousness of His own Son operating in the lives of those who profess to serve Him.

MAN'S ATONEMENT WITH GOD

In the process of God and man becoming one, man has a part to play. Although he possesses no righteousness of his own, it is his privilege to exercise his trust and total dependence upon the One who is able to save him. The parable of the woman with the issue of blood is a perfect example of a soul who exercises faith and trust in Christ as the only remedy.

THE PARABLE OF THE WOMAN WITH THE ISSUE OF BLOOD

> A certain woman, which had an issue of blood twelve years, And had suffered many things of many physicians, and had spent all that she had, and was nothing bettered, but rather grew worse, When she had heard of Jesus, came in the press behind, and touched his garment. For she said, If I may touch but his clothes, I shall be whole. And straightway the fountain of her blood was dried up; and she felt in her body that she was healed of that plague. Mark 5:25-29

This woman was set apart from the crowd and received the blessing of Jesus because she believed the prophecy:

> But unto you that fear my name shall the Sun of righteousness arise with healing in his wings. Malachi 4:2

The woman believed the Old Testament prophecy that there would be healing in the Messiah's wings. The Jewish word, here rendered as "wings", is *kanaph* which means: "the edge of a garment." The children of Israel were required to have a ribbon of blue around the borders of their garments that they may look upon it and remember all the commandments of the Lord (Numbers 15:38-40). Christ's garment had this ribbon. The blue ribbon on the border actually represented the law of liberty kept through the power of Christ. When the woman stretched out her hand she believed that if she could but touch the border of Christ's garment, she would be healed.

The action of faith

> In weakness and suffering she came to the seaside where He was teaching, and tried to press through the crowd, but in vain. Again she followed Him from the house of Levi-Matthew, but was still unable to reach Him. *The Desire of Ages*, p.343

This woman not only believed the promise, but acted on it according to her needs. She sought to reach Jesus, even though it meant diligent searching and then pressing with all her might through the throng. The woman did not feel the divine touch of Jesus immediately but persevered against the obstacles.

Here is a lesson for us. Jesus responds to those individuals who feel their utter need of Him and who strive and persevere to seek *Him* out. Often when we try to get close to Jesus there are obstacles in the way. For example, our employment may rob us of precious time to study God's word but sometimes sacrifices need to be made on our part so that we have the time and energy to seek out Christ. "Let us draw near" (Hebrews 10:22).

She did all that was in her power

> As He was passing, she reached forward, and succeeded in barely touching the border of His garment. But in that moment she knew that she was healed. In that one touch was concentrated the faith of her life, and instantly her pain and feebleness gave place to the vigor of perfect health. *Ibid.*

To barely touch the border of His garment with her finger she must have been fully outstretched on the ground, barely within reach. Faith is more than just believing in your mind – faith is taking action. This woman literally threw herself into the action of her faith. Both her faith and her body were fully outstretched. God will always respond to such faith – the faith of a soul that is fully outstretched and doing all that it can to claim His promise.

The woman had done all she could do to reach Jesus. If she had not put 100% effort into doing her part she would have come short of being healed.

Christ responded to her part

> She had begun to despair, when, in making His way through the multitude, He came near where she was. *Ibid.*

The woman did everything on her part but ultimately she was dependent on Jesus to come near to her; so Jesus came just close enough for her to barely touch the border of His garment.

That day, many people who thronged about Jesus would have been looking for a personal touch from Him. Jesus would have been surrounded by the Jews that went to synagogue each week (the church) – but because many of the Jews felt self-righteous and were striving to attain salvation through their own righteous works, He could not draw near to them and impart the blessing. The Jews had fallen into the deception of believing that corporate salvation would save them – the Old Covenant church system of works. This is why they did not truly seek after a personal relationship with Christ.

A partnership

Without human effort divine effort is in vain. A personal relationship with Christ is a two way thing – the co-operation of the human with the divine. In a marriage both parties are bound to one another by love and they reciprocate their love one to another out of a genuine heart response. It's not a struggle to reciprocate love when you really love someone, in fact, it comes naturally. When we really love God we will discern His great love for us and this will invoke a love response in us to give back to Him what He has given to us – His own life.

She was the only one who received the blessing

> And Jesus, immediately knowing in himself that virtue had gone out of him, turned him about in the press, and said, Who touched my clothes? And his disciples said unto him, Thou seest the multitude thronging thee, and sayest thou, Who touched me? Mark 5:30-31

The woman had been an outcast of society for twelve years because her issue of blood had condemned her as unclean. Christ was thronged by the members of the Jewish Church and yet none of them received the blessing – only the woman whom the church had declared to be unclean was healed because she possessed real faith. Her faith demonstrated that she was a true disciple of Christ. While the church establishment of the day sought the blessings and benefits of Christ, He drew near to an individual. This lesson conveys that church membership does not equal salvation.

WHAT HAPPENS IF WE EXPERIENCE TEMPORARY FAILURE?

> For a just man falleth seven times, and riseth up again: but the wicked shall fall into mischief. Proverbs 24:16

> The steps of a good man are ordered by the LORD: and he delighteth in his way. Though he fall, he shall not be utterly cast down: for the LORD upholdeth him with his hand. Psalms 37:23-24

> There are those who have known the pardoning love of Christ and who really desire to be children of God, yet they realise that their character is imperfect, their life faulty, and they are ready to doubt whether their hearts have been renewed by the Holy Spirit. To such I would say, Do not draw back in despair. We shall often have to bow down and weep at the feet of Jesus because of our shortcomings and mistakes, but we are not to be discouraged. Even if we are overcome by the enemy, we are not cast off, not forsaken and rejected of God. No; Christ is at the right hand of God, who also maketh intercession for us... He desires to restore you to Himself, to see His own purity and holiness reflected in you. And if you will but yield yourself to Him, He that hath begun a good work in you will carry it forward to the day of Jesus Christ. Pray more fervently; believe more fully. As we come to distrust our own power, let us trust the power of our Redeemer... *Steps to Christ*, p.64

FAITH HAS NOTHING TO DO WITH FEELINGS

> Don't look to feelings. Feelings are as variable as the wind. You know that is so. Never pay a particle of attention to them. It is none of your business how you feel. When God says so, it is so, whether I feel so or not.
>
> *General Conference Bulletin*, 1895, p.402

When Christ was upon the cross He bore the weight of all our sins as though He Himself had committed them – His heart was heavy with guilt and condemnation. Despite how He was feeling, Christ pressed through those feelings and believed that His Father had heard and answered His prayer. Whatever circumstance in life, it is your privilege to go boldly to the throne of grace and plead to the Father, "Please lift me back up with your hand," and then continue on in the faith of your new life believing you are forgiven.

GOD SEES THE END PRODUCT

> So shall my word be that goeth forth out of my mouth: it shall not return unto me void, but it shall accomplish that which I please, and it shall prosper in the thing whereto I sent it. Isaiah 55:11

> For I know the thoughts that I think toward you, saith the LORD, thoughts of peace, and not of evil, to give you an expected end. Jeremiah 29:11

> God counts the things that are not as though they were. He sees the end from the beginning, and beholds the result of His work as though it were now accomplished. The precious dead, from Adam down to the last saint who dies, will hear the voice of the Son of God, and will come forth from the grave to immortal life. God will be their God, and they shall be His people. There will be a close and tender relationship between God and the risen saints. This condition, which is anticipated in His purpose, He beholds as if it were already existing. *The Desire of Ages*, p.606

> No master workman looks at a piece of work he is doing, as it is half finished, and criticises that, and begins to find fault with that. There may be faults about it; but it is not finished yet. And while he works on it to take away all the faults, still he looks at it as it is in his finished purpose, in his own original plan, in his own mind.
>
> And if he looked at us as we look at ourselves, and if he were as poor a workman as we, that would be all there could be of it; we could never be of any worth. But he is not such a workman as we, and therefore he does not look at us as we see ourselves. No; he looks at us as we are in his finished purpose. Although we may appear all rough, marred, and scarred now, as we are here and in ourselves; he sees us as we are yonder in Christ... He is the Workman. And as we have confidence in him, we will let him carry on the work; and as he carries it on, we will look at it as He sees it. *General Conference Bulletin*, 1895, p.368

As Christians it is often very difficult to take God at His word and to believe His promise in Micah 7:19, that He will completely subdue (conquer) all our iniquities right here and now while we are living upon this earth. But this is what the word of God promises to do and His word does not return unto Him void but will prosper in the thing whereto He sends it (Isaiah 55:11). In the hearts of those who have received that word, it *will* produce results. And it is these results that God looks upon. He does not see us as we see ourselves – He sees us as finished already.

WHAT DOES IT MEAN TO BE "IN CHRIST"?

> There is therefore now no condemnation to them which are in Christ Jesus, who walk not after the flesh, but after the Spirit. Romans 8:1

To be "in Christ" is to believe that Jesus became you. It is to be conscious that Christ is one with us in all our life's experiences – He feels what we feel just as we feel because He is as ourself. Our life and His life are one. He takes upon Himself our wretched miserable life with all its mistakes and failures, bearing all its sin and guilt for us. In exchange He gives us the very practical life that He has lived – a life that God Himself lived as one with us. This is the life that God accounts to us because this is the life that we will now live. And then there is no condemnation to them that are in Christ Jesus because God cannot condemn His own life.

SAVED BY HIS LIFE

> Ye shall know the truth, and the truth shall make you free. John 8:3

> For if, when we were enemies, we were reconciled to God by the death of his Son, much more, being reconciled, we shall be saved by his life. Romans 5:10

As we lay hold of the simple truth that Christ has lived a perfect life for each and every one of us and that the battle against sin has already been fought and won on our behalf, this understanding will set us free from sin indeed. It is this understanding of the new life Christ offers us which ultimately will save us – not His death. While we are reconciled to God by Christ's death, we shall be saved by His life.

SALVATION IS A GIFT

> For by grace are ye saved through faith; and that not of yourselves: it is the gift of God: Not of works, lest any man should boast. For we are his workmanship, created in Christ Jesus unto good works, which God hath before ordained that we should walk in them. Ephesians 2:8-10

Salvation is a gift. There is nothing that we can do to earn it. All that we can do is believe and receive the gift. He has already created a new life for us in Christ, full of His own good works.

THE GIFT AVAILABLE TO ANY MAN

> Behold, I stand at the door, and knock: *if any man* hear my voice, and open the door, I will come in to him, and will sup with him, and he with me. Revelation 3:20

God is no respecter of persons (Acts 10:34). The free gift of His life is for any man who is willing to receive it. Christ will sit down to share life's experiences with any man that opens the door.

THE INFLUENCE OF A NEW LIFE

> For as ye have yielded your members servants to uncleanness and to iniquity unto iniquity; even so now yield your members servants to righteousness unto holiness. Romans 6:19

While the gift is available to any man, it will only be received by those who are willing to permit the new life in Christ to replace the old life of sin.

Sin is an influence, constantly seeking to sweep us along in its wicked ways. Before discovering our unity with Christ, we were helplessly swept along in its stream. But now we become conscious of the imparted life of Christ as an even more powerful influence in our lives. All that we need to do now is to choose to yield ourselves to its influence, just as we used to yield ourselves to the influence of sin, and that perfect life of Christ will become practically realised in our experience.

OUT WITH THE OLD AND IN WITH THE NEW

> Can the Ethiopian change his skin, or the leopard his spots? then may ye also do good, that are accustomed to do evil. Jeremiah 13:23

> That ye put off concerning the former conversation the old man, which is corrupt according to the deceitful lusts; And be renewed in the spirit of your mind; And that ye put on the new man, which after God is created in righteousness and true holiness. Ephesians 4:22-24

There is an old saying: "Don't try and teach an old dog new tricks." Metaphorically speaking – we need to kill the old dog and get a new one that already knows them. The same principle applies in respect to our old sinful life. Christ has already lived a perfect life for us. All we need to do is choose that life instead of trying to patch up the old one.

> The word of God does not take a man and find out how much of good there is in him, and how much bad there is in him, and then patch the good on in the place of the badness, and take him into heaven that way. You should not put a new patch on an old garment. Christ said so, and it is so. *Ibid.*, p.142

When Christ gives us the gift of His perfect life there are no patches of sin in it. The garment is whole and it is our new life to live.

LET GO AND LET GOD

> Let this mind be in you, which was also in Christ Jesus. Philippians 2:5

Christ has already lived a perfect life for each one of us. Why then should we continue trying to work out our own problems? Sin is our greatest problem. But Christ has already lived a life as ourselves and met each and every one of our trials and He had the victory each time. This life was *OUR* life. If we will let go of the old one and stop trying to work things out ourselves, the life of Christ will *BE* our real life. When we "let go and let God", we will live an entirely new life. It was God in Christ that dealt with all of the daily perplexities and it was God Himself that solved all the problems. When God Himself has lived our life for us, then do we have anything to worry about? The consequences are God's consequences to deal with because He did it, not us. All we need to do is to be honest with ourselves and with God. We must admit that we have tried to live our own lives and that we didn't do a very good job of it. We need to come before God with total sincerity and say, "God, I've tried to live my life. I can't do it right. You do it. I accept the life that you have already made for me in Christ."

OUR NEED IS OUR QUALIFICATION

> When Jesus heard it, he saith unto them, They that are whole have no need of the physician, but they that are sick: I came not to call the righteous, but sinners to repentance. Mark 2:17

The qualification for our salvation depends solely upon need. It has nothing to do with religion or church association. In the days of Christ's ministry, those who received His greatest blessings were those who were outcasts of the established religion or non-Jews.

The following are examples of this:

- The woman with the issue of blood who spent all her money on physicians and was an outcast of society for twelve years. Under Jewish law, any woman with regular menstruation was to separate herself from the congregation until she was pure from her issue. This woman's menstruation never ceased, and for twelve years she was unable to mingle with the people and was treated as an outcast. All her money had been wasted on physicians and in utter desperation she now sought out the true Physician to heal her. Despite many obstacles, the woman diligently sought out Jesus and pressed through the crowd. She believed that the moment she touched the border of His garment she would be healed. Christ sensed her touch of faith and virtue flowed out of Him. Even though He was pressed in on every side by the church, it was the outcast who received His blessing that day. (Matthew 9.)
- The leper of Galilee was the only one brave enough to leave the colony to seek out Jesus. He had heard of Jesus and His works, and faith sprang up in his heart. He convinced himself that he must traverse the mountains and valleys of Galilee until his path crossed the path of Jesus. Beside the Lake of Galilee he sees Jesus healing the sick in the crowd and he is filled with hope. Forgetting himself and fixing his eyes upon Jesus he presses through the crowd, not even registering

the cruel taunts and rough treatment hurled at him. He sees only Christ and casts himself at His feet with the cry, "Lord, if Thou wilt, Thou canst make me clean." Jesus replied, "I will; be thou made clean," and laid His hand upon him. The crowd thronging Jesus had not accepted the leper as part of their church – he was an outcast and they treated him as such. They believed his sin had brought upon him the wrath of God and that he deserved this terrible disease. But the work of Christ in cleansing the leper from leprosy was an illustration of His cleansing the soul from sin. Upon believing Christ's words that his sins had been cleansed and forgiven him, he was healed. The difference between the leper and the church thronging about Jesus was that the leper felt his need of the Great Physician. Such a soul Jesus will never turn away. (Matthew 8.)

- The woman of Samaria who had five husbands and the man she was with was not her husband, listened to Jesus at the well and became one of the greatest missionaries to Samaria. She heard words of life pour out from Christ's lips, "Whosoever drinketh of this water shall thirst again: but whosoever drinketh of the water that I shall give him shall never thirst; but the water that I shall give him shall be in him a well of water springing up into everlasting life." The woman had come for water, and she drank of the *water of life*. Jesus had awoken a sense of need within her for a better life. She had been convicted of sin, and believed on Jesus Christ. In her interest, she forgot her water pot and going back to the city she said to her countrymen, "Come, see a man, which told me all things that ever I did: is not this the Christ?" The Jews and Samaritans were bitter enemies, yet Christ longed to reach this people through one of their own kind. In this woman of questionable reputation, Christ perceived one who would bring the Gospel to her people. (John 4.)

CHRIST'S GREATEST BLESSINGS ARE BESTOWED UPON THE OUTCASTS

- The centurion of Capernaum believed upon Jesus to heal his sick servant and said, "Speak only the word." (Matthew 8.)
- The leper of Samaria was an outcast of society hated by the Jews and the only one of ten healed lepers to return and thank Jesus. (Luke 17.)
- The two demoniacs of Gergesa were tortured souls who ran to Jesus seeking to be released from their demonic captivity. (Mark 5.)
- The Canaanite woman of Tyre and Sidon believed upon Jesus to heal her demon possessed daughter even though Jesus tested her faith and called her a dog. (Matthew 15.)
- The deaf man of Decapolis believed upon Jesus to heal him and became one of Christ's greatest missionaries to his people. (Mark 7.)
- The blind man who washed in the pool of Siloam was healed by Jesus and then cast out of the Synagogue for testifying of his faith in Christ. (John 9.)
- The paralytic of Bethesda was the "worst case" because his disease was self-afflicted. (John 5.)

- Mary Magdalene the devil possessed harlot who was the first to preach a risen Saviour. (John 8.)

GOD'S TRUE CHURCH

> Again I say unto you, that if two of you shall agree on earth as touching anything that they shall ask, it shall be done for them of my Father which is in heaven. For where two or three are gathered together in my name, there am I in the midst of them. Matthew 18:19-20

Only those who feel their utter need of Christ will receive His divine life and make up the true church of God. That is the qualification for membership in His church. Not the great cathedral, not the synagogues, not the meeting places of the various denominations but where two or three are gathered in Christ's name, there is His dwelling place. Only the presence of Christ can constitute a true church.

THE PARABLE OF THE TEN VIRGINS

> Then shall the kingdom of heaven be likened unto ten virgins, which took their lamps, and went forth to meet the bridegroom. And five of them were wise, and five were foolish. They that were foolish took their lamps, and took no oil with them: But the wise took oil in their vessels with their lamps. While the bridegroom tarried, they all slumbered and slept. And at midnight there was a cry made, Behold, the bridegroom cometh; go ye out to meet him. Then all those virgins arose, and trimmed their lamps. And the foolish said unto the wise, Give us of your oil; for our lamps are gone out. But the wise answered, saying, Not so; lest there be not enough for us and you: but go ye rather to them that sell, and buy for yourselves. And while they went to buy, the bridegroom came; and they that were ready went in with him to the marriage: and the door was shut. Afterward came also the other virgins, saying, Lord, Lord, open to us. But he answered and said, Verily I say unto you, I know you not.
> Matthew 25:1-12

A relationship with Jesus Christ cannot be transferred to another person, nor can it be gained through church corporations or affiliation. The oil in the lamp is the life of Christ in the individual. Only those who know Jesus Christ by personal experience will enter in to the wedding feast.

THE INFUSION OF HIS LIFE IS THE WRITING OF THE LAW IN THE HEART

> After those days, saith the Lord, I will put my law in their inward parts, and write it in their hearts. . . . I will forgive their iniquity, and I will remember their sin no more. Jeremiah 31:33, 34

> Then said I, Lo, I come: in the volume of the book it is written of me, I delight

> to do thy will, O my God: yea, thy law is within my heart. Psalms 40:7-8

The law was written in Christ's own heart. His heart was ours. As we receive the infusion of His life through the Holy Spirit, we are receiving the law in our hearts.

CHRIST'S LIFE: A MIGHTY STREAM

> Let judgment run down as waters, and righteousness as a mighty stream.
> Amos 5:24

Our perfect life in Christ is rushing past like a mighty stream. It is our own true life. All we need to do is throw ourselves into it and be one with its current.

GOD'S PROMISE

> For he will finish the work, and cut it short in righteousness because a short work will the Lord make upon the earth. Romans 9:28

> I will hasten my word to perform it. Jeremiah 1:2

The Lord is saying, "I am going to finish the work, I am going to give you my life, I will make this a short work."

DAILY PRAYER

> Consider how I love thy precepts and, quicken me according to thy loving kindness. Psalms 119:159

"Dear Heavenly Father, even though I know I am but *a worm and no man*, I believe you are going to perform your promises in my life today. I open the windows of my soul heavenward so that Christ's life, full of your right-doing, may pour into my earthen vessel like a mighty stream. Whatever the trial or perplexity, I cast all my burdens and cares upon you because I know you have already worked out the perfect solution. You have already lived my life. And I gratefully accept that beautiful gift."

LIVE OUT THY LIFE WITHIN ME

by Frances R. Havergal

Live out Thy life within me, O Jesus, King of kings!
Be Thou Thyself the answer to all my questionings;
Live out Thy life within me, in all things have Thy way!
I, the transparent medium, Thy glory to display.

The temple has been yielded, and purified of sin,
Let Thy Shekinah glory now shine forth from with within,
And all the earth keep silence, the body henceforth be
Thy silent, gentle servant, moved only as by Thee.

Its members every moment held subject to Thy call,
Ready to have Thee use them, or not be used at all,
Held without restless longing, or strain, or stress, or fret,
Or chafings at Thy dealings, or thoughts of vain regret.

But restful, calm and pliant, from bend and bias free,
Awaiting Thy decision, when Thou hast need of me.
Live out Thy life within me, O Jesus, King of kings!
Be Thou the glorious answer to all my questionings.

Section 4

D

Sodom and Gomorrah

Sodom of the Vale, Fairest of Cities;
Her wickedness ascended unto heaven.
Idleness pride and fullness of bread;
She did not strengthen the poor and needy.
God in mercy bore long with Sodom;
Repent, she would not.
Judgment was visited.
Burned with brimstone,
Preserved by ashes,
She remains a witness to the ungodly.

PART 1 - SODOM AND GOMORRAH

Fairest among the cities of the Jordon Valley, Sodom was described as "the garden of the Lord" (Genesis 13:10). Meandering streams wove their way through the groves of the fertile valleys watering the exotic gardens. The well watered plains brought forth a bountiful supply of their produce with very little effort from man. With their wants well supplied and free from having to work the ground, the inhabitants became lazy and self-indulgent. The people worshipped false gods in large and extravagant temples which were elevated upon high platforms. Sphinxes, towers and pyramids were erected in prominent places of the city and surrounded by beautifully landscaped gardens. All were protected by fortified walls.

ABUNDANCE OF IDLENESS

> Behold, this was the iniquity of thy sister Sodom, pride, fullness of bread, and abundance of idleness was in her and in her daughters, neither did she strengthen the hand of the poor and needy. And they were haughty, and committed abomination before me: therefore I took them away as I saw good.
>
> Ezekiel 16:49-50

The inhabitants of the wicked cities were destroyed because they were not preoccupied with labour and had too much free time on their hands. Because of the fertility of the soil everything came too easy to them and people from faraway lands contributed to their existing wealth when they came to buy of their excess produce.

HOSPITALITY

There are a number of traditional Jewish records which testify to the cruelty and inhospitality to strangers by the inhabitants of Sodom. The wicked intention of the Sodomites towards the two angels that appeared to Lot in human form was often carried out (Genesis 19). Visiting merchants were robbed of their wares and strangers seeking shelter for the night were abused and murdered.

SEXUAL IMMORALITY

The custom of the Sodomite men was to visit the groves at regular times in the year and swap their wives and daughters with strangers. This resulted in the breakdown and decay of the family institution as the true identity of the father of the child could never be properly known.

WHY DID GOD DESTROY SODOM?

God has a limit of forbearance with wickedness. For the sake of a righteous few God will deal with the wickedness of the many. Where the continuation of the human race is threatened with extinction through wickedness, God must intervene.

If the wicked influence of Sodom and Gomorrah had not been restrained it would have corrupted all the nations of the earth and threatened the extinction of the human race within only a few generations. Although God bore long with Sodom and the wicked cities of the plain, the wickedness became so rife that He had no choice but to put a check on it for the sake of the rest of the world. The people had been given many opportunities to repent and they had not been left without faithful witnesses.

GOD GAVE TIME TO REPENT

For many years the inhabitants of Sodom and Gomorrah had witnessed the faithful example of Abraham, Lot and Melchizedech. On one occasion the five cities of the plain were attacked by Chedorlaomer the king of Elam and his allies. The kings of the plain were defeated in the battle and the people were carried off captive, including Abraham's nephew, Lot, and his family. Upon hearing word of his nephew's abduction, Abraham armed his servants and with the surrounding tribes pursued after them. Though greatly outnumbered, God fought with him and he was victorious, delivering all the captives. Upon their return, the king of Sodom sought to honour Abraham with the booty from the battle, but Abraham, not wanting to be accused of seeking his own glory, refused the gifts and attributed the victory to God.

> The man of faith pleaded for the inhabitants of Sodom. Once he had saved them by his sword, now he endeavored to save them by prayer.
>
> *Patriarchs and Prophets*, p.139

ABRAHAM INTERCEDES FOR THE CITIES OF THE PLAIN

> Abraham answered and said, Behold now, I have taken upon me to speak unto the Lord, which am but dust and ashes... That be far from Thee, to do after this manner, to slay the righteous with the wicked: . . . that be far from Thee: Shall not the Judge of all the earth do right? Genesis 18:25-27

Abraham delighted in helping strangers and one day while gazing through the door of his tent he noticed three strangers travelling by. Eager to meet their needs, Abraham ran from his tent and pleaded for the strangers to stop and refresh themselves. After a time, Abraham learned that one of the strangers was Christ who then took him into His secret counsel and revealed to him the punishment that was soon to be visited on Sodom and Gomorrah. Remembering Lot and his family who dwelt in Sodom, Abraham pleaded with Christ for the cities to be spared for the righteous that dwelt there. Thinking that there must be at least fifty righteous persons in Sodom he petitioned for the judgment to be waived could that many be found there. Christ agreed. Abraham began to question whether there may be that many and eventually reduced the number to ten. "And [Christ] said, I will not destroy it for ten's sake. And the LORD went his way" (Genesis 18:32-33).

THE PERSUASION OF INTERCESSORY PRAYER

Elijah on Mt Carmel

> And it came to pass at the seventh time, that he said, Behold, there ariseth a little cloud out of the sea, like a man's hand. And he said, Go up, say unto Ahab, Prepare thy chariot, and get thee down, that the rain stop thee not.
> 1 Kings 18:44

During Israel's apostasy in the time of king Ahab, a national judgment had been brought on the land and for three and a half years the clouds withheld their rain. In the contest on the highland of Mount Carmel the people, aroused to the enormity of their guilt, were brought to repentance and Elijah interceded before God on their behalf for the drought to end. Associating himself with the people, he prayed until he was nothing in his own sight. Six times he pressed on in prayer with no token of having been heard, yet he persevered, believing that God was listening to his supplications on behalf of Israel. The seventh time he prayed, a tiny cloud the size of a man's hand arose out of the sea and grew into a thick, black cloud which rolled out into the heavens and drenched the thirsty land with an abundance of rain. Had Elijah ceased his intercession for Israel at the sixth prayer the rain would never have come.

Moses on Mount Sinai

God had brought the Israelites to enter into covenant with him at Sinai. The people promised to worship Him only, but after forty days they fashioned a golden calf and sacrificed before it. Moses was with God in the mount who said to him, "Get thee down; for thy people... have corrupted themselves... I have seen this people, and, behold, it is a stiffnecked people: Now therefore let Me alone, that My wrath may wax hot against them, and that I may consume them: and I will make of thee a great nation" (Exodus 19:7, 9-10).

Instead of giving up, Moses interpreted God's threat as an invitation to intercede for the rebellious nation. In his anger God threatened to destroy them and had Moses not interceded for the people the nation would have been wiped out. Disowning them, God referred to the Israelites as Moses' own people that he had brought out from the bondage of Egypt. Moses, losing all sight of himself, pleaded, "Lord, they are Your people that You have brought out of Egypt and if You destroy them the heathen nations will accuse You of bringing them here to kill them." God was well-pleased with the unselfish prayer of Moses and granted his petition, but the chief instigators in the apostasy were slain. It was necessary for a check to be placed upon the wickedness otherwise the nation would be involved in irretrievable ruin. It was also necessary that this sin should be punished as a witness to the fact that God will not tolerate idolatry.

After the judgment had been executed, Moses again returned up the mount and persevered in prayer with God, pleading, "Oh, this people have sinned a great sin, and have made them gods of gold. Yet now, if thou wilt forgive their sin; and if not, blot me, I pray thee, out of thy book which thou hast written" (Exodus 32:31-32). He did not stop interceding until God gave the assurance that He would go with Israel and lead them into the Promised Land.

Summary

The character of God is such that when we utter selfless prayers for others without giving up, He will do the utmost to save them. On this principle, had Abraham persevered and supplicated a seventh time for Sodom to be spared for the sake of one righteous person, the cities on the plain would have been spared. God would have put a check on the sin in another way.

> The Lord delights in mercy; and for the sake of a few who really serve Him, He restrains calamities and prolongs the tranquillity of multitudes. Little do sin-

ners against God realise that they are indebted for their own lives to the faithful few whom they delight to ridicule and oppress. *The Great Controversy*, p.631

THE DESTRUCTION OF SODOM AND GOMORRAH

Then the LORD rained upon Sodom and upon Gomorrah brimstone and fire from the LORD out of heaven; And he overthrew those cities, and all the plain, and all the inhabitants of the cities, and that which grew upon the ground.

Genesis 19:24-25

While Abraham continued to converse with Christ, the two angels went on their way to Sodom. As evening approached, they reached the city and Lot, who was sitting at the gate, invited them to his home; but they replied, "Nay, but we will abide in the street all night." Lot pressed them greatly until they eventually agreed and went to his home. Shortly after, a large multitude of men from all quarters of the city began to gather outside, demanding that Lot send his visitors out so that they could rape and kill them. Lot went out to try to negotiate with them, but they became more determined. The two angels drew Lot back in and struck the crowd with double blindness so that they could not find the door and departed from the scene in confusion.

Lot was then told by the angels to get his family out of the city. In the early hours of the morning he went in search of his daughters and related to them all the angels had said. But they did not believe the warning and his son-in-laws mocked him. Distressed, Lot returned home without success and as the sun arose the angels hastened him away, saying, "Arise, take thy wife, and thy two daughters, which are here; lest thou be consumed in the iniquity of the city." And it came to pass that when they had brought them out of Sodom to where Christ waited, He commanded them, "Escape for thy life; look not behind thee, neither stay thou in all the plain; escape to the mountain, lest thou be consumed." Hoping to secure refuge in a little city nearby, he pleaded with Christ to spare Zoar. His request was granted and the fugitives fled toward it. Fearful for the fate of her daughters who remained in Sodom and pained at losing her beautiful home, Lot's wife Ada stole one last glance back in the direction of the doomed city and was instantly turned into a pillar of salt.

Later that morning, as soon as Lot had entered Zoar, God rained fire and brimstone from heaven upon the four cities of the plain. Fearing that Zoar may also be consumed, Lot fled to the mountains with his daughters. Here in a cave they found refuge from the apocalyptic inferno.

D4

NABATIYE
AL QUN
Har Meron
1208 m
Zefat
Haifa
HAZAFON
HEFA
Hadera
Nāblus
(Shechem)
TEL
AVIV
Tel Aviv-Yafo
WEST
BANK
HAMERKAZ
Tall 'Asur
1022 m
Ashdod
Jerusalem
YERUSHALAYIM
Ghazzah
aza City)
Al-Khalīl
(Hebron)
STRIP
Yunis
Dead
Sea
afah
Beersheba
ISRAEL
HADAROM
At Tafi
AT TAF

D7

PART 2 - ARCHAEOLOGICAL PROOF FOR SODOM AND GOMORRAH

> And turning the cities of Sodom and Gomorrah into ashes condemned them with an overthrow, making them an example unto those that after should live ungodly. 2 Peter 2:6

The Bible records that approximately 4,000 years ago, in the days of Abraham and Lot, five cities on the plain of the Dead Sea were destroyed by burning brimstone. In the following pages of this book historic texts and archaeological evidence prove the biblical account. These cities have been preserved as a witness to us today. They testify of that time when the world "shall burn as an oven; and all the proud, yea, and all that do wickedly, shall be stubble."

A BRIEF DESCRIPTION OF THE REGION

> The whole land thereof is brimstone, and salt, and burning, that it is not sown, nor beareth, nor any grass groweth therein, like the overthrow of Sodom, and Gomorrah, Admah, and Zeboim, which the LORD overthrew in his anger, and in his wrath. Deuteronomy 29:23

The western plain of the Dead Sea in Israel is home to a number of important historical sites including Qumran, Ein Gedi and Masada. It was in this barren wilderness that King David found a refuge at the small oasis of Ein Gedi in the Judean Desert (opposite page: top left). Today the region is still barren and nothing grows there naturally, but to utilise the land several large shade houses have been erected to create an artificial environment for growing food for sale in the busy markets of Jerusalem.

True to the description of Moses, the region of the Dead Sea is a desolate wasteland. The surface and shores of the Sea are 429 metres below sea level, making it the lowest land elevation on earth. The sea is a further 304 metres deeper and is known as the "Dead" Sea because of the scarcity of aquatic life – the sea is nearly 35% salt. (In contrast, the world's oceans are 3.5 percent on average.) The region's mean temperature ranges between 32 and 39 °C (90 and 102 °F) with average rainfall of 50mm per year. In June and July, temperatures soar up to 47 °C during the day and drop to just under 29 °C in the evening. Winters are also dry and hot with average temperatures around 21 °C during the day and 13 °C during the night.

The Jordon River runs from the Sea of Galilee in the north, down to the Dead Sea 105 kilometres further south. It was at the northern tip of the Dead Sea that the Israelites crossed over the Jordon River from Ammon and entered into the Promised Land. In recent decades the Dead Sea has receded at a record level of 1.5 metres per year. The salt and mud from the Sea is harvested and sold around the world as beauty and natural healing treatments.

EXTRA-BIBLICAL ACCOUNTS OF SODOM AND GOMORRAH

The cities of Sodom and Gomorrah are mentioned in antiquity by several historians. Strabo places the country of the Sodomites near Masada. While Tacitus describes a once fertile plain along the valley of Siddim upon which the five cities were situated. Flavius Josephus locates Zoar at the southern tip of the lake, in Arabia. The prophet Isaiah wrote that when the Media-Persian Empire would rise, the Moabites would flee to Zoar. This intimates that Zoar was a small city on the border of Arabia and Israel where the Moabites could find refuge at the extremes of their own country (Isaiah 15:5).

> It came to pass in the days of Amraphel king of Shinar, Arioch king of Ellasar, Chedorlaomer king of Elam, and Tidal king of nations; That these made war with Bera king of Sodom, and with Birsha king of Gomorrah, Shinab king of Admah, and Shemeber king of Zeboiim, and the king of Bela, which is Zoar. All these were joined together in the vale of Siddim, which is the salt sea.
>
> Genesis 14:1-3

> The country of Sodomites is fiery; for near Moasada (Masada) are to be seen rugged rocks that have been scorched, as also, in many places, fissures and ashy soil, and drops of pitch that emit foul odours to a great distance, and ruined settlements here and there; and therefore people believe the oft-repeated assertions of the local inhabitants, that there were once thirteen inhabited cities in that region of which Sodom was the metropolis, but that a circuit of about sixty stadia of that city escaped unharmed; and that by reason of earthquakes and of eruptions of fire and of hot waters containing asphalt and sulphur, the lake burst its bounds, and rocks were enveloped with fire; and, as for the cities, some were swallowed up and others were abandoned by such as were able to escape. Strabo (XVI 42-44)

> Not far from the lake (Dead Sea) is a plain which according to report was once fertile and the site of the cities, but which was later devastated by lightening and it is said that the traces of their disaster still exist there and that the very ground looks burnt and has lost its fertility. Tacitus, *Histories* V, Ch. 7

> The length of this lake is five hundred and eighty furlongs, where it is extended as far as Zoar in Arabia; and its breadth is a hundred and fifty. The country of Sodom borders upon it. It was of old a most happy land, both for the fruits it bore and the riches of its cities, although it be now all burnt up. It is related how, for the impiety of its inhabitants, it was burnt by lightning; in consequence of which there are still the remainders of that Divine fire, and the traces [or shadows] of the five cities are still to be seen, as well as the ashes growing in their fruits; which fruits have a color as if they were fit to be eaten, but if you pluck them with your hands, they dissolve into smoke and ashes. And thus what is related of this land of Sodom hath these marks of credibility which our very sight affords us. Flavius Josephus, *Wars of the Jews*, Book 3, Chapter 8, Paragraph 4

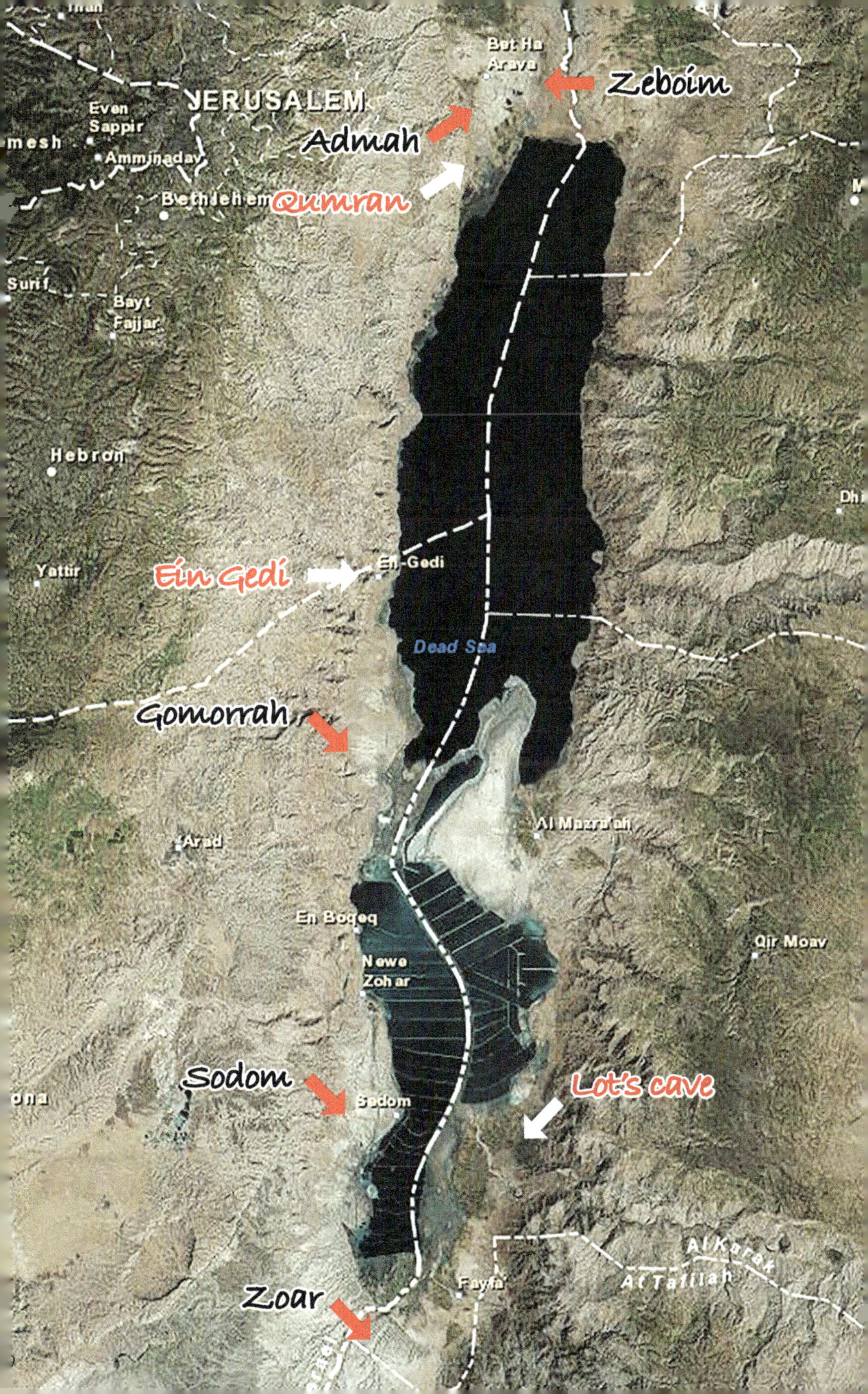

Bet Ha Arava
Zeboim
JERUSALEM
Even Sappir
Admah
Amminaday
Bethlehem
Qumran
Surif
Bayt Fajjar
Hebron
Yattir
Ein Gedi
En-Gedi
Dead Sea
Gomorrah
Arad
Al Mazra'ah
En Boqeq
Qir Moav
Newe Zohar
Sodom
Sodom
Lot's cave
Zoar
Fayfa
Al Karak
At Tafilah

HISTORICAL EVIDENCE FOR SODOM AND GOMORRAH

The cities of Sodom and Gomorrah are mentioned extensively in both the Old and New Testaments. Being the Word of God, we know the Biblical account is historically correct; therefore we are not surprised to find the names of the cities mentioned in other ancient sources, dating to that same time.

THE EBLA TABLETS

In the remains of an ancient royal palace called Tell Mardikh (Ebla) in North-western Syria, such a source has been found.

During the excavations of the palace at Ebla in 1975, the excavators found a large library (royal archive room) filled with tablets dating to 2400-2300 B.C. Nearly 15,000 tablets and fragments were found, but when joined together they constituted 2,500 tablets detailing life in the 300,000 person city of Ebla. They are written in Cuneiform, a language that originated in Sumer, Mesopotamia, and adapted to the language of Ebla's Semitic inhabitants. The Ebla tables are especially important because they include the names of cities and people that appear in the Old Testament, and therefore provide evidence for the historical accuracy of the Bible. The descriptions found in the Ebla tablets match the descriptions of daily life in the time of Abraham.

The Ebla tablets refer to a creation story and a flood story. Also mentioned are names and places which coincided with biblical ones: Esau (Genesis 4), Amorite (Genesis 10), Abraham (Genesis 12), Israel (Genesis 32), Sinai, Jerusalem and Canaan. But perhaps one of the most convincing testaments to the Bible's historical accuracy is the mention of the two "sin cities" – Sodom and Gomorrah (Genesis 10). This is the oldest known text which mentions the names of the five cities.

EVIDENCE OF ZOAR'S EXISTENCE ON THE MADABA MAP

> My heart shall cry out for Moab; his fugitives shall flee unto Zoar, an heifer of three years old: for by the mounting up of Luhith with weeping shall they go it up; for in the way of Horonaim they shall raise up a cry of destruction. Isaiah 15:5

The Madaba Map is part of a floor mosaic in the early Byzantine church of Saint George at Madaba, Jordan. Dated to the 6th Century A.D. the Madaba Map is a map of the Middle East and depicts an area from Lebanon in the north to the Nile Delta in the south, and from the Mediterranean Sea in the west to the Eastern Desert. Among other features, it depicts the Dead Sea with two fishing boats, a variety of bridges linking the banks of the Jordan, fish swimming in the river and receding from the Dead Sea; a lion hunting a gazelle in the Moab desert, palm-ringed Jericho, Bethlehem and other biblical Christian sites. Part of the map contains the oldest surviving original cartographic depiction of the Holy Land and especially Jerusalem. The Madaba Map gives the location of 150 towns, including Zoar at the southern tip of the Dead Sea. Archaeologists have found the map to be a reliable compass of Israel and in recent excavations it has assisted them in confirming the location of lost towns and unearthing the remains of several Byzantine churches.

In ancient times when a city was destroyed a new city was often rebuilt upon its foundations and given the same name. Jerusalem, Jericho and the city of Troy are classic examples of this. According to Isaiah the city of Zoar was a newly built city (only three years old) when he prophesied of Moab's fugitives fleeing there. We can therefore conclude that the Zoar of the Madaba Map was not the original city but a newly rebuilt one at the same location.

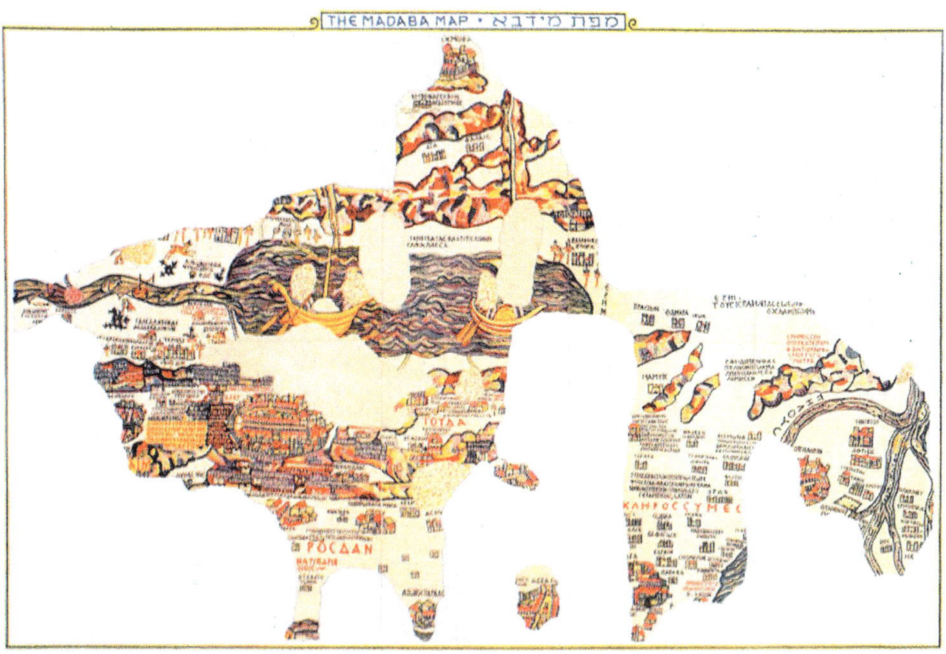

Fig. D12 – Madaba Map.

MASADA

The ancient Roman fortress Masada is situated on top of an isolated rock plateau on the western side of the Dead Sea. Herod the Great built palaces for himself on the mountain and fortified Masada between 37 and 31 B.C. According to Flavius Josephus, the Jewish historian, the Siege of Masada by troops of the Roman Empire towards the end of the First Jewish-Roman War ended in the mass suicide of the 960 Sicarii rebels and their families hiding there. A curse had been pronounced upon Jerusalem in 31 A.D. when the Jews rejected Christ as their Messiah. In 70 A.D. the prophecy of destruction was fulfilled when the city was besieged by the Romans and burnt to the ground. In 73 A.D. the last outpost of the Jewish rebels at Masada was conquered by the Romans. A double curse rests upon Masada as at the foot of the ancient fortress the ashen remains of Gomorrah can still be seen.

14

15

D16

D17

D18

EVIDENCE OF SULPHUR BALLS AT GOMORRAH

> The LORD rained upon Sodom and upon Gomorrah brimstone and fire from the LORD out of heaven. And he overthrew those cities, and all the plain, and all the inhabitants of the cities, and that which grew upon the ground.
>
> Genesis 19:24-25

In the immediate area of the five ashen cities of the plain along the Dead Sea, thousands of golf-ball sized sulphur balls have been discovered. Many of the sulphur balls have burn rings around them which is evidence that they were once on fire. Over the last twenty years many specimens have been collected and taken to laboratories all around the world for analysis.

One sample analysed at Spectrachem Analytical, in Gracefield, New Zealand, revealed a sulphur content of 98.4 percent. Sulphur concentrations this pure exist nowhere else in the world except for the five cities of the plain. The Gillespie Museum of Minerals in Florida contains 20,000 mineral specimens. In their entire collection they have never seen sulphur in such a pure concentration.

The Bible states that *the Lord rained down fire and brimstone from heaven*. Indeed it would appear that these sulphur balls – which exist no where else on the earth except for the remains of the five ashen cities of the plain – are not from this earth. They are a foreign substance that did not originate from earth but *were rained down from heaven.*

SPECTRACHEM ANALYTICAL
SRS 303-AS
*** Semi Quantitative Analysis of undiluted materials ***
Sample: $smq

H-Be	B	C	N	O	F	Na	Mg	Al
%	%	%	%	%	%	%	%	%
0.0	0.0	0.0	0.0	0.0	0.0	0.150	0.220	0.032
Si	**P**	**S**	**Cl**	**K**	**Ca**	**Sc**	**Ti**	**V**
%	%	%	%	%	%	%	%	%
0.127	0.00	98.400	0.311	0.025	0.626	0.000	0.000	0.000
Cr	**Mn**	**Fe**	**Co**	**Ni**	**Cu**	**Zn**	**Ga**	**Ge**
%	%	%	%	%	%	%	%	%
0.000	0.000	0.021	0.000	0.003	0.000	0.000	0.000	0.000
As	**Se**	**Br**	**Rb**	**Sr**	**Y**	**Zr**	**Nb**	**Mo**
%	%	%	%	%	%	%	%	%
0.000	0.000	0.000	0.000	0.015	0.000	0.002	0.000	0.000
Rh	**Ag**	**Cd**	**In**	**Sn**	**Sb**	**Te**	**I**	**Cs**
%	%	%	%	%	%	%	%	%
0.000	0.000	0.000	0.000	0.000	0.000	0.000	0.000	0.000

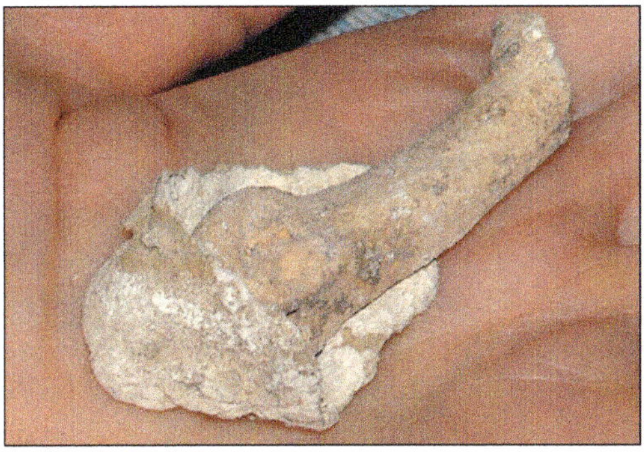

This page:

Fig. D21 – Top left: bone found in sulphur ball.

Fig. D22 – Top right: sulphur ball and next to it is a sulphur ball still in its burned and hardened shell.

Fig. D23 – Right: sulphur ball embedded in a limestone wall that has been burnt to ash.

Fig. D24 – Lower right: sulphur ball with burn ring.

Fig. D25 – Bottom right: sulphur balls in rock.

Fig. D26 – Bottom left: Gillespie Museum houses 20,000 mineral samples. They have never seen sulphur as pure as the sulphur balls collected from the five cities of the Dead Sea plain.

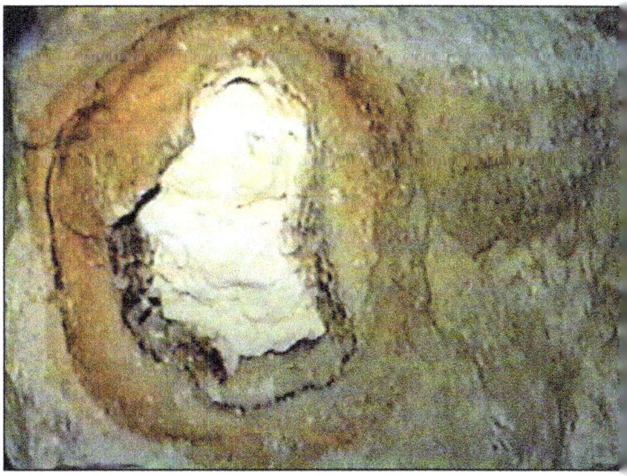

Opposite page:

Fig. D19 – Gomorrah sulphur specimen is compared with natural sulphur.

Fig. D20 – Spectrachem Analytical analysed the sulphur ball specimen from Gomorrah and the test gave the result that the specimen was 98.4 percent pure sulphur.

THERMAL IONISATION

The Bible says that brimstone (sulphur) rained down from heaven upon the five cities of the plain. As the burning sulphur balls were thrust upon the limestone buildings, the extremely high temperatures caused the electrons within the limestone to repel and attract one another. This is called *thermal ionisation* which created a multi-shaded layering of ash and a swirling effect in the buildings (figure D33-D35).

Fig. D28 – Specimen shows signs of having been melted, with the upper portion bubbling and the lower section pooled into a solid.

Fig. D29 – Resembles a bone with marrow in it.

Fig. D30 – Sulphur crystals are a remnant of the consumed brimstone. Very large slabs of sulphur crystals have been found in the area of Gomorrah.

Fig. D31 – A burnt limestone slab which fell away from a burning building was preserved.

Fig. D32 – Sulphur ball burning in a spoon.

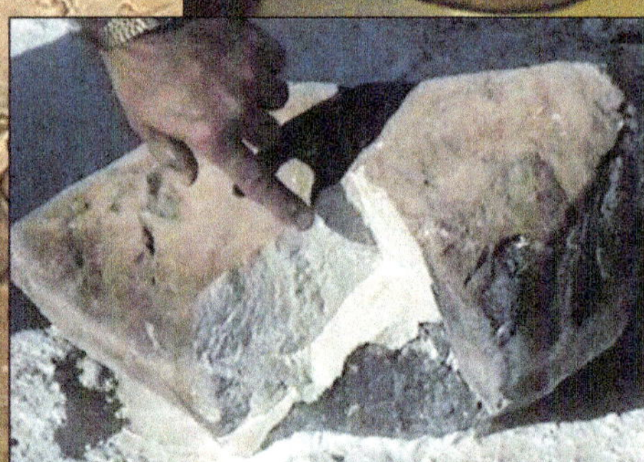

34

35

D.

D.

MAN-MADE SHAPES AT GOMORRAH

Amidst the ashen remains of Gomorrah the appearance of strange man-made shapes can be seen. In the picture top left (figure D36) there is a cylindrical shape on a platform and directly across from it, on a separate platform at the same elevation, the foundation of an identical cylindrical shape can be seen. The two features at one time mirrored one another from across the expanse. Perfect symmetry of this kind does not occur in nature.

Another structure of interest is an enormous platform (see figure D37) built at an elevation for everyone to see. Due to its vast size it may have formed the base of a temple or place of worship. The platform is in an "E" shape and has three legs which extend out from the main elongated body at sharp 90° angles. The three legs of the platform appear to be identical in height, evenly spaced apart and perfectly flat on the surface. Structures which jut out at sharp 90° angles in perfect symmetry, adjacent to one another, do not occur in nature.

The geometric angles, symmetry and regularity of the shapes and structures at Gomorrah are an evidence that this city was designed and built by humans. While the remains have been turned to ash, the structures are sturdy to walk upon. However when a piece of a structure is broken off and crushed in the palm of a person's hand it crumbles into ashes.

D38

D39

SPHINXES

Sphinxes are generally associated with architectural structures such as royal tombs or religious temples. They typically have the body of a lion, sometimes with the wings of a great bird and the face of a human. In ancient Egypt, sphinxes and pyramids were common place and they were also common in Gomorrah. The remains of many sphinxes in various shapes and sizes have been documented at Gomorrah but the most impressive sphinx at the site is photographed in figure D47.

The ashen remains of Gomorrah are laden with sphinx type monuments. The object in figure D47 is similar in size and shape to the famous sphinx at the Giza Pyramids in Egypt (figure D46). It appears to have a human face and the body of a lion with two arms stretched out in front. At the lower left corner of figure D47, a sphinx is positioned on a raised square platform. Figure D40 is of the same object.

D40

D41

D42

D43

D44

D45

46

47

FORTRESS WALLS AND CITY STREETS

Ancient cities were protected by fortress walls. Figure D49 is a photograph of an old fortress wall in Egypt reinforced with buttresses. Figure D48 is a photograph of the ashen remains of what appears to be a fortress wall with buttresses at Gomorrah.

D48

D49

In Canaan double walls were often built for extra fortification of the cities. Some of the city inhabitants would make their home within the walls. Figure D50 (left) is a photograph of the ashen remains of double walls at Gomorrah with slits that look like windows. Figure D51 (right) is an artist's rendition of what the walls would have looked like in the time of Abraham.

D50

D51

Figure D53 (right) is a photograph of an old fortress wall in Israel. Figure D52 (left) is a photograph of what resembles a double wall near Mt Sodom.

D52

D53

54

55

56

D5

D5

TEMPLE AT GOMORRAH

Temple remains at Gomorrah still retain much of their original shape and features (see figure D61 and D63). The artist's reconstruction in figure D62 and figure D64 is Babylonian in style. The Mayans built similar temples and tombs at Chichen Itza in Yucatan (figure D59) and Palenque in Chiapas (figure D60), Mexico.

D59

D60

D61

D62

D63

D64

BUILDINGS AT GOMORRAH

> And Lot lifted up his eyes, and beheld all the plain of Jordan, that it was well watered every where, before the LORD destroyed Sodom and Gomorrah, even as the garden of the LORD, like the land of Egypt, as thou comest unto Zoar.
>
> Genesis 13:10

Square and rectangular buildings with walls built at sharp 90° angles with roof tops are also located at Gomorrah. Figure D57 (opposite page) is a building situated in the middle of a deep trench. The Bible mentions that Sodom and Gomorrah were well watered – the cities may have had many canals running through them like Venice.

PYRAMIDS AT GOMORRAH

Highway 90 runs parallel to the Dead Sea on the west side. Exiting highway 90 and entering into the road that leads to Masada, two pyramids are clearly seen on either side of the road. The pyramid in figure D65 is positioned on a platform on the right side of the road and figure D66 is on the left side. Both pyramids are at strategically visible locations.

D65

D66

PART 3 - THE LAST DAYS

AS IT WAS IN THE DAYS OF LOT

> As it was in the days of Noe, so shall it be also in the days of the Son of man. They did eat, they drank, they married wives, they were given in marriage, until the day that Noe entered into the ark, and the flood came, and destroyed them all. Likewise also as it was in the days of Lot; they did eat, they drank, they bought, they sold, they planted, they builded; But the same day that Lot went out of Sodom it rained fire and brimstone from heaven, and destroyed them all. Even thus shall it be in the day when the Son of man is revealed. Luke 17:26-30

Christ likened the condition of the world before His second coming to the condition of the world before the flood. He also compared it with Sodom and Gomorrah in the days of Lot. The Apostle Paul describes professed Christianity at the end of the world in the same manner. These people had a form of godliness but it only covered a heart as black as coal. A half-hearted Christian is worse than an infidel.

> This know also, that in the last days perilous times shall come. For men shall be lovers of their own selves, covetous, boasters, proud, blasphemers, disobedient to parents, unthankful, unholy, Without natural affection, trucebreakers, false accusers, incontinent, fierce, despisers of those that are good, Traitors, heady, highminded, lovers of pleasures more than lovers of God; Having a form of godliness, but denying the power thereof: from such turn away. 2 Timothy 3:1-5

THE ABRAHAM HOSPITALITY TEST

> Abraham planted a large grove in Beersheba, and he made to it four gates facing the four sides of the earth, and he planted a vineyard in it, so that if a traveller came to Abraham he entered any gate which was in his road, and remained there and ate and drank and satisfied himself and then departed. For the house of Abraham was always open to the sons of men that passed and repassed, who came daily to eat and drink in the house of Abraham. And any man who had hunger and came to Abraham's house, Abraham would give him bread that he might eat and drink and be satisfied, and any one that came naked to his house he would clothe with garments as he might choose, and give him silver and gold and make known to him the Lord who had created him in the earth; this did Abraham all his life. *Book of Jasher,* p.116

LOT BECAME TAINTED BY HIS SURROUNDINGS

Lot had grown up under the godly influence of Abraham and had entered Sodom with the intention to remain true to his faith. Living in the city for many years, his senses became blunted to the unholy influences around him. Through the marriage alliances of his children with the Sodomites, and the wealth secured by commerce, Lot's interests were bound up in Sodom. Had Abraham not interceded for Lot he would have been destroyed with the rest of the inhabitants.

THE EVIL INFLUENCE OF CITY LIFE

> Woe unto them that join house to house, that lay field to field, till there be no place, that they may be placed alone in the midst of the earth! Isaiah 5:8

Lot had chosen all of the plain for his flocks and herds but he pitched his tent towards Sodom and it was not long before he relocated to the city itself. Had he remained in his country retreat he would not have been involved in the ruin of Sodom. The faith that he had received from Abraham would have been nurtured and preserved by a simple lifestyle as a herdsman in the country.

> When every other voice is hushed, when every earthly interest is turned aside, the silence of the soul makes more distinct the voice of God. Here rest is found in Him. The peace, the joy, the life of the soul, is God. *Signs of the Times*

UNEQUAL UNION

> Be ye not unequally yoked together with unbelievers: for what fellowship hath righteousness with unrighteousness? and what communion hath light with darkness? 2 Corinthians 6:14

> Can two walk together, except they be agreed? Amos 3:3

> The wife of Lot was a selfish, irreligious woman, and her influence was exerted to separate her husband from Abraham. But for her, Lot would not have remained in Sodom, deprived of the counsel of the wise, God-fearing patriarch. The influence of his wife and the associations of that wicked city would have led him to apostatise from God had it not been for the faithful instruction he had early received from Abraham. The marriage of Lot and his choice of Sodom for a home were the first links in a chain of events fraught with evil to the world for many generations. *Patriarchs and Prophets*, p.174

LOT'S LINGERING SPIRIT

> But his wife looked back from behind him, and she became a pillar of salt. Genesis 19:26

Lot's wife is often considered foolish because she did not obey God's voice and looked back at the wicked city. But many do not stop to consider that the example of her husband was the cause of her downfall. Had Lot immediately left the city and not lingered (Genesis 19:16-26), his wife would have realised the urgency of the situation and not questioned the commandment, "Look not behind thee."

GOD HEARD THE CRY OF LOT'S HEART

> And while he lingered, the men laid hold upon his hand, and upon the hand of his wife, and upon the hand of his two daughters; the LORD being merciful unto him: and they brought him forth, and set him without the city.
>
> Genesis 19:16

Even though Lot's heart strings were deeply attached to Sodom, God heard his heart's cry for deliverance and fearfully removed Him. Although Lot lingered, not wanting to leave his home and children behind, the two angels laid hold upon him and removed him from the city. He will do the same for us today. But we should first do everything in our power to live in harmony with God's will.

> And turning the cities of Sodom and Gomorrah into ashes condemned them with an overthrow, making them an example unto those that after should live ungodly; And delivered just Lot, vexed with the filthy conversation of the wicked: (For that righteous man dwelling among them, in seeing and hearing, vexed his righteous soul from day to day with their unlawful deeds;) The Lord knoweth how to deliver the godly out of temptations. 2 Peter 2:6-9

SODOM WAS BURNED WITH ETERNAL FIRE

> Even as Sodom and Gomorrah, and the cities about them in like manner, giving themselves over to fornication, and going after strange flesh, are set forth for an example, suffering the vengeance of eternal fire. Jude 1:7

In the Bible, "suffering the vengeance of eternal fire" does not mean that the fire will burn forever. It burns until there is nothing more to consume leaving only ashes – the destruction is permanent and eternal. The lake of fire upon the cities of the plain is a type of the lake of fire in the final judgment of the wicked. Once the fire has consumed the wicked, "they shall be ashes under the soles of your feet in the day that I shall do this, saith the LORD of hosts" (Malachi 4:3). Anyone who is not found written in the book of life will be cast into the lake of fire (Revelation 20:15).

> Turning the cities of Sodom and Gomorrah into ashes condemned them with an overthrow, making them an ensample unto those that after should live ungodly. 2 Peter 2:6

SINNERS CANNOT LIVE FOREVER

Only Christ "has immortality", "but the soul that sinneth, it shall die" (1 Timothy 6:16, Ezekiel 18:4). We can only have eternal life by accepting Christ as our personal Saviour. The existence of those who reject Christ will come to an end.

WHAT HAPPENS WHEN WE DIE?

For the living know that they shall die: but the dead know not any thing, neither have they any more a reward; for the memory of them is forgotten. Also their love, and their hatred, and their envy, is now perished; neither have they any more a portion for ever in any thing that is done under the sun. Whatsoever thy hand findeth to do, do it with thy might; for there is no work, nor device, nor knowledge, nor wisdom, in the grave, whither thou goest. Ecclesiastes 9:5-6, 10

THE DEAD DO NOT REMEMBER

For in death there is no remembrance of thee: in the grave who shall give thee thanks? Psalm 6:5

THE DEAD HAVE NO THOUGHTS

His breath goeth forth, he returneth to his earth; in that very day his thoughts perish. Psalm 146:4

THE DEAD ARE SILENT

The dead praise not the LORD, neither any that go down into silence. Psalm 115:17

There is no consciousness of anything when we die. There are no thoughts and no memories. The dead remain in this state until the resurrection of the good or the resurrection of the wicked.

DEATH IS LIKE SLEEPING

When he was come in, he saith unto them, Why make ye this ado, and weep? the damsel is not dead, but sleepeth. Mark 5:39

Our friend Lazarus sleepeth; but I go, that I may awake him out of sleep. Then said his disciples, Lord, if he sleep, he shall do well. Howbeit Jesus spake of his death: but they thought that he had spoken of taking of rest in sleep. Then said Jesus unto them plainly, Lazarus is dead. John 11:11-14

THOSE IN CHRIST SLEEP UNTIL HE COMES AGAIN

If I go and prepare a place for you, I will come again, and receive you unto myself; that where I am, there ye may be also. John 14:3

Christ was not lying to the disciples when He gave them the promise that He would come again to receive them unto himself. He did not say that they would come to Him in the form of a departed spirit, but they would sleep until His second coming.

> Martha saith unto him, I know that he shall rise again in the resurrection at the last day. John 11:24

Martha's hope for sleeping Lazarus was that he would rise again in the resurrection.

> This is the Father's will which hath sent me, that of all which he hath given me I should lose nothing, but should raise it up again at the last day. John 6:39

THE RESURRECTION OF THE RIGHTEOUS WILL HAPPEN AT THE LAST DAY

> But I would not have you to be ignorant, brethren, concerning them which are asleep, that ye sorrow not, even as others which have no hope. For if we believe that Jesus died and rose again, even so them also which sleep in Jesus will God bring with him. For the Lord himself shall descend from heaven with a shout, with the voice of the archangel, and with the trump of God: and the dead in Christ shall rise first: Then we which are alive and remain shall be caught up together with them in the clouds, to meet the Lord in the air: and so shall we ever be with the Lord. 1 Thessalonians 4:13-18

Paul tells the Thessalonians not to sorrow for the dead because those who sleep in Christ will be raised at the resurrection.

> Henceforth there is laid up for me a crown of righteousness, which the Lord, the righteous judge, shall give me at that day: and not to me only, but unto all them also that love his appearing. 2 Timothy 4:8

> And when the chief Shepherd shall appear, ye shall receive a crown of glory that fadeth not away. 1 Peter 5:4

Christ says that the faithful will receive a crown of glory at His second appearing – not beforehand.

SPIRITUALISM

> When they shall say unto you, Seek unto them that have familiar spirits, and unto wizards that peep and that mutter: should not a people seek unto their God? for the living to the dead? To the law and to the testimony: if they speak not according to this word, it is because there is no light in them. Isaiah 8:19-20

> Satan leads men to consult those that have familiar spirits; and by revealing hidden things of the past, he inspires confidence in his power to foretell things to come. By experience gained through the long ages he can reason from cause to effect and often forecast, with a degree of accuracy, some of the future events of man's life. Thus he is enabled to deceive poor, misguided souls and bring them under his power and lead them captive at his will.
>
> *Patriarchs and Prophets*, p.687

For six thousand years Satan has been studying the lives of every individual and can fairly accurately predict an individual's future by reasoning from cause to effect. Through clairvoyants and tarot cards many are bewitched, not realising they are consulting with evil spirits. When the event predicted happens, their belief in spiritualism is reinforced.

Satan and his angels also use this knowledge to impersonate the dead. When a person is vulnerable through the grief and loss of a loved one, demons take on the form of the deceased and appear to them with perfect representation in voice and mannerism. The bereaved may find comfort in thinking that they are communicating with their lost love one but in reality they are communing with evil spirits. All who do this are severing their connection with God.

ANTI-CHRIST

> Little children, it is the last time: and as ye have heard that antichrist shall come, even now are there many antichrists; whereby we know that it is the last time. 1 John 2:18

> For false Christs and false prophets shall rise, and shall show signs and wonders, to seduce, if it were possible, even the elect. Mark 13:22

> And no marvel; for Satan himself is transformed into an angel of light.
> 2 Corinthians 11:14

Just prior to the close of probation Satan will impersonate Christ as an enlightened being. Satan comes in a manner which will bring all of the different religions of the world together and he will introduce a counterfeit teaching of salvation which all religions will agree with. As anti-Christ, he will teach that through prayer and meditation humanity will reach a higher state of conscientiousness. The human species will evolve to its divine destiny. He says, "You shall be as gods," (Genesis 3:5).

This teaching is the opposite to Christ becoming one with us through the impartation of His life. Rather, it teaches that you are Christ and your own works will save you.

ANTI-CHRIST WILL DECEIVE MANY

> Then if any man shall say unto you, Lo, here is Christ, or there; believe it not. For there shall arise false Christs, and false prophets, and shall show great signs and wonders; insomuch that, if it were possible, they shall deceive the very elect. Behold, I have told you before. Wherefore if they shall say unto you, Behold, he is in the desert; go not forth: behold, [he is] in the secret chambers; believe it not. For as the lightning cometh out of the east, and shineth even unto the west; so shall also the coming of the Son of man be. Matthew 24:23-27

ALL WILL MAKE THE CHOICE

> This gospel of the kingdom shall be preached in all the world for a witness unto all nations; and then shall the end come. Matthew 24:14

The Gospel of Jesus Christ will be proclaimed to the entire world. When everyone has had the opportunity to make an intelligent and informed decision, to accept or reject it, probation will close.

THE CLOSE OF PROBATION

> He that is unjust, let him be unjust still: and he which is filthy, let him be filthy still: and he that is righteous, let him be righteous still: and he that is holy, let him be holy still. And, behold, I come quickly; and my reward is with me, to give every man according as his work shall be. Revelation 22:11-12

When everyone has made their decision their characters will be set in concrete for better or for worse. Their destiny will be fixed. Christ will cease His ministration in the heavenly sanctuary and He will then pronounce the words of Revelation 22.

JUDGED BY HIS WORDS

> If any man hear my words, and believe not, I judge him not: for I came not to judge the world, but to save the world. He that rejecteth me, and receiveth not my words, hath one that judgeth him: the word that I have spoken, the same shall judge him in the last day. John 12:47-48

To those who receive Christ and His word, He will be both their intercessor and their judge. But He will not judge those that reject Him. They will be judged by the word of God. In the final judgment, the very word that the sinner willfully rejected will declare his guilt and condemnation.

CHRIST IS THE ONE WHO JUDGES US

> For the Father judgeth no man, but hath committed all judgment unto the Son: And hath given him authority to execute judgment also, because he is the Son of man. John 5:22, 27

> And He who has given the light, He who has followed the soul with tenderest entreaty, seeking to win it from sin to holiness, is in one its advocate and judge. From the opening of the great controversy in heaven, Satan has maintained his cause through deception; and Christ has been working to unveil his schemes and to break his power. It is He who has encountered the deceiver, and who through all the ages has been seeking to wrest the captives from his grasp, who will pass judgment upon every soul.
>
> And God "hath given Him authority to execute judgment also, because He is the Son of man." Because He has tasted the very dregs of human affliction and temptation, and understands the frailties and sins of men; because in our behalf He has victoriously withstood the temptations of Satan, and will deal justly and tenderly with the souls that His own blood has been poured out to save,--because of this, the Son of man is appointed to execute the judgment.
>
> *The Desire of Ages*, p.210

> But the Lord shall endure for ever: he hath prepared his throne for judgment. And he shall judge the world in righteousness, he shall minister judgment to the people in uprightness. The Lord is known by the judgment which he executeth: the wicked is snared in the work of his own hands. Psalm 9:7-8

> God does not stand toward the sinner as an executioner of the sentence against transgression; but He leaves the rejectors of His mercy to themselves, to reap that which they have sown. Every ray of light rejected, every warning despised or unheeded, every passion indulged, every transgression of the law of God, is a seed sown which yields its unfailing harvest. The Spirit of God, persistently resisted, is at last withdrawn from the sinner, and then there is left no power to control the evil passions of the soul, and no protection from the malice and enmity of Satan. *The Great Controversy*, p.36

God's compassionate nature is shown by the way in which He executes judgment. God does not execute the sinner for His transgressions; He simply lets nature take its course. By their persistence in sin, the guilty place themselves in the path of retribution and reap the consequences of their own actions. The wages of sin is death and when man clings to that sin, he becomes identified with it, and will be destroyed with it.

FOR GOD SO LOVED THE WORLD...

> For God so loved the world, that he gave his only begotten Son, that whosoever believeth in him should not perish, but have everlasting life. For God sent not his Son into the world to condemn the world; but that the world through him might be saved. John 3:16-17

There is no reason at all for anyone to ever suffer the penalty of sin. Christ has already paid the price and offers us the gift of His sinless life in the place of our sinful lives. If we would accept this gift, we would not perish, but have eternal life. But many are too proud to depend upon God for their salvation.

LINE UP OF EVENTS JUST PRIOR TO CHRIST'S SECOND COMING

THE SEVEN LAST PLAGUES

> Therefore shall her plagues come in one day, death, and mourning, and famine; and she shall be utterly burned with fire: for strong is the Lord God who judgeth her. Revelation 18:8

When probation is closed and every case has been decided, the seven last plagues begin. The plagues are localised and not global because of their severity. The earth will be afflicted with the plagues for one prophetic day (one year) and are consecutive. The Bible also refers to the seven last plagues as "the time of trouble".

1. Noisome and grievous sores (Revelation 16:2).
2. Sea becomes as blood and every living thing in it dies (Revelation 16:3).
3. Rivers and fountains of water become blood (Revelation 16:4-7).
4. Power given to the sun to scorch men with great heat (Revelation 16:8-9).
5. Seat of the beast full of darkness (Revelation 16:10-11).
6. River of Euphrates dries up to prepare the way of the kings of the east to come up to Armageddon (Revelation 16:12-16).
7. A great earthquake and hailstones the size of a talent (32.3kg) (Revelation 16:17-21).

THE TIME OF JACOB'S TROUBLE

> For thus saith the LORD; We have heard a voice of trembling, of fear, and not of peace. Ask ye now, and see whether a man doth travail with child? wherefore do I see every man with his hands on his loins, as a woman in travail, and all faces are turned into paleness? Alas! for that day is great, so that none is like it: it is even the time of Jacob's trouble; but he shall be saved out of it. Jeremiah 30:5-7

When Christ ceases to intercede in the heavenly sanctuary (Hebrews 9:11-12) the seven last plagues begin. During the time of trouble, Christ's people drink a bitter cup. Their lives are imperilled because the wicked accuse them of causing the calamities. Although their bread and water will be sure, the people of God will experience hunger and thirst and great discomfort. They will need to depend upon God for their daily needs and protection.

> The seventh angel poured out his vial into the air; and there came a great voice out of the temple of heaven, from the throne, saying, It is done. And there were voices, and thunders, and lightnings; and there was a great earthquake, such as was not since men were upon the earth, so mighty an earthquake, and so great. And the great city was divided into three parts, and the cities of the nations fell: and great Babylon came in remembrance before God, to give unto her the cup of the wine of the fierceness of his wrath. Revelation 16:17-19

> Thus saith thy Lord the LORD, and thy God that pleadeth the cause of his people, Behold, I have taken out of thine hand the cup of trembling, even the dregs of the cup of my fury; thou shalt no more drink it again: But I will put it into the hand of them that afflict thee; which have said to thy soul, Bow down, that we may go over. Isaiah 51:22-23

The people of God drink the bitter cup during the plagues until the beginning of the seventh plague. At this time, Christ removes the bitter cup from them and it is passed into the hands of the wicked who drink it in the battle of Armageddon (Jeremiah 25:15-38).

> LORD, in trouble have they visited thee, they poured out a prayer when thy chastening was upon them. Like as a woman with child, that draweth near the time of her delivery, is in pain, and crieth out in her pangs; so have we been in thy sight, O LORD. We have been with child, we have been in pain, we have as it were brought forth wind; we have not wrought any deliverance in the earth; neither have the inhabitants of the world fallen. Isaiah 26:16-18

This scripture likens the experience of God's people during the time of Jacob's trouble to a woman travailing with birth pains. They fear that some of their sins may not have been confessed and that they have not glorified God in their lives as they should have.

> Thy dead men shall live, together with my dead body shall they arise. Awake and sing, ye that dwell in dust: for thy dew is as the dew of herbs, and the earth shall cast out the dead. Come, my people, enter thou into thy chambers, and shut thy doors about thee: hide thyself as it were for a little moment, until the indignation be overpast. For, behold, the LORD cometh out of his place to punish the inhabitants of the earth for their iniquity: the earth also shall disclose her blood, and shall no more cover her slain. Isaiah 26:19-21

When God gives His covenant of peace to His people the earth shall cast out some of the dead. Then the seventh plague will begin and God will hide the faithful until the indignation be overpassed.

THE SPECIAL RESURRECTION OF TWO DIFFERENT CLASSES OF PEOPLE TOGETHER

> At that time shall Michael stand up, the great prince which standeth for the children of thy people: and there shall be a time of trouble, such as never was since there was a nation even to that same time: and at that time thy people shall be delivered, every one that shall be found written in the book. And many of them that sleep in the dust of the earth shall awake, some to everlasting life, and some to shame and everlasting contempt. Daniel 12:1-2

At the commencement of the seventh plague a special resurrection of two different classes of people takes place.

THE WICKED RAISED

> Behold, he cometh with clouds; and every eye shall see him, and they also which pierced him: and all kindreds of the earth shall wail because of him. Even so, Amen. Revelation 1:7

> But Jesus held his peace. And the high priest answered and said unto him, I adjure thee by the living God, that thou tell us whether thou be the Christ, the

> Son of God. Jesus saith unto him, Thou hast said: nevertheless I say unto you, Hereafter shall ye see the Son of man sitting on the right hand of power, and coming in the clouds of heaven. Matthew 26:63-64

Those who pierced Christ at His crucifixion in 31 A.D., including Caiaphas, Annas and Pontius Pilate, and the most violent opposers of His truth of all ages, will be raised to see Christ coming in the clouds as King and Victor.

THE RIGHTEOUS RAISED

> Here is the patience of the saints: here are they that keep the commandments of God, and the faith of Jesus. And I heard a voice from heaven saying unto me, Write, Blessed are the dead which die in the Lord from henceforth: Yea, saith the Spirit, that they may rest from their labours; and their works do follow them. Revelation 14:12-13

Those who entered into the Covenant relationship with God, receiving the gift of a new life from Christ but who have died believing, are also raised to hear the Covenant of Peace proclaimed from their Master's lips. These people have laboured for the salvation of souls through preaching, writing and the example of a faithful life. Even after they had passed into the grave their legacy continued to benefit others.

FIRST-FRUITS UNTO GOD

> The graves were opened; and many bodies of the saints which slept arose. Matthew 27:52

When Christ arose from the tomb on the resurrection morning, a multitude of captives were raised from their graves with Him as first-fruits unto God. In like manner the righteous resurrected in the special resurrection, only a short time before Christ's second coming, are a first-fruits unto God.

The Special Resurrection

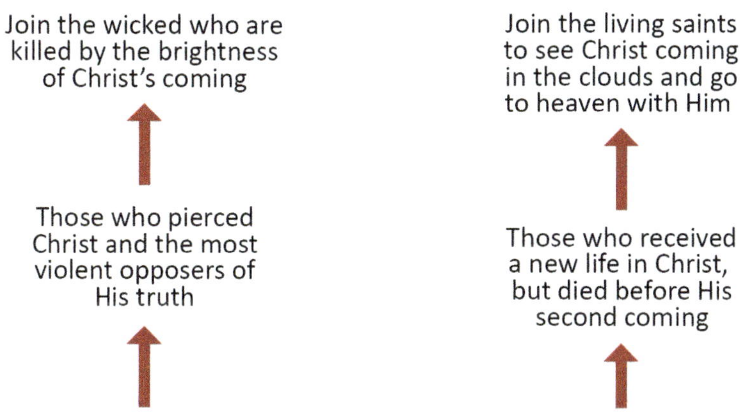

GOD CONFIRMS HIS COVENANT OF PEACE

Gather my saints together unto me; those that have made a covenant with me by sacrifice. And the heavens shall declare his righteousness: for God is judge himself. Psalm 50:5-6

The righteous saints, raised in the special resurrection to behold the coming of Christ in the clouds, join the ranks of the living saints to receive God's covenant of peace. At this time, the law, the declaration of His righteousness, is displayed in the heavens.

JESUS COMES IN A SIMILAR MANNER TO WHICH HE FIRST ASCENDED

When he had spoken these things, while they beheld, he was taken up; and a cloud received him out of their sight. And while they looked stedfastly toward heaven as he went up, behold, two men stood by them in white apparel; Which also said, Ye men of Galilee, why stand ye gazing up into heaven? this same Jesus, which is taken up from you into heaven, shall so come in like manner as ye have seen him go into heaven. Acts 1:9-11

THE SECOND COMING OF CHRIST

For as the lightning cometh out of the east, and shineth even unto the west; so shall also the coming of the Son of man be. Matthew 24:27

Then shall appear the sign of the Son of man in heaven: and then shall all the tribes of the earth mourn, and they shall see the Son of man coming in the clouds of heaven with power and great glory. And he shall send his angels with a great sound of a trumpet, and they shall gather together his elect from the four winds, from one end of heaven to the other. Matthew 24:30-31

Behold, he cometh with clouds; and every eye shall see him. Revelation 1:7

The second advent of Christ is a monumental event that the entire world will see and hear. Both the wicked and the righteous will see Him coming through the clouds. The wicked will be destroyed by the brightness of His coming (2 Thessalonians 2:8) and the righteous will be caught up together with Him in the clouds. When Christ ascends back to heaven with the saints, there will be no living souls left on earth.

CHRIST'S SECOND APPEARING NOT A SECRET RAPTURE

But as the days of Noe were, so shall also the coming of the Son of man be. For as in the days that were before the flood they were eating and drinking, marrying and giving in marriage, until the day that Noe entered into the ark, And knew not until the flood came, and took them all away; so shall also the

> coming of the Son of man be. Then shall two be in the field; the one shall be taken, and the other left. Two women shall be grinding at the mill; the one shall be taken, and the other left. Watch therefore: for ye know not what hour your Lord doth come. Matthew 24:37-42

In the days of Noah, the righteous were left and the wicked were taken. Also in the days of Lot, he was spared with his daughters and the wicked were taken. Applying this principle to the above text it is not speaking of a particular time, but simply stating that one of the women grinding at the mill will be saved and the other will be taken. It is depicting the two different classes who may yet at this time be associating with one another – one will be "left" or saved while the other is "taken" or destroyed.

THE FIRST RESURRECTION

> In a moment, in the twinkling of an eye, at the last trump: for the trumpet shall sound, and the dead shall be raised incorruptible, and we shall be changed. For this corruptible must put on incorruption, and this mortal must put on immortality. So when this corruptible shall have put on incorruption, and this mortal shall have put on immortality, then shall be brought to pass the saying that is written, Death is swallowed up in victory. 1 Corinthians 15:52-54

> Marvel not at this: for the hour is coming, in the which all that are in the graves shall hear his voice. And shall come forth; they that have done good, unto the resurrection of life; And they that have done evil, unto the resurrection of damnation. John 5:28-29

Aside from the special resurrection of a multitude at the beginning of the seventh plague there are two more resurrections which take place at different times. The righteous are raised from the grave at the second coming of Christ and this is called "the resurrection of life" or "the resurrection of the just" (Luke 14:14). The wicked are raised for a short time at "the resurrection of damnation" which takes place a thousand years later.

THE MILLENNIUM

> Blessed and holy is he that hath part in the first resurrection: on such the second death hath no power, but they shall be priests of God and of Christ, and shall reign with him a thousand years. Revelation 20:6

> And I saw an angel come down from heaven, having the key of the bottomless pit and a great chain in his hand. And he laid hold on the dragon, that old serpent, which is the Devil, and Satan and bound him a thousand years. And cast him unto the bottomless pit, and shut him up, and set a seal upon him, that he should deceive the nations no more, till the thousand years should be fulfilled. Revelation 20:1-3

Christ returns to heaven with his people and the earth is left as a desolate waste. Satan and His evil angels are bound to this earth and left to contemplate the consequences of their rebellion against God for a thousand years. The earth is strewn with dead bodies and there is no one for him to deceive.

THE BOTTOMLESS PIT

> I beheld the earth, and, lo, it was without form, and void; and the heavens, and they had no light. I beheld the mountains, and, lo, they trembled, and all the hills moved lightly. I beheld, and, lo, there was no man, and all the birds of the heavens were fled. I beheld, and, lo, the fruitful place was a wilderness, and all the cities thereof were broken down at the presence of the LORD, and by his fierce anger. Jeremiah 4:23-26

The earth is without form and void like a "bottomless pit" during the millennium.

THE BOOKS OF RECORD

> For God shall bring every work into judgment, with every secret thing, whether it be good, or whether it be evil. Ecclesiastes 12:14

> Every idle word that men shall speak, they shall give account thereof in the day of judgment. For by thy words thou shalt be justified, and by thy words thou shalt be condemned. Matthew 12:36-37

> Behold, it is written before me: I will not keep silence, but will recompense, even recompense into their bosom, Your iniquities, and the iniquities of your fathers together, saith the LORD, which have burned incense upon the mountains, and blasphemed me upon the hills: therefore will I measure their former work into their bosom. Isaiah 65:6-7

The sins of the wicked are registered in the "books of record" in heaven.

JUDGED ACCORDING TO LIGHT

> Jesus said unto them, If ye were blind, ye should have no sin: but now ye say, We see; therefore your sin remaineth. John 9:41

> Therefore to him that knoweth to do good, and doeth it not, to him it is sin. James 4:17

> If I had not come and spoken unto them, they had not had sin: but now they have no cloak for their sin. John 15:22

> That servant, which knew his lord's will, and prepared not himself, neither did according to his will, shall be beaten with many stripes. But he that knew not, and did commit things worthy of stripes, shall be beaten with few stripes. For unto whomsoever much is given, of him shall be much required: and to whom men have committed much, of him they will ask the more. Luke 12:47-48

All will be punished according to the way they lived up to what they knew to be right. Those who claimed to be Christians but did not live up to the light that shone upon their pathway from God's word will be more severely judged than those that never had the knowledge that they did.

EVERYONE KNOWS

> For the invisible things of him from the creation of the world are clearly seen, being understood by the things that are made, even his eternal power and Godhead; so that they are without excuse: Because that, when they knew God, they glorified him not as God, neither were thankful; but became vain in their imaginations, and their foolish heart was darkened. Professing themselves to be wise, they became fools. Romans 1:20-22

Everyone in this world has the proof of God's existence all around them in the evidences of His creation, but they do not permit reason to acknowledge Him. At some point in their life, every person is convicted that God is real and His ways are right.

NEGLECTED OPPORTUNITIES

> Pilate saith unto him, What is truth? And when he had said this, he went out again unto the Jews, and saith unto them, I find in him no fault at all. John 18:38

At the trial of Christ, Pilate asked Him, "What is truth?" But before Christ could answer him, he walked away. Many are doing the same today.

REJECTION OF CHRIST IN HIS MESSENGERS

> But into whatsoever city ye enter, and they receive you not, go your ways out into the streets of the same, and say, Even the very dust of your city, which cleaveth on us, we do wipe off against you: notwithstanding be ye sure of this, that the kingdom of God is come nigh unto you. Luke 10:10-11

When Christ's messengers speak a plain "Thus saith the Lord" and the people reject that message, they are rejecting Christ in the person of His messenger. The light of the Bible has been given that all may study for themselves to test the truth of the message (Acts 17:10-11; 2 Timothy 2:15).

CHRIST RETURNS TO THE EARTH

Behold, the day of the LORD cometh, and thy spoil shall be divided in the midst of thee. For I will gather all nations against Jerusalem to battle; and the city shall be taken, and the houses rifled, and the women ravished; and half of the city shall go forth into captivity, and the residue of the people shall not be cut off from the city. Then shall the LORD go forth, and fight against those nations, as when he fought in the day of battle. And his feet shall stand in that day upon the mount of Olives, which is before Jerusalem on the east, and the mount of Olives shall cleave in the midst thereof toward the east and toward the west, and there shall be a very great valley; and half of the mountain shall remove toward the north, and half of it toward the south. And ye shall flee to the valley of the mountains; for the valley of the mountains shall reach unto Azal: yea, ye shall flee, like as ye fled from before the earthquake in the days of Uzziah king of Judah: and the LORD my God shall come, and all the saints with thee.

Revelation 14:1-5

The books in heaven are examined by the saints and at the end of a thousand years they return with Christ. Christ stands upon the Mount of Olives which is cleaved asunder into a great plain. He then raises the wicked for a season.

THE SECOND RESURRECTION

The rest of the dead lived not again until the thousand years were finished.

Revelation 20:5

They shall be gathered together, as prisoners are gathered in the pit, and shall be shut up in the prison and after many days shall they be visited. Isaiah 24:22

The sea gave up the dead which were in it; and death and hell delivered up the dead which were in them: and they were judged every man according to their works. Revelation 20:13

All the wicked who have ever lived on the earth are raised to be judged according to their works.

THE HOLY CITY DESCENDS DOWN FROM HEAVEN

He carried me away in the spirit to a great and high mountain, and shewed me that great city, the holy Jerusalem, descending out of heaven from God. Having the glory of God: and her light was like unto a stone most precious, even like a jasper stone, clear as crystal. Revelation 21:10-11

I John saw the holy city, new Jerusalem, coming down from God out of heaven, prepared as a bride adorned for her husband. Revelation 21:2

A short time after the resurrection of the wicked, the city of Heaven, God's dwelling place, descends from the skies to the earth. God will dwell with His people forever and govern the universe from here.

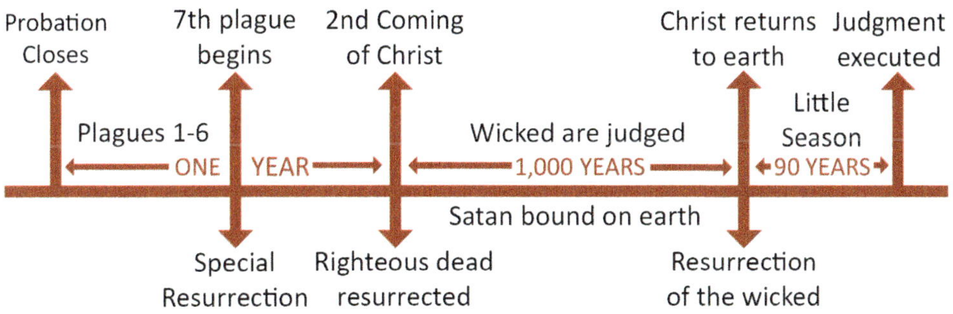

A SEASON

And cast him [Satan] into the bottomless pit, and shut him up, and set a seal upon him, that he should deceive the nations no more, till the thousand years should be fulfilled: and after that he must be loosed a little season.

Revelation 20:3

There shall be no more thence an infant of days, nor an old man that hath not filled his days: for the child shall die an hundred years old; but the sinner being an hundred years old shall be accursed. Isaiah 65:20

With the resurrection of the wicked, Satan is released from his bondage of loneliness and desolation for a prophetic season (90 years) and throws himself once more into the work of deception. The wicked are raised in the same state that they went into the grave. There is no life in them; therefore they do not grow. They are living dead. A child of ten who lives to a hundred years of age will remain a child for that entire ninety year period. (It is around the age of ten that a child begins to make conscientious decisions. For example Christ at twelve years of age recognised His calling. Before this spiritual maturity there is no accountability.)

But the children of the murderers he slew not: according unto that which is written in the book of the law of Moses, wherein the LORD commanded, saying, The fathers shall not be put to death for the children, nor the children be put to death for the fathers; but every man shall be put to death for his own sin. 2 Kings 14:6

Children of the wicked who have not reached spiritual maturity will not be raised in the judgment and held accountable for the sins and decisions of the parents. Many will be left in the grave and it will be as though they never existed.

SOME LEFT IN THE GRAVE

If there is no light, or no opportunity for a soul to live up to the light, they will remain in the grave and not be resurrected to the judgment. However, in 1 Corinthians 7:13-14 and Psalm 139:15-16, Christians are given the promise that their faithfulness will cover others.

A STRANGE ACT

> For the LORD shall rise up as in mount Perazim, he shall be wroth as in the valley of Gibeon, that he may do his work, his strange work; and bring to pass his act, his strange act. Isaiah 28:21

It is in mercy that God executes judgment on the sinner. The presence of His glory and the unselfish spirit of His saints would be torture and he would welcome destruction to be hidden from the face of the One who loved him and died for him.

A SECOND PROBATION

> Let favour be shewed to the wicked, yet will he not learn righteousness: in the land of uprightness will he deal unjustly, and will not behold the majesty of the Lord. Lord, when thy hand is lifted up, they will not see: but they shall see, and be ashamed for their envy at the people yea, the fire of thine enemies shall devour them. Isaiah 26:10-11

> Can the Ethiopian change his skin, or the leopard his spots? then may ye also do good, that are accustomed to do evil. Therefore will I scatter them as the stubble that passeth away by the wind of the wilderness. Jeremiah 13:23-24

Although their sentence has been set, the wicked are permitted a second probation on the earth to demonstrate that if they were given another opportunity to repent they would do the same thing again. This is a testimony to the universe that the sentence soon to be executed is just.

SATAN DECLARES WAR ON THE CITY

> When the thousand years are expired, Satan shall be loosed out of his prison, And shall go out to deceive the nations which are in the four quarters of the earth, Gog and Magog, to gather them together to battle: the number of whom is as the sand of the sea. Revelation 20:7-8

Satan resumes his delusions and convinces the wicked that he is the true king of the earth and that his city has been unlawfully seized by imposters. He works mighty miracles to support his claim and makes the weak strong. He tells them if they can gain access to the tree of life within the city they can live forever. The mighty generals of history, some of whom have never lost a single battle, marshal the throngs into divisions and companies. Comparing their numbers with those within the city they believe they can overthrow it. The inventors and artisans build powerful weapons during the ninety years to prepare for the final combat.

THE CORONATION OF CHRIST

> Thy throne, O God, is for ever and ever: the sceptre of thy kingdom is a right sceptre. Psalm 45:6

As the vast multitude, like the sands of the sea, rally in their companies around the city wall, they are suddenly halted by Christ's appearance upon the walls. At this time the coronation of the Son of God takes place and the righteous rejoice as Christ receives His crown.

THE FINAL JUDGMENT

> I saw the dead, small and great, stand before God; and the books were opened: and another book was opened, which is the book of life: and the dead were judged out of those things which were written in the books, according to their works." Revelation 20:11-12

All are deeply convicted of every sin they have ever committed as His penetrating eye looks upon them. Shame and guilt sweeps over the multitude as the life of Christ and His crucifixion is played out in panoramic view above them. They realise what they might have had but chose instead to put it far from them. All see that God is justified in excluding them from heaven. Falling prostrate to the ground they exclaim, "Great and marvellous are thy works, Lord God Almighty; just and true are thy ways, thou King of saints" (Revelation 15:3).

SATAN JUDGED BY THE WICKED

> How art thou fallen from heaven, O Lucifer, son of the morning! how art thou cut down to the ground, which didst weaken the nations! For thou hast said in thine heart, I will ascend into heaven, I will exalt my throne above the stars of God: I will be like the most High. Yet thou shalt be brought down to hell, to the sides of the pit. They that see thee shall narrowly look upon thee, and consider thee, saying, Is this the man that made the earth to tremble, that did shake kingdoms; That made the world as a wilderness, and destroyed the cities. Isaiah 14:12-17

> Therefore thus saith the Lord GOD; Because thou hast set thine heart as the heart of God; Behold, therefore I will bring strangers upon thee, the terrible

> of the nations: and they shall draw their swords against the beauty of thy wisdom, and they shall defile thy brightness. They shall bring thee down to the pit, and thou shalt die the deaths of them that are slain in the midst of the seas. Ezekiel 28:6-8

Satan acknowledges His sin but then the spirit of rebellion returns and he runs in among the people to inspire them to instant battle. But the wicked now realise that their case is hopeless and they cannot prevail against God. Awakening to Satan's lies, their anger knows no bounds and they rush in upon him to kill him and his agents of deception.

EXECUTION OF THE JUDGMENT

> Death and hell were cast into the lake of fire. This is the second death. And whosoever was not found written in the book of life was cast into the lake of fire. Revelation 20:14-15

> But the fearful, and unbelieving, and the abominable, and murderers, and whoremongers, and sorcerers, and idolaters, and all liars, shall have their part in the lake which burneth with fire and brimstone: which is the second death. Revelation 21:8

> Upon the wicked he shall rain snares, fire and brimstone, and an horrible tempest: this shall be the portion of their cup. Psalm 11:6

As Satan is about to suffer the wrath of the people, God sends fire upon the earth to consume sin; and all those who have attached themselves to sin are consumed. God is not sending the fire to destroy individuals as such; but because of their attachment to sin they have placed themselves in the path of destruction. The entire earth now becomes a seething lake of fire as was the Vale of Siddim when Sodom and Gomorrah were destroyed.

HELL-FIRE IS SENT TO CONSUME SIN

> For, behold, the day cometh, that shall burn as an oven; and all the proud, yea, and all that do wickedly, shall be stubble: and the day that cometh shall burn them up, saith the LORD of hosts, that it shall leave them neither root nor branch. Malachi 4:1

> The works that are therein are burned up. 2 Peter 3:10

The fire is sent to cleanse and purge the earth of everything that man has made and from every trace of sin. Once the earth is purified it will be a clean foundation upon which God will start again.

UNQUENCHABLE FIRE

> He will burn up the chaff with unquenchable fire. Matthew 3:12

> Thou shalt make them as a fiery oven in the time of thine anger: the LORD shall swallow them up in his wrath, and the fire shall devour them. Hebrews 10:27

Unquenchable hell-fire is simply a fire that nobody can put out. Hell-fire burns itself out once there is nothing more to consume.

THE WORM OF LIFE

> They shall go forth, and look upon the carcases of the men that have transgressed against me: for their worm shall not die, neither shall their fire be quenched; and they shall be an abhorring unto all flesh. Isaiah 66:24

The worm of life does not die in the wicked so that every sense of suffering remains until they are entirely consumed by fire.

DURATION OF PUNISHMENT ACCORDING TO GUILT

> If thou sayest, Behold, we knew it not; doth not he that pondereth the heart consider it? and he that keepeth thy soul, doth not he know it? and shall not he render to every man according to his works? Proverbs 24:12

The punishment is according to the light received and rejected. The greater the accountability, the longer the individual will be consumed by the fire. Those who are far less accountable will burn up like a puff of smoke.

SATAN BURNS THE LONGEST

> I will destroy thee, O covering cherub, from the midst of the stones of fire. . . . I will cast thee to the ground, I will lay thee before kings, that they may behold thee. . . . I will bring thee to ashes upon the earth in the sight of all them that behold thee. . . . Thou shalt be a terror, and never shalt thou be any more.
> Ezekiel 28:6-8, 16-19

> He that opened not the house of his prisoners? All the kings of the nations even all of them lie in glory, everyone in his own house. But thou art cast out of thy grave like an abominable branch, and as the raiment of those that are slain, thrust through with a sword, that go down to the stones of the pit; as a carcase trodden under foot. Isaiah 14:14-20

Satan not only suffers the guilt and condemnation for his own sin, but also the sins he has caused God's people to commit. He burns for a very long time.

TURNED TO ASHES

> But unto you that fear my name shall the Sun of righteousness arise with healing in his wings; and ye shall go forth, and grow up as calves of the stall. And ye shall tread down the wicked; for they shall be ashes under the soles of your feet in the day that I shall do this, saith the LORD of host. Malachi 4:1

> When the wicked spring as the grass, and when all the workers of iniquity do flourish; it is that they shall be destroyed for ever. Psalm 92:7

After the fire has done its work there will be nothing left of the individual but ashes. Their destruction will be forever.

A NEW HEAVEN AND A NEW EARTH

> For, behold, I create new heavens and a new earth: and the former shall not be remembered, nor come into mind. Isaiah 65:17

> For as the new heavens and the new earth, which I will make, shall remain before me, saith the LORD, so shall your seed and your name remain. And it shall come to pass, that from one new moon to another, and from one sabbath to another, shall all flesh come to worship before me, saith the LORD. Isaiah 66:22-23

> I saw a new heaven and a new earth: for the first heaven and the first earth were passed away. Revelation 21:1

When God recreates the earth it is even more beautiful than it was at the first creation.

NO MORE SIN AND SORROW

> God shall wipe away all tears from their eyes; and there shall be no more death, neither sorrow, nor crying, neither shall there be any more pain: for the former things are passed away. Revelation 21:4

There is now peace upon the earth. The pain and sorrow of this world is no more.

THE CURSE OF SIN REMOVED

> The wolf also shall dwell with the lamb, and the leopard shall lie down with the kid; and the calf and the young lion and the fatling together; and a little child shall lead them. And the cow and the bear shall feed; their young ones shall lie down together: and the lion shall eat straw like the ox. And the sucking child shall play on the hole of the asp, and the weaned child shall put his hand on the cockatrice's den. They shall not hurt nor destroy in all my holy mountain: for the earth shall be full of the knowledge of the LORD, as the waters cover the sea. Isaiah 11:5 -9

Life returns to the way God initially intended it. Children play safely with the animals and all creation is in harmony.

ONLY ONE REMINDER OF SIN

> And one shall say unto him, What are these wounds in thine hands? Then he shall answer, Those with which I was wounded in the house of my friends. Zechariah 13:6

There will be only one reminder of sin – the scars of the crucifixion in the hands, feet and side of Jesus Christ. He came to this earth as our friend but we crucified Him. Nevertheless, He has forgiven us and wants us all to be in heaven with Him.

Fig. D68 – Kerensa at Gomorrah.

Scripture Index

Reference Index of Quotations

White, E. *Patriarchs and Prophets*, p115.1 [13]
Vigouroux, *Dictionnaire de la bible, Chron*. Arm., I, i, t. XIX, col 107-108 [14]
Names of the Patriarchs http://asis.com/users/stag/patzcode.html [16]
Book of Jasher chapter 6, Lines 17-25 [23]
White, E. *The Desire of Ages,* p. 493.2 [25]
White, E. *Patriarchs and Prophets*, 107.1 [25]
Windsor, S. *Noah's Ark: Its Geometry*, 1995 [38, 39]
Patten, D. *A Debate: The Site of Noah's Ark: At Uzengili (Nisir)* 1995 [40]
Windsor, S. *Noah's Vessel: 24,000 Dead-weight Tons,* 1995 [40, 41]
Windsor, S. *Noah's Ark: Its Geometry,* 1995 [41]
Berosus the Chaldean – Part of the ship in Armenia [46]
Baumgardner, J. cited in *The Noah's Ark Conspiracy* Feature Film Youtube [49]
Windsor, S. *Noah's Ark: Its Geometry*, 1995 [50, 50, 50]
Rosetta, J. – cited in *The Noah's Ark Conspiracy* Feature Film You-tube. [50]
Josephus, F. *Antiquities*, Book 20, Chap. 2, Para. 2 [54]
Compbell Thompson, R. *The Epic of Gilgamesh*, Tablet 11, Column 1, Lines 263- 282 [54]
Windsor, S. *Noah's Ark: Its Geometry*, 1995 [58]
Fasold, D. cited in *The Noah's Ark Conspiracy* Feature Film You-tube, [60]
Windsor, S. cited *The Noah's Ark Conspiracy* Feature Film You-tube [62]
Windsor, S. *Noah's Vessel: 24,000 Dead-weight Tons*, 1995, Vessel Arrangements [68-69]
Josephus, F. *Antiquities*, Chapter 3, Para 6.
White, E. *Patriarchs and Prophets*, p.107.1 [77]
White, E. *The Desire of Ages* p.493.2 [77]
White, E. *Patriarchs and Prophets*, p.214.1 [79]
White, E. *Conflict and Courage*, p.74.3,4 [80]
Wikipedia: Imhotep [87]
Wikipedia: Beni Hasan [96]
Lichtheim, M. *Ancient Egyptian Literature*, Vol.3, The University of California Press 1980, pp.95f [100]
Moller, L. *The Exodus Case*, p. 164 [114]
Spurgeon, C. Sermon: *The Exodus*, December 9, 1855 [116]
White, E. *Courage and Conflict*, p.85.3} [143]
Schofield, C. *Heralding the Loud Cry*, p.138 [143]
White, E. *Signs of the Times*, May 20, 1880 [150]
Bunyan, J. *The Law and the Christian* [153]
White, E. *Patriarchs and Prophets*, p.364.2 [155]
Schofield, C. *Heralding the Loud Cry*, p.107 [163]
White, E. *Patriarchs and Prophets*, pp.343.2, 347-349 [170-172]
White, *Patriarchs and Prophets*, pp.349-358 [172-176]
http://www.israeltourblog.com/tag/the-dead-sea-scrolls-israel/ [207]
Quintillian, *Declarations*, 90 A.D. [210]
Altars, Wikipedia [211]
White, E. *The Desire of Ages*, p.233.1 [215]
White, E. *The Desire of Ages* pp.233 -234.1 [216]
White, E. *Thoughts from the Mount of Blessing*, p.9.1 [221]
White, E. *The Great Controversy*, p.410.1 [222]
White, E. *The Great Controversy*, p.421.3 [222]
White, E. *The Life of Paul*, p.167.2 [226]
Jones, A. *General Conference Bulletins 1895*, p.312.3 [229]

White, E. *Steps to Christ*, p.31.1 [229]
Luther, M. *Commentary on Galatians* [233]
Bunyan, J. *Grace Abounding to the Chief of Sinners* [233]
Spurgeon, C. *Christ in the Covenant* [233]
White, E. *The Desire of Ages*, p.330 [234]
Spurgeon, C. *Christ in the Covenant* [235]
Bunyan, J. *The Work of Christ as Advocate* [235]
White, E. *Patriarchs and Prophets*, p.46.2 [236]
Jones, A. *General Conference Bulletins 1895*, p.270.1 [237]
Jones, A. *General Conference Bulletins 1895*, p.270.3 [238]
Jones, A. *General Conference Bulletins 1895*, p.299.1 [238]
Schofield, C. *A Life that Measures with the Life of God*, pp. 24, 28 [239]
Jones, A. *General Conference Bulletins 1895*, p.301.9 [240]
White, E. *The Desire of Ages*, p.343.4 [241]
White, E. *The Desire of Ages*, p.343.5 [242]
White, E. *Steps to Christ* p.64.1 [243]
Jones, A. *General Conference Bulletins 1895* p.402.5 [243]
Jones, A. *General Conference Bulletins 1895* p.368.1-2 [244]
Jones, A. *General Conference Bulletins 1895* p.142.6 [246]
White, E. *Patriarchs and Prophets* p.139.2 [256]
White, E. *The Great Controversy* p.631.3 [259]
Strabo (XVI 42-44) [262]
Tacitus, *Histories* V, Ch. 7 [262]
Josephus, F. *Wars of the Jews*, Book 3, Chapter 8, Paragraph 4 [262]
Book of Jasher, p.116 [281]
White, E. *Signs of the Times*, August 27, 1896 par. 8 [282]
White, E. *Patriarchs and Prophets*, p.174.2 [282]
White, E. *Patriarchs and Prophets*, p.687.2 [285]
White, E. *The Desire of Ages*, p.210 [287]
White, E. *The Great Controversy*, p.36.1 [288]

Image Credits

© Kerensa Grigson

A8, A11, A12, A13, A24, A25, A26, A39, A55, A56, A57, A58, A59, A92, A93, A94, A95, A96, A97, A98, A99, A103, A104, A105, A106, A107, A108, A111, A112, A113, A114, A115, A116, A118, A122, A125, A126, A127, A128, A129, B1, B4, B10a, B37, B38, B39, B41, B42, B43, B44, B45, B57, B60, B80, B81, B91, B98, B110, C1, C8, C9, C10, C11, C12, C13, C15, C17, C18, C19, C30, C31, C32, C33, C39, C41, C46, C47, C48, C49, C50, C51, C52, C53, C54, C56, C59, C60, C61, C65, C67, C69, C70, C71, C72, C73, C74, C75, C81, C82, C89, C94, D1, D3, D5, D7, D8, D14, D15, D16, D17, D18, D32, D36, D37, D38, D39, D47, D58, D66, D67, D68

NOTE: The copyright owners of the below images may not necessarily endorse the written content of this book.

© Anchor Stone International

A14, A15, A16, A18, A19, A20, A21, A22, A23, A27, A28, A29, A30, A31, A32, A33, A34, A40, A41, A42, A43, A44, A45, A46, A47, A49, A50, A51, A52, A53, A54, A60, A61, A62, A53, A65, A67, A68, A69, A70, A71, A72, A73, A74, A75, A76, A77, A78, A81, A82, A83, A84, A85, A86, A87, A88, A89, A90, A91, A110, A117, A119, A120, A121, A123, A124, B64, C7, C64, C80, C83, C84, C85, C86, C87, C88, D19, D20, D22, D23, D24, D25, D26, D28, D29, D30, D31, D33, D34, D35, D40, D41, D42, D43, D44, D45, D48, D49, D50, D51, D53, D54, D55, D56, D57, D61, D62, D63, D64, D65

© Jim & Penny Caldwell

B89, B92, B93, B94, B95, B96, B101, B102, B103, B104, B105, B107, B108, B113, B115, B116, B118, B119, B120, B121

© Lennart Moller

B5, B27, B28, B29, B30, B31, B33, B34, B35, B59, B66, B67, B68, B69, B70, B71, B72, B73, B74, B75, B76, B77, B78, B79, B82, B83, B84, B86, B99, B114, B117

© Ark Discovery International

A66, B50, B58

© Jonathon Gray

A17, A38, A79, A80, A109, B85, C62

© Wyatt Family

A48, D21, D67

© Dr. Kim Sung Hak

B109

© Simon Brown

D52

© Henry Nissan

A9

© Lieden University

B54

© DePaul University

B23

© British Museum

A100

© Yale

A101

© Brooklyn Museum

B36

US Library of Congress

C21, C22, C23, C57, C58, C63

© Journal of Near Eastern Studies, by Nadine Moeller & Robert Ritner

B53

© Vision Video
C25, C27, C42, C43, C44, C45

© www.biografiasyvidas.com
B24

© Women of the Bible
C5, C6

© Hammond Incorporated
A7a

© Point Technologies
A64

© Egyptsites.wordpress.com
B11, B13

© www.bibleistrue.com
D12

NASA Landsat
A10, B26, B32, B40, B48, B56, B65, B87, B88, B100, B106, D6, D9

NASA MODIS
D10

© OpenStreetMap contributors - www.openstreetmap.org
Map data: Open Database License
Cartography: Creative Commons 3.0
C16, C20

Creative Commons 2.0 - https://creativecommons.org/licenses/by/2.0/
D4 - Geagea
B14 - Flickr: KaDeWeGirl
B15 - Flickr: Vincent Brown
B19 - Flickr: Doug Lawrence
B20 - Flickr: Rick Manwaring
B61 - Flickr: Vyacheslav Argenberg
C40 - Flickr: Upload Bot
C46 - Flickr: Norman Walsh

Creative Commons 3.0 - http://creativecommons.org/licenses/by-sa/3.0/deed.en
B17 - rthiele
B21, B22 - DRN Hawkins
B25 - Maverick149
C14 - Biosketch
C26 - Lizrail
C28 - AntanO
C55 - Nemo Bis
C76 - Durova
C77 - 9old9
D13 - Andrew Shiva
D60 - Jan Harenburg
D11 - kselnick

Creative Commons CC 4.0 - http://creativecommons.org/licenses/by-sa/4.0/deed.en
D59 - Daniel Schwen

Public Domain
A7, A102, B12, B18, B55, C78

Location co-ordinates

Noah's Ark

Noah's Ark 39°26'25.88"N 44°14'5.25"E

Original landing site 39°25'42.67"N 44°13'32.27"E

Tendurek 39°25'15.29"N 44°13'38.10"E

Uzengili 39°26'35.72"N 44°13'46.33"E

Noah's Village

Sagliksuyu 39°37'28.12"N 43°59'36.38"E

Naamah's grave 39°37'56.94"N 43°59'15.25"E

Joseph in Egypt

Famine Stela on Seheil Island 24° 3'29.86"N 32°52'28.47"E

Market Place Saqqara 29°52'9.09"N 31°13'3.46"E

Grain pits Saqqara 29°52'7.12"N 31°12'57.18"E

Step pyramid of Djoser 29°52'17.26"N 31°12'59.45"E

Imhotep Ibis Galleries 29°52'51.72"N 31°12'50.95"E

The Exodus

Nuweiba (Red Sea crossing site) 29° 0'12.04"N 34°39'56.56"E

Pi-Hiharoth 29° 2'51.65"N 34°39'44.81"E

Solomon's Pillar - West side 28°58'11.45"N 34°38'32.86"E

Marah 28°44'7.75"N 34°55'21.67"E

Elim 28°34'10.17"N 34°49'59.89"E

Red Sea encampment 28°31'26.17"N 34°48'23.18"E

Jethro's cave (Al-Bad) 28°29'16.67"N 34°59'57.33"E

Split rock/Rephidim 28°43'36.13"N 35°14'10.28"E

Mt Sinai 28°35'44.53"N 35°20'3.84"E

Mt Sinai Encampment 28°35'3.61"N 35°23'30.99"E

Golden calf pedestal & altar 28°34'53.11"N 35°23'46.32"E

Altar of Moses, pillars & corral 28°35'4.81"N 35°22'43.44"E

Jerusalem

Garden Tomb 31°47'2.35"N 35°13'48.98"E

Crucifixion site 31°47'0.93"N 35°13'50.43"E

Skull face 31°47'1.10"N 35°13'52.45"E

Gethsemane 31°46'46.54"N 35°14'23.00"E

The Dead Sea

Ein Gedi 31°27'19.48"N 35°22'16.88"E

Qumran 31°44'24.40"N 35°27'34.72"E

Admah 31°47'0.96"N 35°28'52.67"E

Zeboim 31°48'18.61"N 35°30'31.91"E

Gomorrah 31°18'35.74"N 35°22'27.03"E

Sodom 31° 4'34.57"N 35°22'44.88"E

Zoar 30°53'26.58"N 35°23'9.13"E

Lot's cave 31° 2'46.32"N 35°30'10.41"E

Masada 31°19'0.52"N 35°21'13.84"E

CPSIA information can be obtained at www.ICGtesting.com
Printed in the USA
BVOW07s1729220116

433544BV00020B/7/P